Achieving Success in Nonprofit Organizations

Achieving Success in Nonprofit Organizations

Timothy J. Kloppenborg and
Laurence J. Laning, Editors

business**expert**
Press

First published in 2014 by
Business Expert Press, LLC
222 East 46th Street, New York, NY 10017
www.businessexpertpress.com

ISBN-13: 978-1-60649-728-9 (paperback)
ISBN-13: 978-1-60649-729-6 (e-book)

Business Expert Press Strategic Management Collection

Collection ISSN: 2150-9611 (print)
Collection ISSN: 2150-9646 (electronic)

Cover and interior design by Exeter Premedia Services Private Ltd,
Chennai, India

First edition: 2014

10 9 8 7 6 5 4 3 2 1

Printed in the United States of America.

We dedicate this book to our good friend and late colleague
Dr. Phil Glasgo. Phil wrote the chapter on
Financial Management in this book.

We also dedicate this book to our families who have
given us great encouragement and support:

Bet, Kate, Nick, and Andy
and
Judy and Caroline

Abstract

This book is aimed at leaders of nonprofit organizations. These leaders include executive directors, managers, board members, pastors, key volunteers, and anyone who wishes to make a difference. The four overarching areas of **living the mission**, **making good decisions**, **getting things done**, and **developing your team** emerged from literature searches, focus groups, and surveys to discover objectively what critical skills and knowledge are most useful to leaders of nonprofit organizations. Experts contribute individual chapters in each of these four areas. This book can be used as a reference for specific skills and knowledge in any of these areas. It can also be used as a text since it covers 16 specific chapters within the four major sections and each chapter has a major case example, assessment questions, and summaries of key concepts.

Keywords

nonprofit management, leadership, strategy, execution, portfolio management, project management, information technology, data-based decision making, executive leadership, executive sponsorship, organization assessment

Contents

List of Figures

List of Tables

Preface

We met over 20 years ago. Laurie was midcareer at Procter & Gamble (P&G), having other work experience and his PhD before joining P&G. Tim was untenured at Xavier University having a few years of business experience. Laurie held roles of increasing responsibility at P&G including introducing data management, leading the implementation of SAP in the supply chain, and applying IT to P&G's new product innovation process. He retired as the chief information technology enterprise architect for P&G globally. He has served his church as Missions Director and worked with other nonprofit organizations in many capacities. Tim completed his U.S. Air Force Reserve career with assignments in transportation, procurement, and quality assurance. He published widely including eight books, consulted and trained with many clients, supervised many student teams who helped nonprofit organizations, and served on several nonprofit boards. Tim retired as a distinguished management professor from Xavier.

With our combined 75 years of corporate, academic, military, consulting, training, board, and volunteer experience, we have a strong desire to "give back" and help nonprofit organizations. We bring a synergy of two professionals from the industrial and academic worlds who have worked together for years and have benefited from our differences and our diverse network of colleagues. To that end, we offer our ideas on topics we know well, and we have recruited 15 experts to share their knowledge and experience in other areas essential to nonprofit management. This book applies the Pareto Principle—that is for each chapter, presenting the core 20% of ideas and techniques that when applied will provide 80% of the benefits to nonprofit leaders.

CHAPTER 1

Introduction

Over 2.3 million nonprofit organizations operate in the United States.[1] They range from neighborhood organizations that meet a few times per year to major universities and foundations that have billions of dollars in assets.

This book is focused on the topics and skills that leaders of nonprofit organizations in the United States have indicated in recent research (conducted by the authors) that they need to understand and master, to lead their organization to success as defined by their organization's mission.

Rather than the co-authors of this book selecting topics that we thought were important for leaders of nonprofit organizations, we elected to do the research and ask the leaders of nonprofits themselves what topics they wanted to know more about. This is an example of data-based research (see Chapter 7—Making Good Decisions Using Data).

Organization of Book

Our research (described in Appendix A) arrived at four strong factors that form the major sections of this book. Each factor has multiple related elements which form the chapters. These four factors are illustrated in Figure 1.1 which is a unifying graphic for this book.

These four factors form what we termed as a "Virtuous Cycle in Nonprofit Organization Success." As you do things well in one section/ factor, it helps to do other things well in other sections/factors. Instead of the traditional negative viscous cycle, this is a very positive or virtuous cycle. In Figure 1.1, the bold arrows show the most frequent direction of influence from one section to another. But also note that each section/ factor has some influence on each other section/factor.

Living the Mission is the focus of Section 1. It explains how to develop and refine your organization's mission over time and to work well

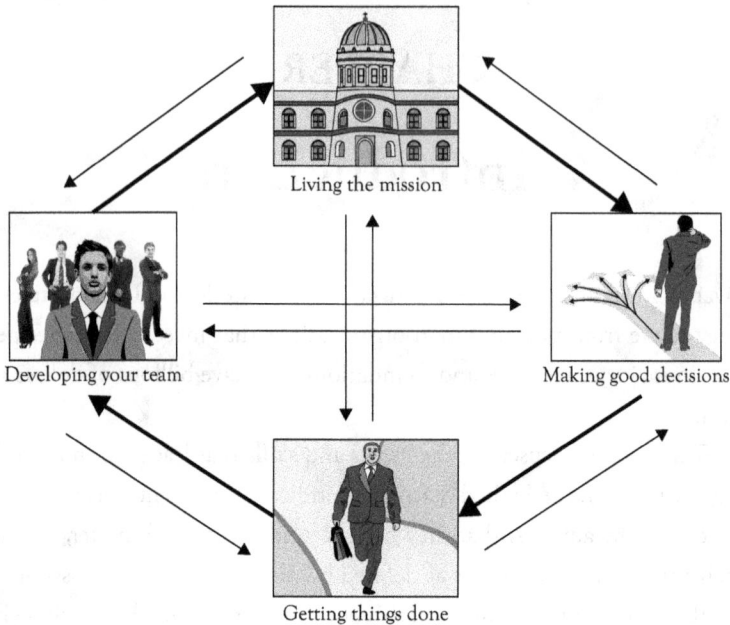

Figure 1.1 A virtuous cycle in nonprofit organization success

with your board. It also explores in depth the key topics of ethics, values, and governance that living a mission must entail. The concluding chapter of this first section develops the critical concept and methods of how to effectively engage with your communities.

Section 2 concentrates on **Making Good Decisions** in running a nonprofit organization. The relevant topics here are how to create successful new products and services through innovation, how to use quantitative and qualitative data to make good decisions, how to establish and manage an excellent portfolio management process, and how to leverage information technology to run an effective organization.

Section 3 illustrates **Getting Things Done** with excellence. This section includes chapters on managing the financial assets of an organization, introducing and managing change in an organization, and managing projects well which includes how to effectively plan projects and how to sponsor projects successfully.

Section 4 focuses on the critical tasks of **Developing Your Team** of people. Topics in this section include human resource management where items like performance reviews, hiring, retention, and succession planning

are covered. Other topics are total quality management and empowerment, using a strengths-based approach for managing your people, and
key insights and learning from employee-owned enterprises that are relevant for all nonprofits.

Nonprofit Organizations in the United States of America

It is helpful to understand some basic statistics for what the population
of nonprofit organizations looks like in the United States. It provides an
important perspective and magnitude of the nonprofit sector in American
life.

According to the latest Nonprofit Almanac 2012 published by the
National Center for Charitable Statistics,[2] some basic statistics on nonprofits in the United States of America are as follows:

1. There are 2.3 million nonprofit organizations operating in the
   United States.
2. There are 1.54 million nonprofit organizations registered with the
   Internal Revenue Service (IRS). This number has grown 24% over the
   past 10 years (beginning in 2010, only nonprofit organizations with
   $50,000 or more in gross receipts are required to file with the IRS).
3. Of the 30 types of nonprofits in the United States, public charities
   are the largest number with 956,000. Public charities represent arts,
   education, health care, human services, and other types of organizations to which donors can make tax deductible donations.
4. Most nonprofits are small. Only 4% of all nonprofits have $10 million
   or more in expenses—primarily hospitals and higher education institutions. 75% of public charities report less than $100,000 in gross
   receipts.
5. In 2010, 9.2% of all wages and salaries in the United States came
   from nonprofit organizations.
6. Nonprofits share of the gross domestic product (GDP) was 5.5% in
   2012.
7. 26.5% of all Americans over the age of 16 volunteer for a nonprofit
   organization.

Key Leadership Challenges for Nonprofit Organizations

Nonprofit organizations present unique leadership challenges. Many of these challenges will be covered in significant depth in each chapter. But it is useful to identify the major unique challenges that confront the leaders in nonprofit organizations. Four of the key challenges are discussed as follows.

First, many nonprofit organizations have limited number of staff resources as well as limited financial resources from which to operate. They must have a scarcity mentality to make ends meet and keep the doors open.

Second, volunteers play a vital role in running many nonprofit organizations. Recruiting, training, and retaining volunteers are no small tasks. Also it is very hard to "fire" a volunteer when someone is just not working out.

Third, the organizational structure of many nonprofit organizations is complex and includes a governing board and a myriad of key stakeholders. Nonprofits do not have the profitability yardstick companies have, so other considerations such as mission take on more importance.

And finally, there is a saying that "no margin means no mission." This means that even though a nonprofit organization's primary goal is not to make money, if a nonprofit does not generate adequate cash and revenue, it will not be able to fund and operate its primary mission. This is often called a dual goal strategy.

Key Features of This Book

This book is written for nonprofit leaders and practitioners working actively in the field. These leaders tend to be well educated within their area, bright, and highly motivated. However, many have not had formal training in business, management, or leadership. The intent of this book is to provide in a concise format the skills and knowledge these leaders most need. To get the most from this book, please take advantage of these key features:

- Each chapter is written by one or two authors who have significant relevant experience in their chosen area of expertise.

- A concise list of learning objectives is shown at the beginning of each chapter.
- Each chapter covers the essential 20% of their topic area that will result in 80% of the overall benefit by applying those concepts and tools.
- A current relevant case study in each chapter highlights a nonprofit organization's use of the topics covered. Every case involves an organization with which the chapter author is actively and directly engaged. Each case ends with a list of key learning's on which you should focus.
- Each chapter ends with a list of five Key Assessment Questions. These questions enable you to assess your organization's overall competency in the topic area of each chapter and develop improvement plans for areas needing attention.

Notes

1. Blackwood, Roeger, and Pettijohn (2012).
2. National Center for Charitable Statistics (2012).

References

Blackwood, A. S., Roeger, K. L., & Pettijohn, S. L. (2012). *The nonprofit sector in brief: Public charities, giving, and volunteering.* Washington, DC: Urban Institute.

National Center for Charitable Statistics. (2012). *The nonprofit Almanac 2012.* Washington, DC: Urban Institute Press.

SECTION 1

Living the Mission

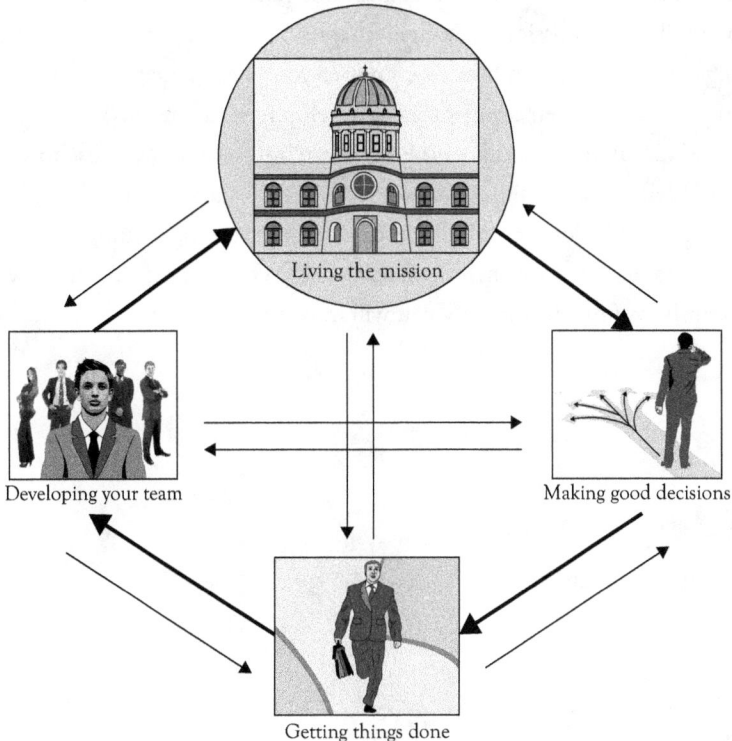

Living the mission

Developing your team

Making good decisions

Getting things done

Living the mission is clearly understanding what programs and services are critical to the communities an organization serves. It is effectively using this knowledge to prepare for the future, guide the present, and appropriately interact and effectively communicate with all relevant constituencies.

The first chapter in this section, Developing and Living Your Mission, describes the usefulness of a mission, how to make it accessible to all stakeholders, and how to measure against it to ensure our organization is on track. The next chapter, "Noses in; Fingers Out": The Board's Role in Achieving Success, provides an overview of responsibilities, functions, and practicalities of serving on or working with the Board of Directors for a nonprofit organization. The third chapter in this section, Walking the Talk: Serving Stakeholders with Ethics, Values, and Good Governance, describes how to combine organizational values, good governance, and an ethical climate to engage leadership, employees, and stakeholders in a manner that maximizes an organization's potential and leads to success in fulfilling its mission. The final chapter in this section, Community Engagement, describes how to empower your staff, target client groups, supporters, and even competitors to develop into full partners.

While all four sections of this book are interrelated, we chose to start with Living the Mission as this hopefully will guide decision making. Living the Mission also ideally leads to getting the right things done in an ethical and effective manner and to many considerations on who will comprise your team and how you will interact with them.

CHAPTER 2

Developing and Living Your Mission

Len Brzozowski

Len Brzozowski—teaches and is a consultant on Strategy and Change through the Sarasota Center for Innovation. He holds advanced degrees in engineering and business strategy from Dartmouth College. His company, Robotron Corporation, was recognized as one of the 50 most innovative small businesses in the United States.

Introduction

This chapter is about the importance of having a clearly defined sense of purpose and direction for your organization. Beyond that, organizations need a sense of purpose that goes beyond the mission statement into specific behaviors and actions so that what the organization actually DOES is connected with that sense of mission. While many organizations have a mission statement, a set of core values (at least on their website), or both, converting those into actions is the key. When you finish this chapter, you should be able to

- assess whether or not your organization's mission is relevant to the world within which you operate;
- assess whether or not your current mission statement is a good reflection of what your organization actually does;
- think more critically about your organizational initiatives that seem contradictory or unrelated to your mission;
- launch a process that improves upon existing programs/ initiatives or creates new ones.

Introduction to the Friars Club

Friars Club logo

The Friars Club of Cincinnati is a Franciscan-based charity. The club has a long history, dating back to when it was formed in 1860 as a Catholic social service organization dedicated to serving at-risk and disadvantaged children through organized sports, and fitness activities. The cornerstone program for the Friars was, and is, basketball.

After the Second World War, the program grew dramatically and several former Friars Club players made it to the NBA as professional athletes. Pride in the program understandably grew as a result. Through its history, the kids were coached and mentored by lay volunteers and Franciscan monks who helped tend to the broader needs of the players (which some would say is the hallmark of the Friars Club organization). Today, many dedicated coaches volunteer their time remembering fondly how the Friars Club made a profound difference in their lives.

Youth at Friars Club practice

In recent years, fund raising has been more problematic, and the club has had to scale back its operations, relying on rented sports facilities in both Catholic and public school buildings. There are currently two paid staff members and a team of deeply passionate volunteers who operate the programs, but the Executive Director and her helpers have many more good ideas than resources. In addition, the organization has been trying to raise money for a new building of their own, but thus far has fallen well shy of their fund-raising goal.

The organization is facing an interesting set of issues. Among them are the following:

- What is retarding their ability to raise money for operations and the building campaign?
- Does the community see the programming as relevant today as it once was?
- How does the organization "re-brand" itself as a relevant 21st century service organization that can attract willing donors to its cause?
- Does it need to rethink the nature of its purpose, and revise dramatically its programs to thrive financially?

This last question is an interesting one. Organizations like Blockbuster, or Borders Books became faint shadows of their former selves as their world changed around them. Competitors like Amazon and Net-flix emerged with new and different business models that made theirs virtually obsolete. In a sense, I think Borders and Blockbuster failed because they became incapable of thinking about themselves as any-thing other than what they were— (a family of brick and mortar outlets where people could drive to browse

Youth at Friars Club practice

and rent or buy movies, music, or books). Their world was changing, and they couldn't accept it and find a way to change until it was too late.

Could this be the same situation facing the Friars Club?

History and tradition can be both strengths and weaknesses. Many at the Friars Club have deep emotional connections based on their own past experiences. This tends to keep present day operations anchored in the proud tradition from its past. There are many compelling reasons why this seems to be sensible. But, the stronger the past tugs at one's heart, the harder it is to look forward and imagine new possibilities.

Let's start with a discussion of the Mission Statement

Oftentimes the mission is so vaguely worded that it isn't useful for making strategic decisions. When ambiguity exists, it can lead to different interpretations (as we will see). In addition, there is no organization on the planet blessed with limitless resources. So, by definition, the strategy flowing from the mission statement must be about MAKING CHOICES about what to do, whom to serve, and how to do it. Most organizations have plenty of good ideas, but since they can't do everything well, they need to choose carefully (and strategically) among the many worthy alternatives. So a good mission statement should be one of the tools that help you decide. Here is the mission statement from the Friars Club:

> *The Friars Club, a Catholic ministry, embracing Franciscan values of community and concern for the poor, bridges the social resource gap faced by at-risk boys and girls through youth sports, educational and enrichment programs to help them develop personal goals and lead successful lives.*[1]

This is a reasonable statement of purpose, but you can see that there are a number of places where ambiguity exists. For example:

- Who are "at-risk boys and girls?" Do they only reside in the inner city? Aren't suburban kids at risk as well, perhaps to different threats?
- What about kids who don't have an interest in sports, or are not athletically inclined? Aren't some of them "at risk?"
- Why should the focus today be mainly about sports? Does this perpetuate a myth to poor inner city kids that sports represent a likely way out of poverty (even though the odds of having a lifelong professional sports career are very small)?
- What "educational programs" are suitable? What should be taught? What are our learning goals? How would we do it? Should there be a classroom-like experience? Who are the "teachers?"

- If the programs are mainly around sports, what are the types of "personal goals" we have in mind—that may lead to "successful lives?" If we can't define them, how can we teach them? And, if we can agree on what these look like, how is it we are deliberately intending to help our children develop them? What does it take to have a successful life? How would we know if our boys and girls are more successful in life in comparison to children who did not experience a Friars Club sports program?

I am not suggesting the mission statement should be revised, but the conversation around what it really *means* is important, and represents the difference between having a statement that simply exists on a website, from one that is a living and breathing tool that guides the organization and those who choose to participate in its ministries.

The Need to Lead With Strategic Intent

One of the things my wife and I always do around the holidays is watch some of the old classic schmaltzy movies that often run at that time of year. You know the ones—with Capraesque values featuring Bing Crosby or Jimmy Stewart. They are filled with characters who organize some charitable activity. Doing something positive for kids is enough to launch the initiative. In their case, there are seemingly no budgets, paid staff, board of directors, 501(c)3 filings, or other elements today's nonprofit executives deal with. It is just about the noble cause, with good people (mostly volunteers) trying to make a positive difference in the lives of others. It feels like good intentions should be enough.

It would be nice to return to such simpler times but in today's complex world, running a nonprofit *should* be more demanding. As stewards of the money our donors provide, we should be constantly seeking ways to improve upon what we deliver to maximize the good we do.

Toward that end, I would like to suggest a strategic thinking and management framework (see Table 2.1) that can help your organization achieve higher levels of performance. While we need ALL of these elements to work together, this chapter focuses primarily on the Mission and Vision sections of the matrix.

Table 2.1 *Strategic thinking and management framework*

Element	Answers the question	Why we need it	Example
Mission	What is our purpose?	Defines our brand. Helps us decide what kinds of programs or investments "fit."	We develop leadership skills in underserved youth enabling them to be successful in life.
Vision	Where are we headed?	Defines what success looks like, implies organizational goals.	To reach 50,000 kids in our region so that they go on to gain a post high school degree, skilled trade, or certification.
Goals	What are we trying to accomplish?	Makes vision understandable, breaks down overall mission/vision into attainable steps.	To serve 5,000 boys and girls each week. To keep them in school, avoiding crime and drugs, and pursuing learning that will position them for life success.
Strategy	How will we get there?	Defines a plan (set of aligned initiatives) to which we are willing to allocate resources (leading to budgets). Forces us to make choices about what we do.	Strategic initiative: create inviting after-school sports program for at-risk urban girls.
Metrics	How will we know if we are succeeding?	Provides objective measures that tell us what's working, and what's not.	To reduce the school dropout rate among our youth to less than 10%.

I am focusing on these two, because many nonprofits I am familiar with fail to think deeply about them, and the sometimes resulting lack of focus adversely impacts these organizations. The purpose of these two ideas combined is to provide a clear sense of purpose (mission) and destination (vision). Note that these two ideas are different, but related. Mission is a statement of why we exist—our noble purpose. The Vision is an aspiration defining where we are trying to go.

Here is one example from Katsuaki Watanabe, Toyota's former chairman. Here is his dream vision:

> *I want Toyota to come up with the dream car—a vehicle that can make the air cleaner than it is, a vehicle that cannot injure people, a vehicle that prevents accidents from happening, a vehicle that can make people healthier the longer they drive it, a vehicle that can excite, entertain, and evoke the emotions of its occupants, a vehicle that can drive around the world on just one tank of gas.*[2]

I love this as a purpose/vision statement. It projects an image of things that are not likely to be possible, but it clearly tells all employees at Toyota what to aim at. It also provides some guidelines for determining where the organization should allocate its resources. You choose the initiatives that you believe will move you closer to that sense of vision.

I have taught managers from Wal-Mart who talked to me about how it works in their organization. Wal-Mart's mission idea is "To make it possible for people to save money so that they can live better lives." That's it. They are not about providing the absolutely best customer service, or the most inviting shopping environment. Save money, Live Better. Simple. Clear. Concise. So, at Wal-Mart it is really difficult to get projects approved if you can't demonstrate that they will reduce cost or improve the life quality of their customers.

Living to such a clear mission requires discipline, and focus. It also requires that you *make choices* about what you will do, whom you will serve, and in what manner.

Perhaps an easy way to visit this issue is to think about Mission as answering four basic questions.

1. Who are we?
2. What do we do?
3. For Whom do we do it?
4. Why does it matter?

An example of this is from Disney. Their mission statement is "We design and deliver the Disney experience, providing happiness to families everywhere."

Who are we?	Disney
What do we do?	Design and deliver experiences in a "Disney Way"
For Whom?	Families everywhere
Why?	To create happiness

The idea of the "Disney Way" relates to a whole host of values and philosophies developed initially by Walt and embraced by the company and all its cast members today.

If done right, this mission idea is useful for deciding what kinds of projects, activities, attractions, or movies FIT with this mission. You don't expect Disney would do a horror film or adult oriented program since they see themselves as providing family entertainment experiences.

My observation is that most mission-based organizations think they do a great job with their mission statement—and believe they have a compelling mission and set of values. But translating these into actions in ways that are aligned across a broad network of paid staff and volunteers is highly challenging. This is partly due to the lack of alignment within the organization and the difficulty in translating the mission into everyday action.

I am not convinced all nonprofits spend enough time thinking about their mission and all its implications.

They typically do have a large number of deeply dedicated people who are personally drawn to some aspect of what they *feel* the organization represents. This abundance of good intentions does not necessarily translate to effective mission execution, especially when each individual

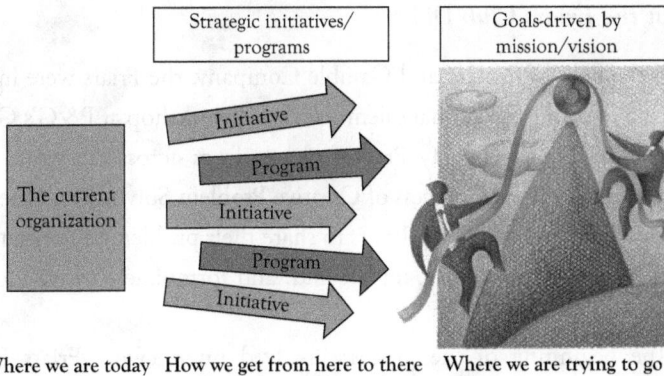

Where we are today   How we get from here to there   Where we are trying to go

Figure 2.1 How mission and strategy work together

interprets the mission in a way that is meaningful to themselves, but not necessarily to the majority of other team members.

In some cases, the mission statement is an afterthought, filled with ambiguous words and phrases that may sound good, but do not offer much help as a compass pointing the direction to go.

As suggested in Figure 2.1, to make a mission/vision useful, it must be translated into a series of strategic initiatives that move the organization closer to the goals implied by its mission. These initiatives are intended to move the organization from where it is today, toward the future goals. The idea is that the organization's future is deliberately *different* (and hopefully better) than what it experiences today. There is no status quo in a changing world. You are either getting better or worse. You get to choose.

For your organization to achieve its best outcomes, *all* of the elements in the Strategic Thinking and Management Framework pyramid need to work together. When we write down our mission, values, or strategy in a concise way, the words we use can mean different things to different people. The result is we all *feel* as though we are executing the strategy and living in accordance with our values, but in reality, we are not well aligned.

So how do we build a deeper level of understanding among all stakeholders about our purpose and direction? That is the topic I would now like to mainly address.

Let's return to the Friars Club case and look at how they tried to rethink their sense of purpose and direction.

What the Friars Club Did

With the help of Procter and Gamble Company, the Friars were invited to bring their organizational dilemmas into a workshop at P&G's Global Innovation Center. Twenty Procter people from across the world were assembled to learn the process of Creative Problem Solving[3] and they, for two intense days invited the Friars to share their problem as they and the P&G team tried to dissect, understand, and formulate creative ideas to solve it.

The beginning of the process involved interviewing Friars Board members, the Executive Director, some coaches, parents, former youth players, and school principals as the team tried to understand more fully the current challenges.

After the interviews, the teams tried to summarize their new insights. One of them developed the Mind Map[4]—as shown in Figure 2.2 (shown also with an idea card developed during the session), "How Might We (HMW) create programming that enriches the 'whole' kid?"

For them, this mind map was a significant breakthrough. It calls on them to broaden their focus to care in a more holistic way for the youth who participate in their programs. Thinking about how to expose them to new things, and engaging with parents were new insights that led to some interesting conversations about organizational purpose and program content.

As the teams went through their analysis, about 400 different ideas were generated. After assessing, and sorting them, these were gradually

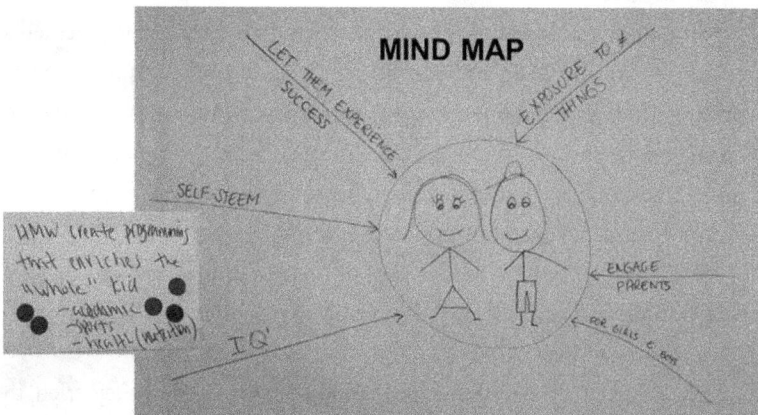

Figure 2.2 Mind map based on stakeholder interviews, Friars Club strategy workshop

digested and condensed down to a set of strategic initiatives that included the following areas:

- Building and Communicating the Brand
- Mission That Connects with Others
- Growth Through Impactful New Programming
- The Building
- Alternative Funding Strategies
- Engaging Parents
- Partnering to Build Momentum
- Attracting and Developing Staff

Each of these thematic areas was built out (see Figure 2.3) providing execution ideas as well as broad initiative goals.

At this time, the Friars Club Board is evaluating the outcome of this workshop and making its choices about future direction.

In my view, it was extremely helpful to have included not only Friars Club members, but a number of "outsiders" who were able to bring a more objective perspective to the discussions. I recall one moment during

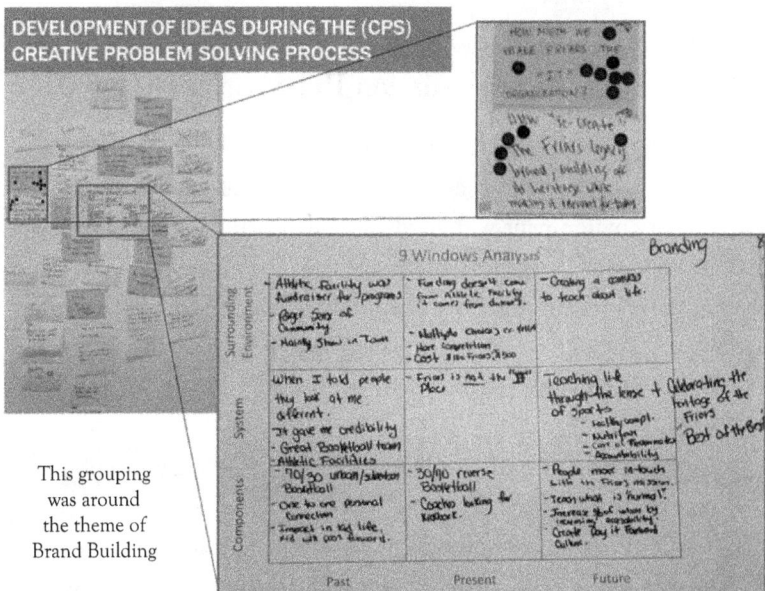

Figure 2.3 How ideas are grouped and expanded upon during a creative problem solving workshop

the workshop when one participant asked the question, "Why do we need coaches? We could teach the older kids to coach the younger ones." Now at first, the idea seemed preposterous to some of the Friars Club members who were there. They have always had coaches. If you have a team, you need one. Don't you? Here is where the mission statement comes in. When considering this question, it helps to look at the Mission Statement for guidance. "Is sports an end goal or a means to an end?" Is the main goal to provide *youth sports programs* or to *help [kids] develop personal goals and lead successful lives?* If you consider it as the former, then replacing coaches with less experienced youth may not be a great idea. If it is the latter, however, then one might consider youth coaches as a great way to teach leadership, caring, planning, and mentoring skills.

The Creative Solving Process used by the Friars Club was an intense experience that required considerable preparation.

The remainder of this chapter provides some tools and templates your organization can use to facilitate the starting discussions about whether you are clear on where you are heading, and how you want to get there. It starts with a re-evaluation of your mission purpose in the context of what is happening today. The next step is to consider whether what we actually DO every day seems consistent with the intent of the mission.

Is Our Mission Relevant?

The first step in assessing the relevancy of your mission and strategy is to stop for a moment, and ask your team to think about and identify the current environment within which you operate. Figure 2.4 is called a Context Map.[5] There are many versions of this in the public domain, and the topics might be altered depending on the nature of your organization's activities. Here is one template[6] I have personally found helpful:

So, here is how you use the map:

1. Create seven charts on a wall (one for each of the red bullet points on the context map).
2. Assemble a team of people from your organization. Make the group diverse and eclectic. (Include paid staff, board members, volunteers, people you serve, family members, civic leaders, and so forth.)

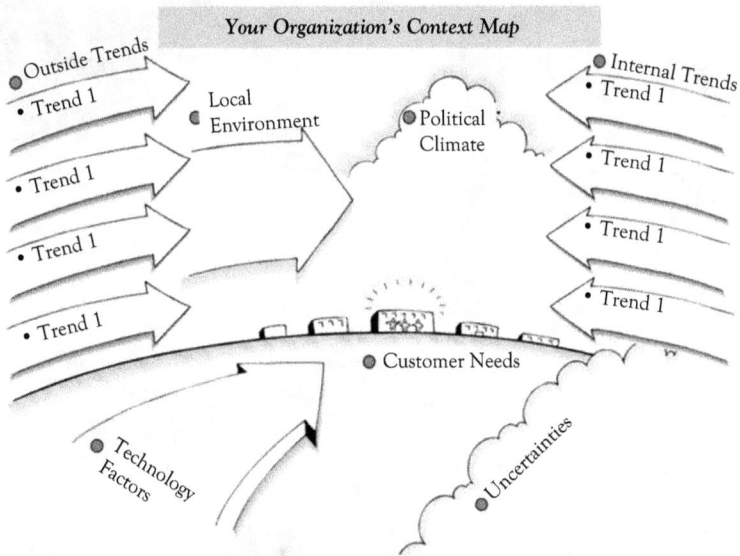

Figure 2.4 Context map template

3. Explain that you want to develop a "big picture" of the environment within which your organization operates.

4. Ask them to choose one section at a time. Invite people to write privately on post-it notes what are the most significant trends, drivers, or forces in relation to each of the categories listed. (People can list as many as they wish.) When they are finished, ask them to read each post-it aloud, and put it on the wall. Do not allow debate about the idea or permit discussion about each response—allow only questions for clarification. If there are some exact duplicates, you can discard them.

5. Once all the post-its are up, give everyone five sticky dots and ask them to place their dots on the five most important items on the wall.

6. When the voting is complete, transfer the most important ones to the context map.

7. Move on to another section and repeat steps 4–6 until all the sections of the map are complete. When you get to the two TRENDS sections, allow the group to choose which categories of trends they think are most important, and work on those. You might think about growth trends, social forces, local events, demographic trends, or any others the group feels really matter.

Figure 2.5 Sample completed context map template

When finished, your context map[7] might look something like Figure 2.5.

The final step in this process is to ask the group to speak aloud about the major new insights or ah-ha's they acquired as a result of this exercise.

Coaching point: *When I have done this with groups, the section they struggle most with is "CUSTOMER NEEDS." Normally people presume that they know what their constituents want. If you do not have "customers" in the room with you when you do this exercise, you might consider a pre-work assignment where some of your colleagues interview some "customers" in advance and summarize their key findings on one sheet of paper.*

Another Coaching point: *Some of your colleagues may argue that this exercise lacks rigor and should be more fact based. If that is the culture of your organization, then you might consider another pre-work assignment where people are asked to research some of the context map categories, collecting interesting charts, graphs, or tables as they see fit. My personal bias is to do the exercise without this pre-work, soliciting the raw, instinctive ideas from the assembled team. Keep a running list of "Wish we Knew's" during the mapping session. Then, if people feel that more research is needed on some areas, assign the research afterward.*

Here would be a good time to break for lunch or even for the day, allowing some time for all these new insights to soak in. (If you break, be sure to keep the Context Map so you can re-display it when the group reconvenes.)

The next step in this process is to revisit the organization's mission statement. In this session, you should have a copy of the mission statement and core values up on the wall somewhere. When the group comes together you can break them into subteams of 3–5 people and ask them to answer these questions in their group:

1. Which key trends, drivers, needs, and forces found on our Context Map does our current mission statement
   a. address well?
   b. seem counter to?
   c. miss altogether?
2. Are there some words or phrases in the mission statement that seem ambiguous or confusing?
   a. How might we improve the wording?
3. How does our mission statement overall, serve the customer needs as we understand them?
   a. How might we revise it to make it more powerful?

When the groups complete their discussions, invite them to share their reflections and capture their key findings.

Using a mission statement template of your choice, ask the group to finalize the proposed wording changes.

Coaching point: *In doing work like this, it is useful to choose a mission statement template that helps all the teams formulate their wording revisions in a way that can be easily compiled and integrated. There are many templates you can choose here, but the one I like a lot is the one presented earlier:*

Write your MISSION by answering these four main questions:

1. *Who are we?*
2. *What do we do?*
3. *For Whom do we do it?*
4. *Why does it matter?*

Do We Live What the Mission Represents?

I like to think of the mission statement as an INTERNAL ALIGN-MENT TOOL, helping all of us inside the organization to make choices about what we do, whom we will serve, and how we will do it. The better we are aligned internally, the easier this becomes.

But THINKING about what to do and actually DOING it, are two entirely different things. What matters is not so much what we think, but what we project to the outside world. Some people would call this our BRAND.

If Mission is what we use internally to focus ourselves, then the BRAND is the flip side of that same coin. If we do it right, the BRAND and the MISSION should be pretty well aligned. In the end, the Brand is less about what we put on the brochure, and more about WHAT WE DO. Our "customers" assess our brand based on how they see us act. Disney can put anything they want in a TV commercial, but if we go to Walt Disney World and do not have a "happy" or "magical" experience, then we tend to think of the advertising as fraudulent, and their brand image is greatly diminished.

Our Brand makes a promise of what we will deliver to those who choose to participate with us. We need to be sure they all see and feel it.

Here is an exercise to help you assess whether you align well, or not so much:

1. Invite in a group of employees (who were not engaged previously in your mission statement/context mapping workshop), "customers," community members, volunteers, and so forth.
2. Ask them to write down what they think your mission statement actually is, based on how they see your organization in the real world.
3. Ask them to write down:
   a. What most impresses them about your organization?
   b. What they would most like to see you change about what your organization does or how it operates?

Coaching point: *Depending on the make-up of your focus group, not every-one may be familiar with the term "Mission Statement." You might consider* *asking them to simply write down what they believe your organizational "Purpose" is. Or you could ask them our questions: What do we do, Who do we do it for, and Why does it matter? Choose the question format that best suits the audience.*

With this new feedback in hand, you should share it with the leadership team who helped build the context map and mission statement, inviting them to reflect on the discrepancies that may exist between intent and perception.

How Do We Produce Better Alignment?

Having heard the candid input from the "outside" world, it becomes possible to create a GAP Analysis, between how we see ourselves and how others see us. The template in Table 2.2 is provided for that purpose.

The *Mission Element* column uses the three key sections of our mission statement template. The *How We See Ourselves* column should reflect how our organizational leaders see us based on how they interpret the mission statement. *How We Are Perceived by Others* comes from the focus group responses. The *Key Gaps* column lists the main ah-ha's that come from comparing the preceding two columns. And finally, the *What We Can Do About It* column lists the strategic initiatives that could potentially close the identified gaps.

The value of this analysis is that it drives us to be deliberate about acting strategically in accordance with our true purpose. It reinforces

Table 2.2 Brand/mission gap analysis template

Mission statement:		Brand-mission gap analysis		
Mission element	How we see ourselves	How we are perceived by others	Key gaps	What we can do about it
What we do?				
Who we serve?				
Why it matters?				

Table 2.3 *Sample completed brand/mission gap analysis template*

Brand–mission gap analysis

Friars Club mission statement: *The Friars Club, a Catholic ministry, embracing Franciscan values of community and concern for the poor, bridges the social resource gap faced by at-risk boys and girls through youth sports, educational and enrichment programs to help them develop personal goals and lead successful lives.*

Mission element	How we see ourselves	How we are perceived by others	Key gaps	What we can do about it
What we do?	Provide youth sports, educational and enrichment programs	We provide youth sports programs	Little recognition that we provide non-sport oriented enrichment and education	– Engage parents and youth in program planning. – Improve communications (newsletter, web, social media).
Who we serve?	At-risk girls and boys	We serve at-risk and suburban youth, we offer nothing for kids who are not interested in sports	Non athletic programming? Do we need different programs for our two main youth audiences?	– Expand -portfolio of program offerings non sports teaching, leadership, life skills). – Program expansion in suburban zip codes to generate money needed to support inner city activities.
Why it matters?	Bridges the social resource gap, enabling youth to develop personal goals, preparing them, for life success	Kids can have fun. (popular comment from. suburban, respondents) and develop their sports skills. Inner city respondents like that we give their kids a place to play as schools are cutting back on. extracurricular sports activities.	Little recognition that we are seeking to develop leadership, provide educational enrichment, or teach life success skills. There may be differing needs between our two athlete audiences.	–Add youth mentoring program to help at-risk kids – Launch assessment tool to measure program impact – Improve communications (newsletter, web, social media)

that our mission is not a good-intentioned wish, but a conscious decision about what we want to be, who we wish to serve, and what benefits we strive to deliver. Mission is about making choices, and then backing them up with strategic initiatives (What We Can Do About It), that apply resources in ways intended to produce specific outcomes that make our organization more effective.

Table 2.3 is a sample BRAND–MISSION GAP ANALYSIS using the Friars Club as a hypothetical example.

The main point of this exercise is to generate the "What We Can Do About It" column containing viable initiatives that might help move your organization forward in pursuit of your vision, consistent with your mission purpose. You still need to put resources against and execute them, but it gives you a way to challenge your own status quo, asking deeper questions about what you are really trying to accomplish.

As you lead your team through this set of exercises, it should stimulate many interesting and powerful conversations about what matters, and what you are really trying to accomplish. By the time you are done, you should end up with a powerful list of ideas that are worthy of action. There will likely be plenty of work ahead, but it really helps to have a solid foundation around a common purpose and goals.

Key Assessment Questions

Here are some questions for you to consider within your own organization:

1. Do you feel the mission statement is useful and appropriate for your organization in making decisions about which initiatives, investments, and programs are most important?
   a. Is it relevant in the face of the environmental forces, trends, and needs you see today in your community?
   b. Does it help clarify what choices you are making about who you will serve, and how?
2. To what degree is your mission clearly understood by members of the Board, your paid staff, and key volunteers?

    a. Would your constituents ("customers") be able to guess your intended mission purpose based on how they see the organization operate on a daily basis?

3. How strong a case can you make that your organization actually delivers on the "brand promise" implied by your mission?

    a. Do you have evidence supporting whether you are delivering what you say you will?

4. Are there initiatives or programs that you have that do not seem to be aligned with the mission?

5. How can we launch a process that improves upon existing programs/initiatives or creates new ones and how can we determine whether it is successful?

Notes

1. Friars Club (2010).
2. HBR Interview (2007, July–August), p. 10.
3. Basadur (2010).
4. Buzan (2012).
5. Gray (2010); Grove Consultants International (2012).
6. Adapted from Grove Consultants International.
7. Gray (2010).

References

Basadur, M. (2010). *How we do it*. Retrieved from Basadur Applied Creativity: www.basadur.com/howwedoit/An8StepProcess/tabid/82/Default.aspx

Buzan, T. (2012). *Mind maps: A powerful approach to note-taking*. Retrieved August 10, 2013, from Mind Tools: http://www.mindtools.com/pages/article/newISS_01.htm

Friars Club. (2010). *Our mission*. Retrieved August 15, 2013, from Friars Club of Cincinnati: http://www.friarsclubinc.org/about.html

Gray, D. (2010). *Context map*. Retrieved September 2, 2013, from Gamestorming: http://www.gogamestorm.com/?p=366%20NOTE

Grove Consultants International. (2012). *Context map*. Retrieved July 12, 2012, from The Grove Consultants International: http://store.grove.com/product_details.html?productid=7

HBR Interview. (2007, July–August). Lessons from Toyota's Long Drive: An interview with Katsuaki Watanabe. *Harvard Business Review* (Reprint R0207E), p. 10.

CHAPTER 3

Noses In, Fingers Out

The Board's Role in Achieving Success

Dick Aft

Dick Aft is President of Philanthropic Leadership, a consulting group that offers personal support to volunteer and professional leaders of nonprofit organizations. His 14-year term as President of the United Way of Greater Cincinnati completed 40 years as a nonprofit executive in 9 different cities. He serves on the boards of professional, arts, educational, and health-service organizations.

All too often, the roles and responsibilities of Board of Directors and their members are viewed as distinct from, rather than integral to, all functions of nonprofit and faith-based organizations. Boards share a unique, but equal responsibility for the success of organizations that they serve. Similarly, when Board members are at their best, they function within *A Virtuous Cycle in Nonprofit Organization Success* (see Figure 1.1) and, therefore, contribute significantly to the achievement of the missions of their organizations.

The purpose of this chapter is to help readers

- work more effectively as a member of a Board;
- compare traditional Board responsibilities with "out of the box" Board roles;
- identify the characteristics of Board members that would best serve your organization;

- establish performance standards for members of Boards;
- use skill-building exercises to help Boards with which you are involved.

Helpful tools for readers and the Boards with which they are involved are also included in this chapter. They provide easy ways to put these tools into practice. One is a simple exercise for Board members to communicate and learn about the variety of ways in which they are involved in the organization. Another is the Love Your Neighbor Center example that offers each reader an opportunity to consider ways to increase Board members' participation and effectiveness.

Introduction to the Love Your Neighbor Center

The Love Your Neighbor Center is known to everyone in the neighborhood as "C." This nonprofit organization was created with the mission of providing daytime and evening services to the elderly residents of its neighborhood.

For decades, "C" served the neighborhood's large population of older adults who wanted a place to gather during the day and enjoy recreational activity during the evenings. Nightly Bingo games attracted scores of them to the Center. Prizes were donated by local merchants. Operators of the games were "C" volunteers. Income from Bingo offset most of "C's" program expenses.

The neighborhood was changing quickly. Families with young children were moving in replacing the older residents. With fewer older people in the neighborhood, the space needed for daytime recreation decreased and "C" was able to open a child care center to meet the needs of its new residents. But, change in the ages of neighborhood residents was resulting in a decrease in the number of people who had interest in playing Bingo. Income was dropping fast. Expenses were remaining the same.

Two key questions faced the "C" Board: What steps would be necessary to balance the budget? What changes in the mission of the center need to be considered?

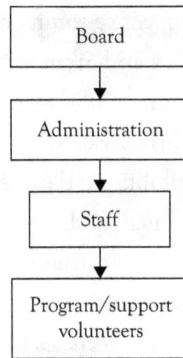

Figure 3.1 Hierarchical table of organization

Roles and Responsibilities of Boards

Noses in. Fingers out!" That is the concise way that Dr. George Pruitt, President of Thomas Edison State College, often describes Board members' responsibilities. Traditional levels of responsibility within nonprofit and faith-based organizations are presented in Figure 3.1 as a hierarchical table of organization

This format is meant to portray relative authority, but omits responsibility. By its "top-down" structure, it also perpetuates a myth about the relative importance of various responsibilities with organizations.

Ten traditional responsibilities of Boards have been identified by BoardSource[1] as follows:

1. **"Determine the organization's mission and purpose.** It is the Board's responsibility to create and review a statement of mission and purpose that articulates the organization's goals, means and primary constituents served." This is often done at special annual or biennial meetings. Productive agendas include the following:

   a. A review of the environment in which the organization operates

   b. Information about the organization's program objectives and impact

   c. Consideration of feedback from key stakeholders, including such groups as clients, staff, funders, and Board members

    d. Retrospective and prospective comments from the Chief Executive

    e. A review of the Mission and Strategic Plans of the organization

    f. Revisions of the Mission and Strategic Plan, as appropriate

2. **"Select the Chief Executive.** Boards must reach consensus on the Chief Executive's responsibilities and undertake a careful search to find the most qualified individual for the position." Moreover, the Board needs to establish and maintain teamwork with its Chief Executive that is based upon clear designations of the responsibilities of each.

3. **"Provide proper financial oversight.** The Board must assist in developing the annual budget and ensuring that proper controls are in place." The function is usually led by an individual or committee with experience and capacity in financial management. Beyond general fiduciary responsibility, this aspect of the Board's responsibility should anticipate increased governmental scrutiny not unlike the Sarbanes-Oxley requirements of corporate board members.[2]

4. **"Ensure adequate resources.** One of the Board's foremost responsibilities is to provide adequate resources for the organization to fulfill its mission." As a minimum, all Board members of nonprofit and faith-based organizations are expected to make financial contributions to the organization. Many employers match such giving by their employees. The percentage of Board members who financially support the organization is a common question asked by most grant-making organizations. Beyond personal giving, Board members should participate in organizational fund-raising campaigns and open doors for the Chief Executive and other staff to meet with prospective contributors.

5. **"Ensure legal and ethical responsibility and maintain accountability.** The Board is ultimately responsible for ensuring adherence to legal standards and ethical norms." This includes any statements disclosing any conflicts of interest that could affect the board members' abilities to carry out their responsibilities. **NOTE:** *Disclosure is informational and generally does not require more than abstention from voting on Board matters that involve conflicts.*

6. **"Ensure effective organizational planning.** Boards must actively participate in an overall planning process and assist in implementing and monitoring the plan's goals" (see 1 on previous page).

7. **"Recruit and orient new Board members and assess Board performance.** All Boards have a responsibility to articulate prerequisites for candidates, orient new members and periodically evaluate their own performance." In general, Boards seek to involve people with keen interests in the work of the organization. Attention is usually given to the degree to which financial, political, or programmatic stakeholders should serve as Board members. The gender, racial, ethnic, income, age, education, and geographic diversities should also be considered.

8. **"Enhance the organization's public standing.** The Board should clearly articulate the organization's mission, accomplishments, and goals to the public and garner support from the community." People who are not on the Board will often reach conclusions about the organization based on information from Board members. Many organizations equip their Board members with informational "handouts" or 30-second "elevator speeches" to support Board members' fulfillment of this responsibility.

9. **"Determine, monitor and strengthen the organization's programs and services.** The Board's responsibility is to determine which programs are consistent with the organization's missions and to monitor their effectiveness" (also part of 1 on page 31).

10. **"Support the Chief Executive and assess his or her performance.** The Board should ensure that the Chief Executive officer has the moral and professional support he or she needs to further the goals of the organization." The office of Chief Executive, **regardless of the person who occupies it**, is seen by most people as the leader of the organization. Just as partners in business partnerships, Boards and Chief Executives of nonprofit or faith-based organizations have some distinct responsibilities. They also share some. It is important that all of these responsibilities be reviewed regularly and communicated openly. Boards generally conduct annual performance and compensation reviews of their Chief Executives. Many Boards, with their Chief Executives' involvement, also conduct annual reviews of Board performance. These questions are critical to both:

    a. What performance improvements should be made to increase the organization's ability to achieve its Mission?

b. How might the Board and Chief Executive change their behaviors to increase the capacity of one another and the organization to continuously improve performance?

Twenty-First Century Board Responsibilities Are Moving "Outside the Boxes"

The increased importance placed on the work that nonprofit and faith-based organizations carry out on behalf of their constituents has resulted in addition of responsibilities for many Boards:

1. **Maintaining transparency.** The concept of "transparency" for non governmental organizations (NGOs) was first articulated in post-Soviet countries during the 1990s. In brief, this kind of transparency calls for open access to all but confidential personnel and client records. In many cases, disclosure of financial and governance information required by Federal reporting Form 990 may not satisfy the public's perceived right to know.

2. **Reporting measurable impact.** Until the end of the 20th century, most organizations identified themselves by *what* they did. Today, Boards are increasingly responsible for seeing that their organizations report the *impact* of their work on community conditions or the lives of the people they serve.

Some Board Members Perform Nontraditional Functions

Organizations' size or culture often determine whether additional responsibilities are carried out by staff or by Board members. Many organizations expect Board members to roll up their sleeves and become engaged in voluntarily doing work traditionally done by paid staff members. Examples include child care on "Mother's Day Out," serving meals in homeless or elderly multiservice centers, or pouring concrete foundations for new homes. The growing number of community service partnerships and collaborative efforts often requires more professional staff time than is available. Many of the community-level meetings have come to welcome volunteer representatives of nonprofit and faith-based organizations. In additional to adding value to the organization's operations, these functions contribute to Board members' fulfillment of their traditional responsibility. For many, they also contribute to the joys of volunteer service.

Regardless of the ways in which each Board member fulfills his or her role, the smoothest performance of the total organization occurs when every person within the organization, including Board members, understands his or her own responsibilities and those of others.

Exploring the Nontraditional Involvement of Your Board Members

Your Board may find value in this simple exercise.

First—Reproduce Figure 3.2 on a flip chart or white board.

Second—Ask each member of the Board to put his or her name into the sector of the chart that represents their current involvement with the organization.

Third—Discuss

  a. the values and limitations of involvement beyond Board membership;
  b. issues that may arise related to involvement beyond Board membership;

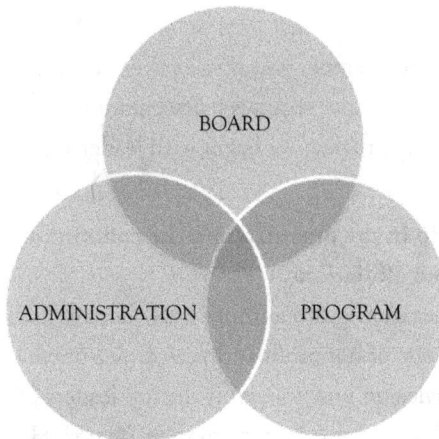

Figure 3.2 Sectors of board member involvement

c. any need to adopt Board policies regarding conflicts of interest that might result from the involvement of Board members in non-Board roles.

Members' Characteristics and Attributes Influence a Board's Capacity to Fulfill Its Responsibilities

Characteristics

Does your Board include people who understand the needs of your clients from personal experience? Does the Board include at least one member who could introduce your Chief Executive to important grant-makers? Can key stakeholders identify people on the Board whom they can call when they have questions?

Questions such as these need to be kept in mind when reviewing Board membership, especially by those responsible for identifying and recruiting new members. In addition, every member of a Board **must** be committed to the organization's mission.

In his classic nonprofit exploration, *Managing the Non-Profit Organization*, Peter Drucker helps us understand why these rules exist. "Mission and leadership are not just things to read about, to listen to." he wrote. "They are things to do something about. Things that you can, and should, convert from good intentions and from knowledge into effective action, not next year, but tomorrow morning."[3] Belief in this must begin with each and every Board member.

Not every Board member will possess every characteristic, but excellence in Board performance requires representation of all of the following characteristics. Like Drucker, we begin with leadership:

- **Leadership in the organization, the community, business or personal affiliations.**
  Many times during this author's experience as a United Way CEO, leaders of nonprofit and faith-based organizations sought advice on how to recruit the top leaders of businesses, foundations, and government to their Boards. How to do it? Get them involved before they become leaders. Opportunities

for talented people to develop their leadership skills arise as much where they volunteer as at their place of employment.

Drucker's view of leadership serves as good advice for nominating committees as they search for Board candidates with fully developed leadership skills. He observes that service opportunities in nonprofit and faith-based organizations help people become leaders. "Developing yourself begins by *serving*." he says. "Leaders are not born, nor are they made—they are self-made."[4]

- **Capacity to give or get** substantial contributions.
  Some Boards follow the "pay to play" axiom, requiring members to make substantial financial contributions. Most nonprofit and faith-based organizations do not. Rather, they ask their Board members to make financial commitments consistent with their ability and to solicit the financial support of others.

  It is not unusual for organizations to specify amounts of money that each Board member is expected to "give *or* get." Many Boards ask their members to "give *and* get" financial support. Above all, Board members must be mindful that most funding organizations request and consider information on the percentage of Board members who make financial contributions to the organization. All Board members are expected to give.

- **Diversity and inclusiveness.**
  Just as "variety is the spice of life," diversity is the spice of organizational leadership. Most nonprofit and faith-based organizations are responsible to represent that thinking of more than one constituency. Survival of each organization is built upon the Board's understanding of the diverse perspectives that are required to do its job.

- **Connectedness to others in the community whose knowledge and support of the organization are important.**
  You are known by the company you keep. Many outsiders who are important to your organization look at Board lists to see whom they know. Connectedness of that nature can result in increased access to financial and other support. Equally important is connectedness to outside individuals and organizations that have a stake in your achievement of your mission.

All nonprofit and faith-based organizations share several stakeholder groups. They include clients who are directly served by the organization, publics that directly or indirectly benefit from the services or the organization, individuals and organizations that give time or money to the organization, and regulating organizations. Other stakeholders may include groups such as religious organizational affiliates, governmental organizations, community foundations, labor unions, and staff members.

Finally, essential and self-explanatory characteristics of all Board members are a commitment to attend and participate in most, if not all, meetings, a willingness to represent the organization in the community, and personal and professional integrity.

Attributes

The Australian nonprofit support organization named "**conscious governance**" suggests a number of Board member attributes that will offer balance to the Board's decision-making capacity. Among them are the ability to ask probing questions, the conscious seeking of truth, a willingness to accept intuition, an understanding of risks and consequences, an ability to consider multiple scenarios, and a willingness to confront facts and mistakes. Board members should ask strategic questions. (Why are we doing this, how expansive will this be for our organization, and how does it fit within our vision and strategic plan?), one or more Board members who are ready to raise ethical considerations (Are there any issues of rights, obligations, fairness, or integrity in what we plan or do?), and one or more who closely monitor compliance issues (What do our constitution, relevant laws, funding guidelines, and any relevant code of ethics require from us?). They should value Board members who are not easily influenced by others, are not always dependent on a collegial atmosphere, and who seek independent verification of information provided to them.[5]

> Seldom are the memberships of nonprofit or faith-based organizations' Boards ideal. The very best Boards, however, continuously seek to improve members' fulfillment of responsibilities. Also, they include people whose characteristics and attributes give energy, balance, integrity, and Mission focus to their important work.

Living the mission
Needed services are provided.
Individuals, families, neighborhoods
and communities are better off.

Caring about people
Success is celebrated.
Coaching and guidance become
common place.
Fear of change is lessened.

Getting things done
Individuals and organizations
collaborate.
Accountability is expected.
Respect is earned.

Making good decisions
Realities are understood.
New approaches are tried.
Impact is increased.

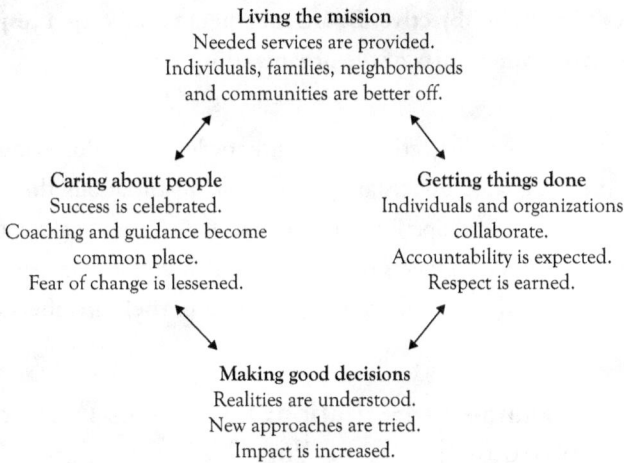

Figure 3.3 Results when all parties do their jobs

Board Roles, Responsibilities, Characteristics, and Attributes Within the *Virtuous* Cycle

Fulfilling its responsibilities is the Board's way of enhancing each non-profit and faith-based organization's *Virtual Cycle*. When the Board does its unique job, and administrators, program staff, and other volunteers do theirs, good things happen as shown in Figure 3.3.

Some Common Myths—True or False?

The Board is the most important group in any nonprofit or faith-based organization. FALSE.

Most people equate certain types of responsibility with importance. In his "New York Times" feature, Peter Bryant observed, "So when a leader walks into the room, everyone else's status goes down, everyone's certainty goes down, everyone's autonomy goes down."[6] But, that is not the case with nonprofit or faith-based organizations. **Each group: Board members, administrators, program staff members, and volunteers are of importance to the total function of the organizations. The work of each is important!**

In order to remain objective, Board members must keep a respectful distance from other parts of the organization. FALSE.

Some of the most objective and most knowledgeable Board members gain valuable understanding of their organizations through past or current participation in other areas of organizational responsibility. "Noses in. Fingers out." are rules that communicate *ways* **Boards should work, not the involvement of their members.**

Case Example Organization: Challenges Faced by the Board of the "Love Your Neighbor Center"

A Concise Illustration of a Board's Role in Achieving Success

After reviewing the balance sheet of the Love Your Neighbor Center, known locally as the "C," you would be positive that it was a nonprofit organization. It was. After observing Board members' search for a financial miracle, you might think that the "C" was faith based. That is for each reader to decide.

Like the Boards of many organizations, the "C" Board confronted operating budget problems. By observing a brief portion of "C's" Board meeting, then reviewing the telling statements made by those at the meeting, the reader can take part in this Board's effort to achieve success. Don't be surprised if you find that simply increasing income will not resolve the problems. It seldom does.

NOTE: While this mini-case presentation is based on the actual experience of an organization, its name has been changed.

That evening's Board meeting was being conducted over coffee at the "C." The Chief Executive had excused himself so that he could fill in for the volunteer Bingo caller who had just moved from the neighborhood.

The Board Chair opened the meeting. "This month's business is the same as last month's business. But this month, things are worse," he said. "Unless we find a way to increase income from our Bingo games, we'll have to close the child care program."

"Some of us contribute money to the 'C'," said a long-time Board member. "Isn't that enough?"

"Time and time again, we've voiced our hopes that our Chief Executive would solve this problem, but he hasn't," commented another.

The youngest Board member wondered if she should speak directly with the program staff member responsible for the Bingo program. "I could probably get better results than our Chief Executive is getting," she added.

Having no interest in finances, the oldest Board member slept.

Another Board member said nothing. He hadn't spoken since the Board voted down his motion that his son, a sociology professor, conduct a survey of neighborhood needs for "C" services.

Having overheard the discussion, the young woman serving coffee, a volunteer with a child in "C's" child care program, put down her tray. She startled Board members by asking a question. "Why don't you ask us parents of children in the 'C's' child care programs for our thoughts about how to solve your problem?"

"Out of order!" said a Board member. "Have her removed!" whispered another. "Just a minute," said Board Chair. "She may have a point. I'd like us to listen to her thoughts."

Thus ensued a discussion that resulted in a turnaround for the "C's" program and budget. It resulted in a change of Mission, Board membership, program, and financial support. **BINGO!**

How well does your Board deal with the issues such as those faced by the Love Your Neighbor Center Board?
"C" Board member: "Today's major item of business wasn't new: how to increase attendance at the 'C's' Bingo's games."

- Does the Board's agenda reflect changing times and changing stakeholders?

  Change, of course, is constant. But it's also a business necessity. In response to complex and fast-moving marketplace realities, companies increasingly have no choice but to make sometimes drastic changes.—Deborah Schroeder-Saulnier[7]

  "C" Board member: "Some of us contribute money to the 'C'."

- Do all members of the Board make financial contributions?

  You can't do the Lord's work if you are broke. Service on a Board requires some amount of financial support by every member. Without evidence of 100% Board giving, many foundations won't let you in the door.—Danny Ransohoff[8]

"C" Board member: "Time and time again, we've discussed our hopes that our Chief Executive would solve this problem, but he hasn't."

- Are regular discussions held with the Chief Executive regarding job performance issues?

The Board is responsible for giving good advice and ultimately taking action if things get out of whack.—Terry Lee[9]

"C" Board member: The youngest Board member wondered if she should speak directly with the program staff member responsible for the Bingo program.

- Should members of the Board speak directly with program staff members when dissatisfied with a supervisor's management of program?

No. The greatest temptation of most outdoor ministry boards is to micro-manage the day-to-day operations of the organization. The temptation is great because the love for the ministry is great and board members feel a tremendous sense of responsibility for making sure that everything goes well. Unfortunately, the actions of the board often have the opposite effect, creating a climate of confusion and mistrust between board and staff. Conflicts between a board and the staff executive are frequently focused on the confusion over the role of each within the life of the organization. When board members become overly involved, it's normal for staff to feel undervalued and not respected for the expertise and experience they bring to the job. It also disrupts the normal flow of communication and decision-making between everyone involved.—Mark D. Burkhardt[10]

"C" Board member: Having no interest in finances, the oldest Board member slept.

- Does every member of the Board share the Board's fiduciary responsibility?

Not every Board member can be a financial wizard. Every Board member, however, needs to be a financial inquisitor.—BoardSource[11]

"C" Board member: He hadn't spoken since the Board voted down his motion that his son, a sociology professor, conduct a survey of neighborhood needs for "C" services.

- Do Board members annually complete and abide by Conflict of Interest disclosure statements?

Often people are unaware that their activities are in conflict with the best interests of the nonprofit so a goal for many organizations is to simply raise awareness and cultivate a 'culture of candor.' It is helpful to take time at a board meeting annually to discuss the types of situations that could result in a conflict between the best interests of the nonprofit —and the self-interest of a staff member or board member.—National Council of Nonprofits[12]

"C" Board member: "Why don't you ask us parents of children in the 'C's' child care programs for our thoughts about how to solve your problems?"

- Have you defined your organization's key stakeholders? Do you reach outside the Board for opinions and ideas that might increase the relevancy of mission and program?

One of the first steps in marketing for the nonprofit institution is to define [its] markets, its publics.—Peter Drucker[13]

"C" Board member: "She may have a point there. Let's talk about it."

- Are Board discussions open to new perspectives? Is it possible to question the things that have "always been done that way?"

In many transformation efforts, the core of the old culture is not incompatible with the new vision, although some specific norms will be. In that case, the challenge will be to graft new practices onto the old roots while killing off the inconsistent pieces.—John P. Kotter[14]

"C" Board: "Thus ensued a discussion that resulted in a turn-around for the 'C.' It resulted in a change of mission, Board membership, program, and financial support."

- What changes in the mission statement of organizations with which you are involved would be consistent with the changes going on around it? What changes in the Board's membership or budget would be appropriate? How might staff effectiveness be increased?

Every nonprofit organization should measure its progress in fulfilling its mission, its success in mobilizing its resources, and its staff's effectiveness on the job.—John Sawhill and David Williamson[15]

So much for the Board's role in achieving success. Keep in mind that exercises like these prompted Peter Drucker to often observe: "Plans for change are nothing until they degenerate into work." He wrote: "It is indeed simple to make nonprofits effective. It does not require miracles—it needs will and work."[16] And the work begins with each organization's Mission. Read on!

Key Assessment Questions

1. What things should your Board review each year to be sure that it is fulfilling its responsibilities?
2. What words would you use to describe the relationships among and between your Board members, your Chief Executive officer, and your organization's key stakeholders? (What words would you *like* to use?)
3. How does your Board continuously learn to better carry out its responsibilities?
4. What characteristics or attributes would you use to describe your organization's Board?
5. How would stakeholders who are not represented on the Board describe its characteristics or attributes?

Notes

1. BoardSource (2003).
2. Independent Sector (2008).
3. Drucker (1990b), p. 49.

4. Drucker (1990b), p. 222.
5. Leadership Tools (2013).
6. Bryant (2013).
7. Schroeder-Saulnier (2009).
8. Known for his ability to capture paragraphs of advice in short sentences, Dr. Daniel J. Ransohoff was both Special Projects Director of the United Way of Great Cincinnati and a member of the faculty of the University of Cincinnati's College of Design, Architecture, Art and Planning from 1958 until 1993.
9. Schultz (2001), p. 162.
10. Burkhardt (2013).
11. BoardSource (2013).
12. National Council of Nonprofits (2013).
13. Drucker (1990b), pp. 73–84, 89–94.
14. Kotter (1996), p. 15.
15. Sawhill and Williamson (2013).
16. Drucker (1990a).

References

BoardSource. (2003). *Basic responsibilities of nonprofit boards*. Retrieved April 12, 2013, from BoardSource: http://www.boardsource.org

BoardSource. (2013). *Fiduciary responsibilities of board members*. Retrieved April 11, 2013, from BoardSource: http://www.boardsource.org

Bryant, A. (2013, March 24). Corner office: David Rock. *New York Times*, p. 28.

Burkhardt, M. D. (2013). *Board micromanagement*. Retrieved April 15, 2013, from Evangelical Lutheran Church in America: http://www.elca.org

Drucker, P. F. (1990a). Lessons for successful nonprofit Governance. *Nonprofit Management and Leadership, 1*(1), 7–14.

Drucker, P. F. (1990b). *Managing the non-profit organization*. New York, NY: Harper Collins.

Independent Sector. (2008). *Sarbanes-Oxley Act and implications for nonprofits*. Retrieved April 15, 2013, from The Independent Sector: http://www.independentsector.org

Kotter, J. P. (1996). *Leading change*. Boston, MA: Harvard Business School Press.

Leadership Tools. (2013). *Conscious governance*. Retrieved April 12, 2013, from Leadership Tools: http://www.conscious-governance.com/nonprofit-leadership-tools.html

National Council of Nonprofits. (2013). *Conflict of interest*. Retrieved April 12, 2013, from National Council of Nonprofits: http://www.councilofnonprofits

Sawhill, J., & Williamson, D. (2013). *Measuring what matters in nonprofits.* McKinsey Quarterly.

Schroeder-Saulnier, D. (2009). *Organizational effectiveness,* responding to change with agility. Retrieved January 3, 2010, from Right Management: http://www.linkageinc.com

Schultz, S. E. (2001). *The board book.* New York, NY: American Management Association.

Helpful Sources of Additional Information on the Board's Role in Achieving Success

"Capacity Building Tools for Faith-Based and Community Organizations," Achive.acf.hhs.gov/programs/ocs/ccf/resources/toolkit.html

"Free Management Library" (Online Integrated Library for Personal, Professional and Organizational Help), www.Managementhelp.org

GuideStar, "Three Fundraising Realities Every Board Member Must Face" (2013), http://www.guidestar.org/rxa/news/articles/2013/fundraising-realities-for-board-members.aspx

Blue avocado, practical productive and fun food for thought for nonprofits, "The Trouble with 'Passion for the Mission'" (2013), http://www.blueavocado.org/node/806

CHAPTER 4

Walking the Talk

Serving Stakeholders With Ethics, Values, and Good Governance

Ann Marie Tracey

Ann Marie Tracey is Co-Director of the Cintas Center for Business Ethics and Associate Professor of Legal Studies and Business Ethics at the Williams College of Business, Xavier University. She previously served as an assistant U.S. attorney, an Ohio Common Pleas Court judge, and Chair of the Ohio Ethics Commission.

Introduction

Nonprofit organizations, whether faith-based or service-oriented, are driven by a commitment to principles or clients. Such altruism and good intentions are great foundation components for a values-based culture in your organization. A nonprofit's faith or service orientation, though, will not ensure an ethical culture or good governance. Nonprofits face all the challenges that for-profit organizations face, and then some. The news media is replete with stories of a wide range of unethical and even criminal behavior occurring in the nonprofit venue. Many factors can facilitate this, ranging from a vague mission or purpose to the economy and technology.

The good news is that by implementing strategies to maintain a workplace culture of strong ethics, you can reduce the risks of unethical behavior and amplify the benefits of maintaining a values-based organization. A values-based culture starts with good governance; it is an essential component to good functioning. It is the way an organization engages its leadership, employees, and operations in a manner that influences behavior and how "business is done."

In the for-profit corporate world, governance must focus on the fiduciary duty to owners and *share*holders. Nonprofit organizations are not so constrained. They can readily widen their circle to embrace *stake*holders such as clients/members, the community, funding sources, and volunteers. By serving them in an ethical culture with shared values, your organization can not only fulfill its mission, but maximize its success as well.

Purpose

The purpose of this chapter is to help you

1. *Articulate the Benefits* of establishing good governance and a values-based, ethical culture;
2. *Recognize the Challenges* to maintaining a values-based culture that nonprofits face;
3. *Implement Proactive Strategies* to succeed in establishing a values-based organization that will enhance its performance while fulfilling its mission.

Introduction to Talbert House

What is the "Value of Values" in an increasingly challenging and rapidly changing environment? Cincinnati, Ohio's Talbert House confronts this question head-on. A provider of addiction-related services, Talbert House faces a daily diet of regulatory, legal, and funding challenges with respect to its 32 programs and more than 80,000 clients. It has integrated key components discussed in this chapter to develop and maintain an ethical, values-based organization. Its success and leadership in addiction and mental health services clearly addresses the import of values-based governance in a nonprofit organization.

The State of Ethics at the Workplace

It is tempting to think that service-oriented nonprofit or faith-based organizations will not face ethical challenges, and will not experience employee misconduct or downright criminal behavior. Certainly the organization's mission will cause employees and volunteers to align their actions with the organization's mission. Would that this were true! Any type of organization is subject to unethical or even illegal conduct, including nonprofits. Every day there are reports of embezzlement and theft from every kind of nonprofit organization, ranging from the YWCA, churches, schools, memorial funds, and children's softball leagues. A 2010 estimate places the annual loss to the nonprofit sector as a result of fraud at $85 billion.[1]

Noncriminal but still unethical conduct can also infiltrate a nonprofit and detract from its mission. Some relate to contracts, such as employees receiving "incentive payments," *that is*, kickbacks, from contractors and vendors, or engaging in self-dealing. Such practices can lead to pricey contracts and substandard products or services. Deceptive fund-raising practices, conflicts of interest, illegal campaign contributions, health and safety violations, credit card abuse, and anti-competitive practices can cause real headaches for an organization and undermine its culture. Other less troublesome, but still problematic behavior occurs and can be detrimental: using company resources for private purposes, Internet abuse, misusing company time, bullying, and lying.

Every 2 years the Ethics Resource Center (ERC) conducts the National Business Ethics Survey (NBES), a nationally representative survey of employees in the United States at all levels with respect to their view of ethics and compliance in their workplace. Its latest survey[2] produced what the ERC deemed "extreme" results: "ethics in corporate America are in transition." While fewer employees reported witnessing misconduct, and more reported it, there were important negative indicators:

- 45% of workers observed misconduct; 65% reported it.
- Retaliation against whistleblowers is at an all-time high.
- More employees reported perceived pressure to compromise their standards.
- More employees view supervisors' ethics negatively.

In addition, 42% of employees responding to the survey reported that their business had a weak ethics culture, the highest level since 2000.

The survey revealed that the economy and technology (especially social media) played an important role in this shift, in surprising ways:

- There is an inverse relationship between the economy and ethical conduct. As the economy improves, and people feel more optimistic, misconduct and failure to report it *increase*.
- Active social networkers are "much more likely" to feel pressure to compromise ethics standards than those that are less active online. They also more readily tolerate questionable activities, like keeping copies of confidential work documents. (And less active social networkers are more likely to face retaliation for reporting misconduct.)

And, as an NBES supplemental report revealed, "the younger the worker, the more likely they are to feel pressure, observe misconduct, and experience retaliation for reporting." The youngest workers were "significantly more likely to experience" retaliation for reporting misconduct than older workers.

Erosion of ethics in the workplace can have a profound impact on the organization. It can face criminal investigations and prosecutions (in either the victim or perpetrator role), financial loss, and collateral damage to employees in the form of poor employee morale, staff turnover, and decreased productivity. Unethical behavior affects the organization externally as well. Reports of misconduct swiftly erode its public "face." Loss of reputation can sink any nonprofit or faith-based organization in a heartbeat. Dependent on community support, volunteer involvement, and financial contributions ("no margin, no mission"), nonprofits simply cannot afford a tarnished reputation. In sum, the drawbacks of unethical conduct in the workplace are profound.

The Benefits of Maintaining a Workplace Culture of Strong Ethics

There is a direct correlation between organizational culture and misconduct: where the ethics culture is weaker, the level of misconduct is more prevalent. The good news: prioritizing ethics and shared values can minimize unethical conduct and greatly enhance a nonprofit's success. As the NBES report also notes, "If business leaders will take heed of these findings and make ethics a business priority, they can have a dramatic impact on the conduct of their workforce."

The benefits of creating and maintaining an ethics and values-based organization are many. They include

- protecting the integrity of finances and the quality of goods and services;
- sustaining and enhancing employee morale and productivity;
- aligning all organizational members with its mission and values;
- developing and maintaining a reputation for transparency and trustworthiness;
- building and retaining quality, mission-focused employees, and board members;
- increased donations to fund the mission;
- mitigating risk.

To reap these and other rewards, it is essential that the nonprofit organization identify obstacles to an ethical, values-based climate. It must then develop proactive strategies to integrate ethics, values, and good governance in the way it does business every day.

Challenges to Maintaining a Values-Based Culture

Nonprofit organizations face the same challenges to a values and ethics-driven culture as do for-profits. These include limited resources (time, money, and personnel), a competitive marketplace, a troublesome economy, too much power placed in one person, and a changing regulatory environment, to name a few. There can also be a lack of board of director involvement and insufficient oversight. Employees are reluctant to report problems or bad behavior.

Nonprofit organizations also may share many challenges that small businesses encounter, such as limited staff and an operating budget too small to have a compliance/ethics officer. Smaller companies may not devote sufficient resources to internal controls and financial oversight. Managers in smaller organizations also may lack the knowledge to develop an adequate strategy to promote an ethical culture.

Many factors can interfere with an organization's "living" its mission and integrating its values, regardless of whether it is a Fortune 500 company or a small nonprofit. These can include the following:

- Lack of leadership
- Weak corporate culture
- Vague mission or purpose
- Lax hiring and training practices
- Not making ethics and values a top priority
- Failure to identify risk
- Inadequate review and oversight
- Complex organizational structure
- A "hands off" board
- Inadequate (or no) policies regarding self-dealing, vendor relationships, and company resources
- No strong antiretaliation policies

While all organizations may share many ethics and related challenges, nonprofits can encounter others that are unique to them. First, there is the tendency to believe that because the organization is nonprofit, everyone is on board with the organization's mission and therefore behavior will always support it. Because clients have legitimate, critical needs, management or employees may rationalize questionable behavior, such as improperly providing a diagnostic code so that health insurance will cover a client's essential treatment. There also may be a belief that the mission is more important than following "the rules"; the ends justify the means.

Concerns extend beyond the nonprofit's employees. Unlike forprofits, volunteers are often integral to a nonprofit's functioning, yet lack formal orientation or training. At the same time, they may have access to funds and confidential information without the proper screening or knowledge to handle either. Board members may have their hearts in the right place but lack the necessary expertise to ensure good governance and financial responsibility. There may be a complicated regulatory environment, such as Talbert House experiences in the health-service industry.

In addition, the difficulty of operating in a tight economy hits nonprofit organizations particularly hard. Sources of funding are through private individual/agency contributions, and governments (tax levies) where there is too much demand and too few resources. There is external scrutiny and accountability, making ethical conduct and strong governance even more important.

Proactive Strategies for an Ethics and Values-Based Organizational Culture

Obstacles can thwart attempts to establish and maintain a values-based entity. However, organizations can take steps to develop and maintain practices that incorporate mission, vision, and values into the way it does business. A "mission statement," declares the core purposes and values the organization espouses. (*See* Len Brzozowski's Chapter 2 of this book, Developing and Living Your Mission; it is a great resource for defining your organization's mission.) After that, cultivating an ethical culture begins with developing clear policies, continues with hiring and training employees, and extends to leadership in the executive office or boardroom, even if the latter is simply an available spot in a church lunchroom.

Key Strategies on Which to Focus

1. Clear Policies and Expectations

   In addition to what is contained in the mission statement, it is critical to articulate agency-specific well-defined expectations concerning employee behavior. These should be both aspirational and instructive. The latter should include what constitutes misconduct, how to report it, and firm nonretaliation policies when employees communicate concerns.

2. Employee Hiring, Orientation, Training, and Promotion
   • *Hiring.* Many organizations now "hire for character." Doing background checks and verifying recommendations and resumes are initial steps. Then add another tool to your ethics arsenal: interview to assess a candidate's grounding in ethics and values. How would he or she address a particular

thorny scenario if it confronts them? Would they consult others? How would his or her individual values factor into the decision if it differed from their supervisors' or from company policy? What if there were conflicting organizational values or directives?

- *New-employee orientation.* This is an opportunity to make crystal clear the organization's values and priorities with respect to expectations. Optimally, a member of upper management delivers this message. The conversation should not only define inappropriate conduct, but also reporting it (when, how, and to whom) and an absolute ban on retaliating against anyone who reports misconduct.

- *Ongoing training.* When was the last time you read your employee handbook or reviewed your orientation materials? You are not alone! Different perspectives and influences, not to mention complex industry and government requirements, are among the reasons that ongoing "compliance, ethics, and values" training is essential. It should be specific to the organization and industry, as well as to the employee's position. Role-play, scenarios, discussion groups, and sharing ethical dilemmas employees encounter are great ways for employees to "flex their ethical muscles." View training as an opportunity to emphasize and promote your organization's values and expectations with respect to conduct.

- *Evaluating and promoting employees.* Integrating ethics and compliance into every employee evaluation and promotion underscores the message that upholding your organizational values is a high priority.

3. Risk Assessment

Ethics and compliance challenges and landmines differ for each organization. Each organization needs to know, understand, and prepare for the areas posing the greatest risks to ethical conduct and legal compliance. For a large service provider in the health industry like Talbert House, to-the-letter compliance with Medicaid requirements is critical. Typical areas that pose risks of unacceptable or unwelcome conduct pertain to Internet and social media usage, privacy, government regulation, handling of money, contracts with vendors or clients, and financial accounting and reporting. Make sure your level of oversight is appropriate for each of your risk areas.

4. Management

   Sound stewardship by management and board members is essential to good governance and a values-based organization. *See* Dick Aft's discussion of the *Board's Role in Achieving Success* in Chapter 3 of this section. Everyone watches the leader in an organization; this is no different with nonprofits. Consequently, it is critical that management "walk the talk": they must exemplify ethical and values-based behavior "in word and deed." This is especially important in smaller operations, as are many nonprofits, where management is more visible to everyone in the company.[3]

5. Communication and Trust

   Two-way open communication and trust are essential not only to set the tone and relate the organization's values and expectations, but also to learn what is occurring "in the trenches." In a large organization, supervisors are critical to assessing the ethical climate, and employees are more likely to report problems to supervisors than to upper management. Both employees and volunteers need to know their input is encouraged and will be accepted without negative repercussions.

6. Prompt Action/Consistent Discipline

   When a report of misconduct occurs, it is essential to take swift action to investigate the conduct and determine the facts. Immediate and appropriate action must follow, with dismissal of any employee engaged in any illegal, financial, dishonest, or otherwise important breach of your organization's policies and values. The importance of the misbehaving individual to the organization is immaterial; if they can't be trusted, they can't work there. If another employee reported the conduct, a best practice is to provide feedback to the reporter. While usually you cannot discuss personnel action, you can relate that the organization conducted an investigation, made findings, and took appropriate action. This underscores for the employee that he or she did the right thing by reporting and that misconduct is unacceptable.

Incorporating each of these proactive strategies will provide your organization with a solid base to accomplish your mission, maintain your reputation, and serve your stakeholders.[4]

Ethics, Values, and Good Governance at the Talbert House

Talbert House provides mental health and addiction-related services to over 80,000 clients in six counties every year. Five service lines comprise its "external" face: Adult Behavioral Health, Community Care, Court and Corrections, Housing, and Youth Behavioral Health. By identifying risks and developing proactive strategies for maintaining a values-driven culture, the Talbert House finds it can better serve its mission and clients.

Talbert House faces the same challenges as do both for-profit and nonprofit organizations: paying competitive salaries to professional staff, turnover, "paperwork" that can overwhelm (just the 7,000 employment applications/year are daunting), including the board of directors in its governance, and reliance on both private and public dollars for funding. At the same time, Talbert has some additional challenges. It is large, operating 32 programs in as many different locations, with over 850 professional and support staff. As an addiction treatment and prevention agency receiving both public and private dollars, it faces constant scrutiny. Some clients use Talbert services as part of court-ordered treatment, or for transition from prison. Clients frequently present with a myriad of diagnoses and social and financial issues. Billing issues abound with new Medicaid reimbursement protocols.

Talbert House has confronted head-on the "thought trap" that because it is a service organization it will not have ethics issues. Instead, its strategic approach to ethics, values, and governance is designed to instill and deserve confidence in its operations.

Mission Vision Values

The touchstone of Talbert's governance approach is the set of principles that guide everything Talbert does: "Mission, Vision, Values." According to long-time President/CEO Neil Tilow, these values permeate the organization and "embody what we try to do." Using a strategic plan that incorporates this theme, Talbert House has grown from an organization with $18 million annual revenue in 1996, to one with $57 million in revenue in 2013.

The Talbert House mission is clear and consistent: "to improve social behavior and enhance personal recovery and growth." Adds Neil, increasingly it is to "solve tough social problems." Its vision is to be a high-quality regional provider of addiction prevention and treatment services. There is a mission and 10 core values around which everything revolves. Of course, stating core values does not translate unaided to embedding them in the organization. To accomplish this, Talbert House takes a number of crucial steps.

Employees and "Mission Vision Values"

As discussed in Chapter 14 of this book with respect to HRM activities, Creating Value Through Human Resources,[5] strategic alignment of management and employees in support of the organization's mission, vision, and strategic objectives is essential. At Talbert House, management team members train each new employee to Mission Vision Values and discuss this core with them in new-employee orientation. Key issues and also career paths within the organization are discussed. There are 10 key values to which staff members are trained at each of its facilities as shown in Table 4.1.

Table 4.1 Ten Talbert House values

Advocacy
Coblioration
Comprehenive
Diversity
Integrity
Innovation
Personal growth
Quality
Safety
Spirit
Stewardship

Several of the Values pertain directly to achieving success in a nonprofit or faith-based organization. These include collaboration, that is, "aligning and partnering with individual, community and other organizations"; stewardship, that is, "long term stability through sound financial performance"; innovation, "finding new and creative alternatives to meet client and community needs"; and spirit, "foster(ing) employee energy, creativity and caring." More ethics-centered values include diversity, defined as "everyone's uniqueness is valued." Integrity is defined as "ethics in personal, professional and business behavior and respecting individual rights." CEO Tilow specifically discusses with each new management team member stewardship, spirit, integrity, and quality. Some values have more relevance to the type of preventive and addiction services Talbert House provides, for instance, advocacy and "safety of programs and facilities."

Values and Strategic Planning

Mission Vision Values flows through to the Talbert House strategic plan, which is reviewed and revised every 3 years. (Long-time board member and former Procter and Gamble executive Fred Joffe brought the P&G strategic planning process to Talbert House.) Every employee, every board member, and about 100 volunteers are surveyed with respect to the plan and how it relates to the mission. A social psychologist leads focus groups in the 10 service areas and speaks to about 100 clients and about 40 employees. Throughout the process the question asked is "where should our priorities be?" States Neil, "It is about having an organization that is unafraid to ask the tough questions." That willingness has brought Talbert House from worrying about making payroll and a net worth in 1982 of $40,000 to one of $27 million in 2013 and importantly, usually about 90 days cash on hand.

Values and Compensation/Employment

For Talbert House vice presidents and its management team, all bonuses are gauged from Mission Vision Values. For its CEO, about 75% of a bonus relates to the strategic plan and its alignment with Mission Vision Values, based on results. Neil emphasizes that values and ethics are critical to continuity of employees; staff turnover is costly and affects quality of service and efficiency. Without the core values, the employee will simply not fit into the organization.

Ethics and Compliance Training

About 12 years ago Talbert House incorporated the compliance process, including ethics and fraud, into its employee orientation. Neil is involved personally, and advises new employees, "Never make the money funny. If we screw up, we'll take our lumps and move on." Neil says integrity issues are probably the main reason shift workers are fired. Maybe they asked a client for money to change a report, or falsified when a client came into one of the court-related residential facilities. Two went to prison. Employees hear about this in the orientation process; it makes an impression.

Talbert House established a "whistleblower" system about a decade ago and encouraged all employees to report concerns. The good news: employees used it. The "bad" news: the first complaint was filed against Neil himself. Neil tells new employees about it: an employee was troubled that there was overbilling for services on a contract. The complaint was investigated and resolved: the contract was a "fixed-cost for services" contract, and not the "cost reimbursement" type of contract about which the employee was concerned. The process worked, and an employee who might have quit or been demoralized learned he or she could report concerns, would be heard, and would face no repercussions.

Talbert House Lessons Learned

There are several key "Lessons Learned" from the Talbert House approach to cultivating a culture of ethics, values, and compliance:

1. Articulating mission/vision/values and making them central to planning and decision making provides a pathway to serving stakeholders successfully.
2. Align employees, management, and board with your organization's vision, mission, and strategic objectives.
3. A nonretaliatory system of reporting misconduct or employee concerns brings problems to light and enhances trust.

4. Using mission/vision/values in hiring, promotion, and competition promotes the strategic plan and company values.

5. Top management must articulate mission, vision, and values that they themselves model.

6. As Neil says, "Fix the problem, don't mask the problem."

Conclusion

"Sound, ethical practices are an important, common-sense business card"[6] not limited to publicly traded companies. They are an essential part of a nonprofit's strategy for building a values-based and successful organization that effectively accomplishes its mission and thrives. Establishing good governance and a values-based, ethical culture builds employee morale and trust, enhances your organization's reputation, and facilitates serving stakeholders. To get there, a nonprofit executive must recognize the challenges of a competitive economic and regulatory climate, and develop proactive strategies to anticipate and address them. With a great ethical culture in place, you and your organization will be in an optimal position to fulfill the mission and be making good decisions, the subject of Section 2 of this book, next.

Key Assessment Questions

1. Are top managers engaged in underscoring and clearly communicating values and expectations?

2. Does my organization have an effective approach for addressing industry-specific ethics and compliance risks?

3. Does our organization have clear policies with respect to conduct and reporting misconduct?

4. Do we hire, evaluate, and promote based on alignment with organizational ethics and values?

5. Do we have a clear, two-way means of communicating expectations and concerns with our employees? Do we listen and act upon employee concerns?

Notes

1. EisnerAmper Accountants and Advisors (2010).
2. Ethics Resource Center (2013c).
3. Fiorelli and Tracey (2008).
4. While not the focus of this chapter, it is noteworthy that these strategies are consistent with those for an effective compliance program under the Federal Sentencing Guidelines. Having such a program not only can prevent misconduct, but also influences whether an organization should be prosecuted, and if convicted, what sentence the judge will impose.
5. Creating Value Through Human Resources, Chapter 14.
6. Fiorelli and Tracey (2008).

References

Boardsource. (2013a). *Board source.* Retrieved October 3, 2013, from www. boardsource.org

Boardsource. (2013b). *Ten basic responsibilities of non-profit boards.* Retrieved October 3, 2013, from http://www.nonprofitalliance.org/system/res/6/ original/10_basic_responsibilities_of_nonprofit_boards.pdf

EisnerAmper Accountants and Advisors. (2010). *Non-profit not immune to fraud.* Retrieved April 22, 2010, from http://www.eisneramper.com/non-profits-fraud-0410.aspx

Ethics Resource Center. (2013a). *Publications.* Retrieved October 3, 2013, from http://www.ethics.org/page/publications

Ethics Resource Center. (2013b). *Generational differences in workplace ethics.* Retrieved October 3, 2013, from http://www.ethics.org/nbes/files /2011GenDiffFinal.pdf

Ethics Resource Center. (2013c). *National business ethics survey of social networkers, new risks and opportunities at work.* Retrieved October 3, 2013, from http:// www.ethics.org/nbes/files/SocialNetworkingFinal.pdf

Fiorelli, P., & Tracey, A. M. (2008). *The "Value" of "Values" in small business: Compliance and ethics programs for "the rest of us," 33 U. of Dayton L. Rev. 204.* Retrieved October 3, 2013, from http://heinonline.org/HOL/ Page?handle=hein.journals/udlr33&div=13&g_sent=1&collection=journals

Miller, L. (2003). *Ethics: It isn't just the big guys.* Retrieved July 24, 2003, from BloombergBusinessWeek Small Business: http://www.businessweek.com/ stories/2003-07-24/ethics-it-isnt-just-the-big-guys

CHAPTER 5

Community Engagement

John Mooney

John Mooney served 27 years as a local-government manager. Since retiring, he has served as interim director of a nonprofit in crisis and as volunteer management consultant for two other nonprofits—6 years with the John XXIII Institute. He holds master's degrees in theology and public administration and a PhD in philosophy.

Introduction

Every organization, for-profit or not-for-profit, is a profoundly social entity, concerned with its various communities. Its mission states the social impact it is committed to make, whether dominating the burger market or educating orphans. Its vision articulates what kind of internal community it must be to accomplish its mission, whether a "world-class" auto manufacturer or a neighborhood-rooted service provider. Its strategies, structures, and systems are ways of organizing its *internal community* (stockholders in for-profits, board, and management and non-management employees) and interacting with its *external communities* (suppliers, collaborators, volunteers in nonprofits, clients, competitors, regulators, donors, and so forth) to successfully pursue that mission and vision.

If community is a defining concern of all organizations, it is especially so for not-for-profit organizations, for at least three reasons. First, our mission and objectives typically aim to benefit communities well beyond those with direct financial interests in our organization. Second, since our activities generally produce small profits, if any, our financial survival depends on investments by the broader community. Third, since we typically cannot match the monetary compensation offered by for-profits, our employees must derive significant nonmonetary benefits from their work. Thus, as already discussed in the Introduction, not-for-profit organizations must be especially proficient in engaging all their stakeholders, all their associated communities, both internal and external.

We will focus here on four key communities for our organizations, one internal (employees) and three external (clients, financial supporters, and network partners). Chapter 1 has already discussed the board's role as an important bridge between the organization and its external communities, and this chapter's reflections should complement the insights especially of Chapters 4, 11, 14, and 16.

Purpose

This chapter aims to help you do four key things:

1. Empower your staff to develop from mere employees to full team partners.
2. Empower your target groups to grow from mere beneficiaries to full program partners.
3. Inspire your supporters to move from mere donors to full capital partners.
4. Strengthen your impact by inviting "competitors" to become full network partners.

Introduction to the John XXIII Institute (Instituto de Acción Social Juan XXIII)

The John XXIII Institute (Instituto de Acción Social Juan XXIII) was founded in 1961 as the social-action arm of the Jesuit's Universidad Centroamericana in Managua, Nicaragua. It is politically nonpartisan and religiously non denominational in its programs, clients, and employment. Its central challenge has always been: how, amid Nicaragua's dramatic chances, to provide low-income Nicaraguans with integrated human-development programs, to increase the well-being and capacities of "persons-in-their-local-communities" in a sustainable way?

Engaging Our Internal and External Communities

"Community" is a tricky word. Its broad sense refers to a wide variety of social groupings (a living or work group, a racial or ethnic group, a religious group, a neighborhood, an entire city, and so forth). In classical sociology, however, each stable, intentional human association is a *Gemeinschaft* ("community"), a *Gesellschaft* ("society"), or in most later formulations somewhere on the spectrum in between. As he pioneered the distinction in terms of pure types, German sociologist Ferdinand Tönnies (1887) said that a "community" was a human association whose goal was the very interpersonal relationship among its members, as in marriages, families, and friendships. A "society" had a goal that lay beyond those relationships, as in football teams, factories, and hospitals. We could say that "communities" work to stay together, while "societies" stay together to work.

Thus most not-for-profits are primarily societies, because our missions focus us on something beyond the relationship among our members. Nevertheless, this chapter argues that all successful organizations engage all their stakeholder communities in the *broad* sense with a keen attention to their communal dimensions in the *classical* sense. We could say that, internally, such organizations are "community-rich societies," "community-rich workplaces." Successful organizations also form community-rich connections with their external stakeholders (clients, financial partners, and so forth). In the words of Meg Ryan to Tom Hanks in "You've Got Mail," business is always personal. In the words of Immanuel Kant and Martin Buber, a person is never just a means or a function. Forming community-rich societies is not some dispensable moral nicety but an essential key to organizational success.

Engaging Our Internal Community: From Employees to Team Partners

I suspect few general meetings of employees take place without some manager saying that "our employees are our most valuable resource." Even if sincerely meant, such declarations are not precise and strong enough.

Management consultant John Pickering defines a "high-performance organization" as one that produces *high-quality goods and services* that represent *high value to our clients and stakeholders* and also maintains *solid financial functioning*. Such an organization is impossible, he insists, unless every employee's job description includes not only her specified *task* (e.g., health-clinic physician) but also a share in the organization's *management* and *leadership*. Thus, she and the clinic's other staff members must share in the work of management, making sure the organization's work plan is done on time and within budget. They must also share the work of leadership, scanning the internal and external environments to identify threats and opportunities, and ensuring that the clinic's work plan continues to align with its vision and mission. Each job's relative share of management and leadership responsibilities will vary, with formal leadership jobs having a larger part. Yet, for the organization to perform best, everyone must embrace all three functions, as illustrated in Figure 5.1. For short, we could call this the "distributed-leadership model."

In fact, leadership is only a half-virtue. The whole virtue is devotion to community (its mission and its members) and has both an initiating and a responsive pole, leadership, and followership. *All* members of a high-performance organization, whatever their official job titles, must have this devotion to that work community, exercising each of its two poles as appropriate. Our clinic doctor will normally take the lead in determining treatment plans, but she may also be the first to notice that the clinic needs vans, not cars, in its fleet. The driver will normally take the lead in picking up clients in a timely way, but he may also be the first to notice that many people from the same neighborhood have a bad rash on their faces.

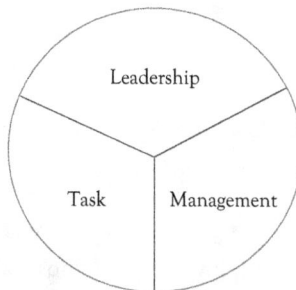

Figure 5.1 Common three-part job structure in distributed-leadership organizations
Source: John Pickering.

Formal leadership roles are absolutely critical and devilishly difficult, perhaps especially in the distributed-leadership model. An organization of any complexity needs a coordination structure with a clear center, a sure principle of unity. We all know of once vibrant organizations falling into centrifugal chaos when the charismatic founder, whose personal leadership made leadership structures seem unnecessary, retired or died. Thus, formal leaders are needed to articulate and model distributed leadership so that it feels credible and safe for other employees to engage, and then they must ensure that everyone is accountable for making distributed leadership work toward the common mission.

Becoming this kind of leader is not a matter of clever techniques but of genuine personal conviction, perhaps even conversion. To credibly talk about "we," a leader must genuinely think, feel, and act "we." He must view his co-workers as free, intelligent, adult partners in their common mission, not as extras in his self-serving drama. This means forming a "community" with them within their "society" framework.

Management guru Tom Peter's classic 1994 video, "The Management Alliance," tells the story of four organizations (an auto-parts factory, a sausage factory, a famous motorcycle manufacturer, and a high school) that achieved remarkable results by adopting a distributed-leadership model. As Peters said, he began the project thinking that he was studying 4 leaders but ended up studying 4,000.

How does an organization achieve this distributed leadership? Surprisingly, a number of successful businesses (including Wegmans, Southwest Airlines, Marriott International, and HCL Technologies) answer: by putting employees first, customers second. Marriott's Executive Vice President Mike Jannini says: "Take care of your employees and they will take care of your customers."[1] Vineet Nayar, CEO of HCL Technologies, one of the world's largest IT outsourcing firms, and author of *Employees First, Customers Second* (2010) says that "by employees first you can actually deliver your promise of customers first. If you do not put the employee first . . . there is no way you can get the customer first."[2] Putting employees first means

- careful hiring;
- thorough and continuous training in their jobs and the organization's culture;

- resources needed for their jobs;
- timely coaching and feedback (positive and corrective);
- maximal information sharing in all directions;
- the freedom and expectation that they own their three-part job;
- positive and fun workplace;
- appropriate support for their personal lives;
- appropriate recognition and compensation.

This "employees first" approach is not a return to the "job for life" paternalism sometimes found in the past, where you had to pilfer the till or murder your boss to get fired. That cheap version of "loyalty" confused a community-rich workplace with a "pure community" in which, as in the proverbial family, "they always have to take you back." Rather, "employees first" reflects the mature loyalty of shared adult responsibility for our mission. Community-rich workplaces remain primarily societies: I retain the right to belong only as long as my position is needed for its mission and can be afforded by its resources, and then only if I am adequately fulfilling the position's requirements. But, once those three conditions are met, the organization remains loyal to me.

A final word of caution. A not-for-profit organization might assume it has a genuine workplace community simply because of the nobility of its mission. History is strewn with counter-examples.

Engaging Our External Communities: From Clients to Program Partners

With some notable exceptions, commercial organizations often treat their clients as mere product consumers. While marketing research no doubt tries to discern clients' unmet needs, it also seeks opportunities to create "needs." We have read about this in Vance Packard's *The Hidden Persuaders* (1957) and lived it with hula-hoops, mini-skirts, and the latest iPhone.

Our organizations, similarly, can reduce our clients to mere service consumers, and abstract ones at that. We can assume we understand what our clients need, often abstracting an individual client from her community in which those needs arise and within which they are usually best met. Treating clients as service consumers creates an unequal provider–recipient relationship, reduces the clients' sense of agency and responsibility, and deprives our organization of critical program information. Treating clients as individuals separate from their communities makes improvements in the broader target community impossible or unsustainable. More fundamentally, it ignores the fact that, in human affairs, the dyad of person-in-community is the irreducible unit of analysis. The atomic individual and the faceless collectivity are false and dangerous abstractions.

These dangers can be minimized by treating those we serve less as clients and more as program partners—in fact, our *first* program partners. As with efforts to create a community-rich internal workplace, we cannot move people from clients to program partners by mere words or gimmicks. We must genuinely think, feel, and act in a new way.

Intimately related to recognizing our clients as program partners is how we frame their needs. The "sustainable livelihood" model of human development wisely focuses on the target group's entire livelihood framework (resources as well as deficits, on all levels from personal to international), not simply on their needs. Again, the focus is on whole persons in their entire community network.

Starting from these perspectives, we can invite those we serve to become our program partners as follows:

- Regularly seeking their perspectives on what they need from our service programs, through informal discussions and formal research methods, ideally in their community context. Again, the focus should be on their entire "livelihood" framework, not just on their needs.
- Including real, not token, representatives from our target groups on our advisory committees and our board.
- As much as possible, making members of our target groups part of program implementation teams. Though inter- and intragroup jealousies can make selection of representatives tricky, this can develop group leadership, stretch dollars, and make programs more sustainable.
- In program assessments, getting as much feedback from the target group as possible. Both quantifiable-outcomes and client-satisfaction surveys can be helpful.

Engaging Our External Communities: From Donors to Capital Partners

As noted earlier, our organizations generate little if any program income (a point we'll re-examine in a bit). Thus, we depend heavily on donors and grantors for most of our capital and operating funds. It is easy to feel caught in permanent state of mendicancy.

For details on fund-raising, see the link (in References) to Thomas L. Seiler's excellent article, "Roadmap to Fundraising Success," published on the website of the highly respected Center on Philanthropy at Indiana University.

Focusing here rather on the connection between fund-raising and community engagement, the following points are central:

- The basic strategy is not just to attract one-time donations or even repeat donors, though those remain important. Rather, it is also and especially to attract committed partners willing to share their human and financial capital to further our mission because it has also become theirs. In fact, probably the best way to get financial partners is to genuinely enlist their other skills as volunteers.
- This is more about friend-raising than fund-raising. Any of us who has become a committed volunteer or donor for an organization knows exactly how it happened: we were seduced! We were seduced by the importance of the need, the beauty of the mission, the intelligence of the plan for getting there, and the quality and commitment of the staff leading the effort. As in all other cases of consensual seduction, the line between giving and receiving becomes blurred. As Seiler says, the organization and the financial partner should discover a "mutual exchange of values." The financial partner feels like a real member of the organization's community.
- Even for committed capital partners, perpetual giving can be wearing. Thus, echoing the Introduction to this book, we need to demonstrate to them, as the John XXIII Institute calls it, a program of "hope with market efficiencies." We need to

lower costs, increase revenues, and ensure a match between the sources and uses of funds (e.g., not funding a continuing staff position with one-time funds). If we have program income, we should try to increase it without injuring our clients or violating our mission. If we don't have program income, we should try to do so, but with the same proviso. We should have a goal of approaching financial self-sustainability as much as possible. Chapter 10 discusses such financial issues in detail.

- If we begin to focus on capital partnerships rather than merely on donations and donors, we might find yet unnoticed possibilities of financial alliances with organizations that already engage our clients as customers, clients, employees, and so forth.

Engaging Our External Communities: From Competitors to Network Partners

Assuming that our organization serves a worthy mission in an effective manner, defending its survival is a good thing. However, hyperdefensiveness can prevent us from networking with other organizations that also serve our target group. Together, we could form a more united and stronger community of providers, with better and more efficient services for our target group and greater clout to boot.

The following suggestions on networking apply to competitors in both the strict sense (e.g., another childhood education program) and the broad sense (e.g., government regulators or a program competing for the same donors):

- The most natural and safe place to meet potential network partners is at professional conferences and meetings concerning our type of work or our target group. Attending such gatherings is not a luxury but an organizational requirement.
- When we have found reasonable and trustworthy dialogue partners, we should explore areas of common interest (a common problem or opportunity, prudent information and resource sharing, complementary services to our target group, joint projects and grant applications, and so forth).

- We should keep an eye open for government regulators of our programs who really want to help. That's why many of them went into government.

Community Engagement at the John XXIII Institute

To understand the Institute's engagement with its internal and external communities, we must appreciate its four major transitions since being founded in 1961.

The programs in its first 24 years were staffed and funded by the Universidad Centroamericana to help the neediest in Nicaragua, which still today has the second lowest per capita income in the American hemisphere, after Haiti, and a string of natural and social crises of which the 1972 earthquake that destroyed much of its capital is emblematic. Yet those early programs were designed with limited input from the local communities served and with little thought to their sustainability.

In 1986, with a greatly reduced staff, it began working with religious orders and the new, inexperienced local and national government agencies to assist those areas most impoverished by the events that led to and followed from the Sandinista revolution against Somoza.

In 1990, the post-Sandinista government's drastic reduction in anti poverty programs led the Institute to rely more on international partners for funding and to work directly with local communities to help design and implement programs that they themselves could sustain. These included community health programs, community pharmacies, teacher education, cooperatives, construction of community facilities, and disaster preparedness, all based on up-front community organizing.

In 1998 after Hurricane Mitch, the Institute seriously started building homes. The Institute built 20% of all the country's Mitch replacement homes. And it kept building homes; by 2012, it had built more than 3,600. By the end of the century, its housing and medical/pharmaceutical programs had become major forces in Nicaraguan human development.

Finally, in its 2011–2015 Strategic Plan, it confronted the migration of international development assistance away from Latin America to Africa, Asia, and Eastern Europe and the effects of the world financial crisis on its long-time financial partners in Europe. That plan focused

Figure 5.2 John XXIII's two key programs, Primero la Vivienda and Comunidades Saludables

on Nicaragua's major needs and the Institute's major strengths, as well as on the need to become as financially self-sustainable as possible. Fortunately, two of Nicaragua's greatest needs (housing and health) coincided with its strongest (and only revenue-producing) programs. Thus, the plan re-affirmed "*Comunidades Saludables*" (Healthy Communities) and "*Primero la Vivienda*" (Housing First) as its "core businesses," whose logos appear in Figure 5.2.

The internal and external communities discussed previously played major roles in those four transitions, as the following, necessarily selective and simplified account illustrates.

The Institute's Internal Community: Its Team Partners

The 1986 transition illustrated the tough workforce decision many organizations have to make at critical junctures. Confronted with literally revolutionary changes in Nicaraguan society, the Institute's new director re-focused its mission and formed a much smaller and mostly new staff better able to meet those challenges. By the proven durability of that mission change and the skill, adaptability, and commitment of that new staff (some of whom still work for the Institute), it clearly was a wise, if wrenching, decision.

The current team's trust, commitment, and balance of skills and ages have allowed the Institute to adjust quickly to new resource crises and societal needs. Its formal leaders radiate a devotion to its mission and members. They have created a team culture that is mission-centered, industrious, and disciplined, but with all the warmth and humor of Nicaragua. The younger members bring new energy and technology skills that have greatly enhanced the Institute's productivity and processes. Team members call each other *compañeros* (companions) and mean it.

The Institute has always put a high premium on **education, training, and information sharing** so that team members can fully own their jobs, important because they are often sent alone to distant localities to manage key elements of a program. This investment has paid off in all the major transitions and in ongoing program development.

During the **2009–2012 transition**, the Institute's formal leaders honestly shared detailed information about the challenges with all their team members (including the cleaning lady), genuinely sought their input, and visibly suffered through the tough personnel decisions. As a result, there was never a morale problem but instead a renewed (if more sober) hope, determination, and creativity.

The Institute's External Community: Its First Program Partners

All the Institute's programs start with a **community-organizing phase** that carefully assesses the needs of the affected persons-in-community and strengthens the capacities of both the persons and the community to make and implement decisions in a sustainable way. And, when a program is complete, the community is asked for careful written and oral feedback. The 1986 transition occurred only because the Institute staff drove through war-torn areas and really observed and listened to what persons and communities said they needed. The Institute' first program partners also take co-responsibility for the **implementation and sustainability** of the programs. Families help build their own homes. Communities help construct their new water systems, schools, and medical posts, and they set up committees to maintain them. Committees sustain the programs in community health, disaster preparedness, micro-lending, and cooperatives. Staff almost never speaks of "helping" their program beneficiaries but rather of "accompanying" them, so the communities can sustain programs after the Institute ends its active program presence.

The Institute's External Communities: Its Financial Partners

The Institute has had many **institutional financial partners** from Europe and the United States, including both government agencies and nongovernmentall organizations (NGOs), several for 20 or 30 years. They have continued because of the Institute's timely completion of projects within budget, thorough reporting, and ongoing communication even now that several have suspended grants due to the world financial crisis that began in 2007.

After the 2009–2012 transition, the Institute seriously began seeking **new financial partners** to move its key programs toward financial self-sustainability. Once again, necessity proved itself the mother of invention. The Institute got three Nicaraguan *municipios* to make first-time investments in housing for their citizens. In a country without a strong tradition of corporate or individual philanthropy, it is planning with the Universidad Centroamericana itself and a large Nicaraguan corporation to build housing for their employees. Continuing to carry mortgage loans with necessarily low interest ties up its money, so the Institute negotiated a deal with a local micro-lending organization to provide loans for some housing services. It began developing the Alliance for Low-Income Housing in Nicaragua, seeking both Nicaraguan partners and also local financial partnership teams in U.S. cities with large Nicaraguan populations and through Jesuit networks in the United States, Canada, and Germany.

The Institute's External Communities: Its Network Partners

For people and organizations with limited funds, networking is a natural instinct, a way of life. The preceding section on financial partners already exemplifies the Institute's networking. Two other examples are worth citing.

Like many other organizations in "developing" countries, the Institute has long welcomed "**delegations**" of private citizens from "developing" countries to come and see its work first hand. Such first hand experiences have won the Institute many new partners.

The Institute's community pharmacy program is a fascinating example of **networking with vendors, regulators, client networks, and potential competitors and political opponents**. Joining with two other large Nicaraguan NGOs to form COIME, the Institute became part of a network with 350 pharmacies instead of just its original 80. COIME's bulk-purchasing power allows the Institute to sell domestically produced drugs at about 54% of their price in private pharmacies. Through an independent quality-control program begun with the University of León in 2005, it forced domestic pharmaceutical companies (and their national government regulators) to reduce quality defects dramatically. Despite resistance from many directions, COIME worked with the Ministry of Health to win passage of a 2010 law recognizing and regulating community pharmacies.

Summary of Key Lessons the Institute Has Learned

1. The importance of a clear mission in making all decisions.
2. The payoff from training, empowering, and informing staff as fully as possible.
3. The power of involving clients as partners in planning, implementing, evaluating, and sustaining programs.
4. The importance of moving toward financial self-sustainability by involving new partners eager to engage their personal and financial capital.
5. The power of networks.

Conclusion

We have examined the pivotal role communities play in the life of not-for-profit organizations, in both the broad and the technical senses of "community." We can transform our internal community of employees into full team partners, who share management and leadership responsibilities in a way that makes us a high-performance organization. We can transform our external community of clients into our first program partners, who experience increased empowerment as persons and as communities by sharing implementation responsibilities. We can transform our external community of donors into capital partners, with a reframing of fund-raising that helps us recognize new categories of partners. Finally, we can transform our external community of competitors into network partners, creating a broader and stronger community in support of our target groups.

The next chapter, Innovation—Creating New Products and Services, leads off this book's second section (Making Good Decisions) and discusses how to realize some of the transformations discussed in this chapter.

Key Assessment Questions

(For all five questions, the follow-ups are: if "yes," how can we enhance it? If "no," why not and how can we make it happen?)

1. Does our whole organization (the board and both management and nonmanagement employees) share a deep devotion to the organization (its mission and members)?
2. Does it believe in distributed leadership? Is that belief reflected in our structures, systems, policies, and work plans?
3. Does it treat our target groups as our first program partners, empowering them as persons-in-their-communities to help in the implementation and improvement of our programs?
4. Does it treat our donors as full capital partners, instilling a devotion to our mission and engaging all their talents as well as their money? If reframed this way as friend-raising before fund-raising, what new financial partners do we become aware of?
5. Does it treat our "competitors" as potential network partners, broadening and strengthening the community in service of our target groups?

Notes

1. Carey (2008).
2. Moore (2012).

References

Carey, W. P. (2008). *Employees first: Strategies for service.* Retrieved June 26, 2008, from Know WPC: http://knowledge.wpcarey.asu.edu/article.cfm?aid=437

Fleming, J. H., & Asplund, J. (2007). *Human sigma: Managing the employee-customer encounter.* Gallup Press. Retrieved October 5, 2013, from http://businessjournal.gallup.com/content/102037/human-sigma-book-center.aspx

International Fund for Agricultural Development. (2013). *Sustainable livelihood.* Retrieved October 5, 2013, from IFAD's website: http://www.ifad.org/sla/

Mooney, J. (n.d.). *Information on Instituto de Acción Social Juan XXIII.* Retrieved from www.juanxxiii.org.ni or jmooney7@verizon.net

Moore, K. (2012). *Employees first, customers second: Why it really works in the market.* Retrieved May 14, 2012, from Forbes: http://www.forbes.com/sites/karlmoore/2012/05/14/employees-first-customers-second-why-it-really-works-in-the-market/

Peter, T. (2013). *The leadership alliance.* Retrieved October 5, 2013, from http://www.youtube.com/watch?v=R03GJpGCoeE

Pickering, J. (2007). Building high performance organizations. In T. Newell, G. Reeher, & P. Ronayne (Eds), *The trusted leader: Building the relationships that make government work* (pp. 127–155). Washington, DC: The CQ Press.

Pickering, J. (2013). *High-performance organization model.* Retrieved October 5, 2013, from http://www.highperformanceorg.com/biographies/john-pickering.html

Seiler, T. L. (2013). *Roadmap to fundraising success.* Retrieved October 5, 2013, from http://www.philanthropy.iupui.edu/files/course_resources/roadmap_to_fundraising_success.pdf

SECTION 2

Making Good Decisions

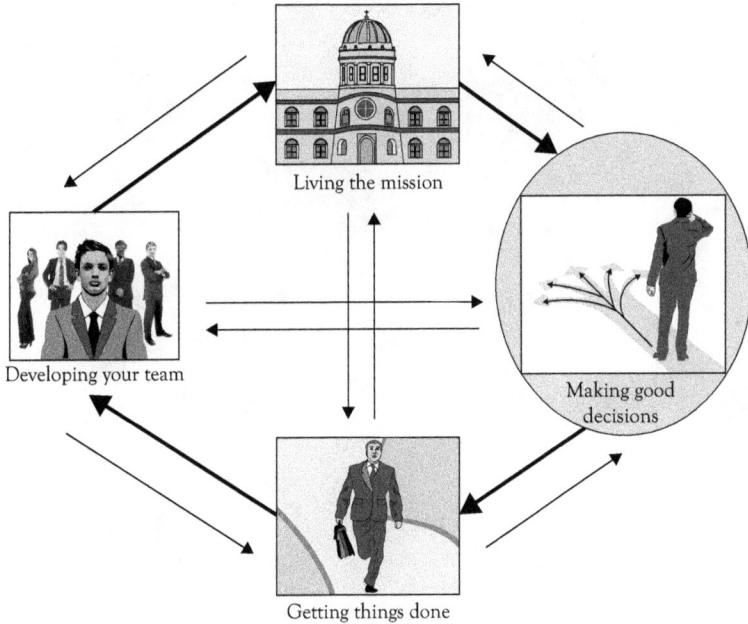

Living the mission

Developing your team

Making good decisions

Getting things done

Making good decisions is the ability to leverage the information you have access to, both qualitative and quantitative information, and combine it with good judgment to take decisive action in areas important to your organization.

The first chapter in this section, Innovation—Creating New Products and Services, outlines how you decide what new products and services are needed to fill the unmet needs of your consumers, customers, or clients and how to develop and market them. The second chapter focuses on data-based decision making. Specifically it illustrates both quantitative and qualitative analysis techniques that are essential to making choices based on objective data analysis. The next chapter, Portfolio Management, shows you how to develop, maintain a portfolio of projects and other work, and how to effectively select and oversee the right projects to achieve your organization's mission. The last chapter in this section, Leveraging Information Technology, demystifies the use of computers to run your daily operations as well as capture and manage large volumes of data to make good decisions.

CHAPTER 6

Innovation

Creating New Products and Services

Rashmi Assudani and Laurence J. Laning

Rashmi Assudani, PhD, is currently Department Chair & Associate Professor at Department of Management & Entrepreneurship at Xavier University, Cincinnati, Ohio. She earned her doctorate degree from McGill University in the area of innovation and strategy, and has her graduate and undergraduate degrees from The Netherlands and India. Over the last several years, her research and teaching has been in the area of innovation. On this topic, she has presented at various national and international conferences including TEDx, London Business School, Academy of Management and European Group of Organization Studies; and has published her work in various journals. Her most recent endeavor in this area was a student trip that she led to India, the focus of which was to examine innovation and entrepreneurship at the top as also bottom of the economic pyramid.

Laurence J. Laning, PhD, Laurence retired from Procter & Gamble after 29 years in IT. He was the Chief IT Global Architect for P&G in his last 5 years with the company. He is currently the Missions Director at Northminster Presbyterian Church in Cincinnati. He is an adjunct professor in Xavier University's College of Business. He is an active consultant for YourEncore Inc. and Xavier's Leadership Center.

Introduction

The world in which we live continues to change, and the needs of the people continue to evolve. Therefore, it is imperative for organizations to understand these unmet needs and meet these needs with new products and services. Innovation can be defined in this context as creating new solutions for unmet needs or problems, as well as creating new processes to solve existing problems.

Specific to nonprofit organizations, which are facing competing demands for their resources and which are experiencing changing stakeholder needs, the process of innovation has the potential to allow these organizations to fulfill their mission and to grow over time. Collaborative partnerships with other organizations, including other nonprofits and for-profits, present new opportunities to organizations to benefit from innovation capabilities and resources that may be available outside of their organization's traditional boundary.

The objectives of this chapter are as follows:

1. Introduce the concept of innovation and why this is relevant especially for nonprofit organizations.
2. Explain the process of innovation.
3. Discuss parameters and required resources for selecting projects that will help reach your innovation goals.
4. Introduce the concepts of collaborative partnerships and open innovation and describe how you can leverage resources outside your own organization to accomplish innovation.

In order for an organization to provide new offerings (products and services), it needs resources and capabilities to develop these new offerings. However, the reality is that organizations are limited in their scope to respond to unfamiliar markets and unique (and changing) user needs. Part of the reason for this limitation can be attributed to routines that have been established in these organizations as a way of doing something. These established routines result in a mental model, a certain accepted way of doing business, in organizations. Disrupting these mental models is a necessary precondition to initiate innovation. Further, organizations need resources—human, financial, or both, among others—to innovate, and resources in current times are increasingly limited for most (if not all) organizations.

Therefore, extending beyond the traditional borders of the organization to access resources not available within the organization itself and forming collaborations with potential partners is an evolving necessity. Such an activity system has potent resources available for generating new services and new products, initiating new processes, or both. Exposure to different partners also has the potential to alter routines and mental models.

One such collaboration is between for-profit and nonprofit organizations. This case study articulates the journey of a new social initiative that one multinational enterprise (MNE) embarked upon. The success of this new initiative is attributed, at least partly, to the collaboration with different partners, including nonprofits, which put their collective effort behind finding locally relevant solutions.

Introduction to "Support My School"

Since education is considered one of the primary drivers of economic and social change, in January 2011, a social initiative in India, called "Support My School," was designed to revitalize rural and semi-urban schools to ensure that education reaches every child. Coca Cola, along with the support of several other organizations, was the primary driver of this initiative. Since India is a relatively young country and education is one of the primary drivers to achieve social and economic potentials in this country, the "Support My School" social initiative strategically lines up with the long-term sustenance of organizations such as Coca Cola as they practice business in countries like India. Without the growth in economic potentials and without the growth in human capital, organizations that are envisioning an engaged long-term presence in other countries are likely to find themselves in a stalemate.

Several studies revealed that lack of basic amenities like Toilets, Access to Water, and Basic Infrastructure creates an unwelcome environment in schools, which has led to a higher rate of absenteeism and finally resulting in dropouts. Girl children in such areas have suffered the most. These studies estimated that over 50% of rural schools in India have non-functional or no toilets. As the girl entered her adolescence, involuntarily she sat at home just because there were no proper, separate toilets for girls in rural schools. Lack of proper water and sanitation facilities in schools in rural India continues to remain a huge challenge.

This unique need sparked an innovative thought to initiate a social initiative "SUPPORT MY SCHOOL."

Key questions facing the leaders of the "Support My School" initiative were as follows:

1. How can we develop schools that are healthy and active learning centers?
2. How can we provide better access to sanitation, water, playing facilities, libraries, and computer centers to these schools?
3. How can we do all this to enhance school attendance and reduce dropout rate?
4. How can we enhance our resources to achieve these objectives?

Innovation Defined

It may seem obvious that innovation is required for an organization to thrive and be successful in the future. However many nonprofit organizations invest very limited or no resources in creating future products and services. Often nonprofit organizations are totally consumed with supporting their existing products and services and running their day-to-day operations and sometimes struggling to do that.

An insightful definition of innovation is creating something original, new, and important.[1] The very nature of innovation is being proactive and anticipating the needs of your customers, consumers, and clients that are either unmet or being met poorly by the current products and services in the market.

We have defined innovation earlier in this chapter. There are some related terms surrounding innovation and it is useful to understand their definitions and how they relate to innovation. The terms we will examine are invention, improvement, and research and development. We will explore closed and open innovation later in this chapter.

Invention refers to the creation of an idea or method itself, while innovation is more concerned with applying inventions to unmet needs and launching it in the marketplace.[2] Innovation does depend on creative solutions to existing or new problems or issues. Improvement is focused on doing something we are currently doing but doing it better. Innovation is often focused on doing something new or different. Finally, research and development refers to a group of activities in a business designed to develop new products or services or to discover and create new knowledge that will enable new products and services to be developed based on these new discoveries.[3]

How Do You Innovate?

This is one of the most interesting and challenging questions as it relates to innovation. Is there a structured process for ensuring innovation? What kind of an environment would an organization need to ensure continued innovation?

Innovation is not magic. It is often hard work. It is knowing who your target customer or consumer is and really understanding their unmet needs in depth in tangible clear ways. Then the tough part comes, that is, creating cost-effective products and services that not only meet but delight your target consumers in the areas of these unmet needs. The insights needed to develop these new products and services often comes from having an in-depth knowledge of your area, your customers, consumers, and clients, and the science and politics of your area of work.

Research into best practices for creating new products shows that the following factors correlate highly with performance in creating successful new products and services:

- Strategic areas defined—areas of strategic focus are identified.
- The role of new product development is included in business or service goals.
- Goals for new products or services are clearly defined.
- There is a clearly articulated innovation strategy for the business or service.
- There is a long-term commitment to innovation.

There are proven work processes that are effective in managing the creation of new products and services. The most common process for a single innovation project is a "stage-gate" process. An example is shown.[4]

The five stages

DISCOVER	DESIGN	QUALIFY	READY	LAUNCH
Promising consumer proposition	Integrated business proposition	The Initiative	Prepare market launch	Execute market entry

The four gates

	1	2	3	4
Key decision	Staff it?	Design complete? Start implementation?	Criteria met? Launch plan agreed?	Ready for launch?
Milestone	Project establishment	Project commitment	Launch plan agreement	Launch authorization

**Figure 6.1 P&G's SIMPL process—an idea-to-launch stage-gate®
model**

Not all organizations will need as thorough or rigorous a set of processes
for innovation, but this example highlights the key issues that must be
managed for innovation to be successful and not left to chance.

Figure 6.1 shows the basic stages and decision gates in a five-stage
stage-gate model.

Stage 1: DISCOVER—Promising Consumer Proposition
Stage 2: DESIGN—Integrated Business Proposition
Stage 3: QUALIFY—The Initiative
Stage 4: READY—Prepare Market Launch
Stage 5: LAUNCH—Execute Market Entry

These five stages describe different phases a new product or service goes
through as they are developed and tested to see if they will be successful
in the market. Moving from one stage to another stage is a process of
managing risk. If a new product or service fails in one stage, it should be
stopped and not be permitted to move on to the next stage.

Therefore there are key decision points or "gates" between each stage
(i.e., Gates 1–4). The four decision gates are as follows:

Gate 1: After DISCOVER Stage—Staff It? (Project Establishment)
Gate 2: After DESIGN Stage—Design Complete? Start Implementation? (Project Commitment)

Gate 3: After QUALIFY Stage—Criteria Met? Launch Plan Agreed? (Launch Plan Agreement)

Gate 4: After READY Stage—Ready for Launch? (Launch Authorization)

At each gate there is a go/kill decision point. The work in each stage delivers measures that are used to make the decision to go or not, at each gate decision point. By passing each gate and proceeding to the next stage of work, you are managing risk and doing the work to assure you that the new product or service will be successful in the market. It is unrealistic to think that every new product/service project will be successful. In fact, some of the best decisions made are to NOT deploy or launch a new product or service that has not proven itself by exceeding the launch criteria established in the stage-gate process.

The key question posed in each decision gate is central to the work that needs to be done in the stage preceding that gate. For example in Gate 1, what data would you need to have from the DISCOVER stage for you to be comfortable in staffing this project? In Gate 2, what data and results would you need to see before you would declare the design of the product or service complete?

The review process at each decision gate is a very important part of having a successful stage-gate process. The organization's key decision maker is responsible for making objective and data-based decisions on whether an innovation project will proceed to the next stage of work or be killed.

How Do You Wisely Invest Your Innovation Resources?

Innovation is a set of processes that need to be established and managed over time. There are two different levels of work processes that need to exist in some form to have an effective innovation process:

1. One level of work process focuses on innovation strategy, project selection, and resource planning.
2. A more detailed level of work processes exists once you have selected an innovation project and you need to develop and manage the risk of this specific project. This is normally done using a stage-gate work process.

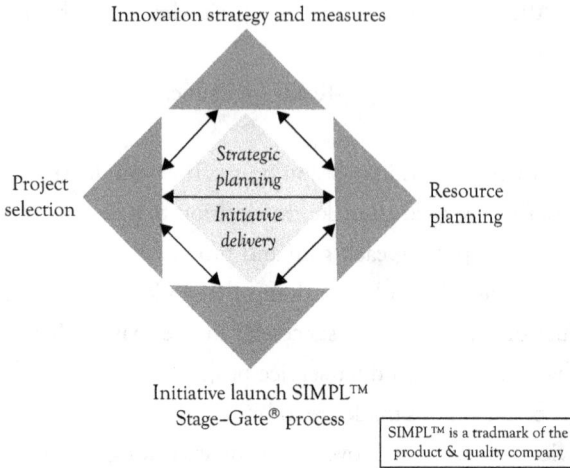

Innovation strategy and measures

Project selection

Strategic planning

Initiative delivery

Resource planning

Initiative launch SIMPL™
Stage–Gate® process

SIMPL™ is a tradmark of the product & quality company

Figure 6.2 P&G's initiatives management diamond—guiding the business's new product efforts

Figure 6.2 illustrates the four major points in what can be called the "initiatives diamond" that shows the major processes for these two levels.[5]

Focusing on the first level of work processes, innovation project choices are a special case of Portfolio Management (see Chapter 8). Some of the key questions that need to be addressed to make innovation choices are as follows:

1. What percentage of your total resources will you dedicate to innovation? It is useful to have some set percentage of your resources focused on creating new products and services. This percentage will depend on many factors such as what resources are required just to keep the day-to-day operations going successfully. What is your total staff headcount?. And do you have the people with the right skill set to be successful at innovation activities?

2. Will you have dedicated resources focused on innovation or ask people to add innovation to their current responsibilities? There are pros and cons to both models. What is more important is that an organization has an explicit innovation portfolio and that they manage this innovation portfolio carefully and with some rigor.

Once you have the resource question addressed, the choice among alternative portfolio projects is best made using objective criteria such as the following:

- Which project(s) will have the greatest impact or payoff in an important area for the organization? Can you estimate the quantitative impact or payoff so that you can assess how well this project will enable you to reach your stated goals?
- Which project(s) do we have the "technical right to succeed with" because we have the background, experience, and resources (both people and money) to be successful in this area? Or we are partnering with the right organizations that bring some of these key factors with them.
- Which project(s) do we have the right mix of people available now to work on this project?

Using these criteria, you can evaluate alternative project portfolio choices and make the right choices for your innovation program. Chapter 8 on Portfolio Management has a more extensive discussion of ways to manage effectively a portfolio of projects.

Collaborative Partnerships

Previous sections illustrated internal processes for innovating. Partnerships with external stakeholders such as distributors and suppliers are equally important to ensure that innovation reaches its consumers. Such partnerships are even more important for products/services that require nontraditional distribution and suppliers.

For example, many for-profit organizations which have embraced innovation in their mission not only for reasons of their financial bottom line, but also to meet with the other two expectations in triple bottom line (to deliver upon good for the people and planet), have established collaborative partnerships with nonprofits and NGOs (nongovernmental organizations). Triple bottom line is a concept known as people, planet, and profit. It represents a set of values to measure organizational success.

To accomplish this, for-profits have looked at establishing collaborative partnerships with nonprofits and NGOs.

For example, Danone[6] launched its Danimal yogurt in South Africa, for reasons related to their social mission. This yogurt was enriched with nutrients that kids in South Africa were deficient in. While it was a great idea to meet this unmet need and Danone conducted intense research to develop a product that met this unmet need, it was equally important to find ways to distribute this product to its end user. Danone's success to distribute Danimal to its end users was partly attributed to its collaboration with nonprofit organizations which could help Danone reach its end users via nontraditional distribution channels.

Unilever adopted an innovative approach to distributing its products to its consumers in emerging markets. These consumers were in small towns and villages which were spread out over large geographic areas. The typical distribution channel with established retailers was not an option since such infrastructure did not exist in these places. In order to increase market penetration, Unilever engaged micro-entrepreneurs in door-to-door selling so that their products could get to these hard-to-reach places. While this resulted in enhanced financial returns to Unilever, this innovative distribution channel required a trained pool of labor. Therefore, Unilever, with help from local NGOs and local governments, trained and developed a large pool of women entrepreneurs to support such distribution. This innovative model would not have reached such success without the collaboration between Unilever, local NGOs and local government.

Closed and Open Innovation

Closely tied to the topic of collaborative partnerships is a discussion on open innovation. Over the past decade, the concept of open innovation has been developed and adopted by many companies as an additional approach for developing new products and services. Open innovation is a concept that was created by Henry Chesbrough, a professor from the University of California, Berkeley.[9]

In simple terms, closed innovation is the traditional model of Research & Development (R&D) where a company hires the best people they can find with the right technical knowledge and skills and focuses on creating proprietary knowledge and products and services. The company owns the intellectual property and focuses on being first to market with these new products and services to capture the dominant market share and related profits.

Open innovation on the other hand recognizes that a firm should use resources beyond its own organization as sources for innovation. For example, in the early 2000s, Procter & Gamble recognized that it could not reach its commercial goals for volume and profit using only its own internal R&D staffs.[10] P&G created a program they termed Connect & Develop (vs. Research & Develop) or C&D. This C&D program was very successful and leveraged global resources and ideas available on the World Wide Web or Internet.

There are two basic types of Internet services useful for firms utilizing an open innovation strategy. First, there are sites where fully developed solutions and products/prototypes exist for sale such as Yet2.com. In these situations, you need to evaluate if these solutions meet your needs and are cost-effective to acquire.

The second type of services available globally is where you state your research/innovation challenge to a global network of subject matter experts (e.g., incentive) and typically you declare an award to the best proposed solution. In this situation, this global network of experts is aware of your research problem and a number of experts will self-select themselves to work on and propose a solution to your problem(s).

Both types of services greatly expand the reach of your organization to find ideas through others to provide a new product or service. The number of highly qualified experts available globally through these types of services is vast and can expand your organization's capability several fold to innovate beyond the capabilities of your own people.

Open innovation is being more broadly used in for-profit organizations than nonprofit organizations currently. However, given the potential of open innovation concepts to expand the ability of nonprofits to innovate by leveraging global resources, it is important that nonprofit leaders understand and find opportunities to apply open innovation approaches to their organizations' work.

One such example of open innovation is with Embrace, a 503c nonprofit organization, which has developed an innovative solution to the biggest problem that many babies in developing countries face, especially those who are in areas that don't have access to innovations in modern medicine.[11] One of the biggest problems these babies face is hypothermia: they are not able to regulate their own body temperature, and therefore cannot stay warm. In fact, room temperature for these small infants feels freezing cold. Four million babies die within their first month of life. Those that do survive often develop lifelong health problems such as early onset of diabetes, heart disease, and low IQ.

Embrace developed an innovative solution at a fraction of cost of a typical incubator, so this incubator was financially feasible for these families. To make this product a reality from the vision to its actual product form, Embrace relied on a variety of sources including charitable donations and social venture funds.

Innovation at "Support My School"

The Objectives of "Support My School"

The campaign adopted a multipronged objective approach. The objectives included sensitizing the community by raising awareness to revitalize schools in rural and semi-urban India with an emphasis on proper sanitation, access to water, and sporting facilities. The objectives also sought to make Support My School a platform for the community to make a difference. The campaign was built around the following pillars to create maximum impact: Build mass awareness on importance of water and sanitation and how it impacts education, engage communities and schools in providing solutions, bring all stakeholders on a common platform, reach out to at least 10 million people, and raise funds to directly support at least 100 schools.

The Impact Quotient

Over 100 schools across 10 states now lay claim to better access to sanitation, water, playing facilities, libraries, and computer centers. The intervention in each of the schools targeted was designed to convert the schools into healthy and active schools. The elements that were sought to be added in the schools were improved access to water, sanitation facility for girls and boys, providing playgrounds and sports equipment, rainwater harvesting project, developing the environment in the school campus, library and teacher training (Pearson Foundation), and computer center and Internet (Tata Teleservices Limited).

Other stakeholders such as Pearson Foundation joined the campaign as a partner in July 2011 to develop and implement a strategic pillar of the campaign, that is, setting up libraries and to conduct teacher training. Tata Teleservices Limited joined the campaign in October 2011 through its project learning to help set up computer centers and Internet in targeted schools, which did not have any.

How Did All This Happen?

An idea remains an idea till the time it is implemented, and a successful execution requires garnering support from various stakeholders (refer to Figure 6.3), and designing and enacting the project plan.

Garnering Support

A network of partnership between for-profits (for example, Coca Cola India and NDTV) and nonprofits (for example, Sulabh International,

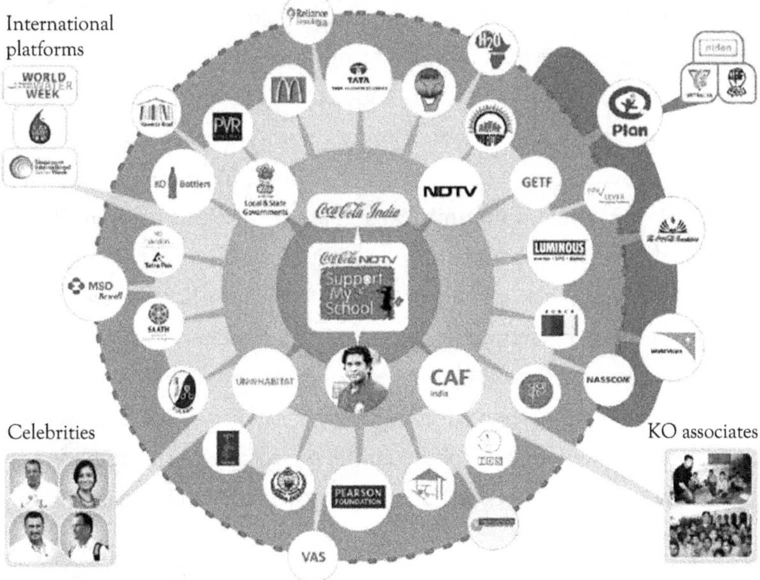

Figure 6.3 Power of partnerships

Charities Aid Foundation [CAF], and Saath) was instrumental in this innovative idea's implementation. Support from policy makers and opinion leaders added to this momentum. Local and national media's attention to this social initiative encouraged many more stakeholders to join in.

Project Implementation

Since the scope of the project was very large (India has a very large rural and semi-urban population and access to these locales is not very easy. Moreover, language and cultural differences abound across different parts of the country.), it was necessary to scope out the project into clusters for its better management.

With pledges of over a million dollars in hand, Charities Aid Foundation (CAF) led the implementation of these schools through a network of grassroots NGOs. A clustered approach was adopted for execution of the project, with each cluster comprising 5–8 schools. This cluster strategy helped economize the cost of implementation and also increased the impact in the region. These clusters then became the unit of impact for the campaign. It was an efficient way to deliver upon the project and allowed for the project scope to be as large as this one.

A separate grassroots NGO was allocated for each of these clusters. These NGOs were vetted through a formal process and had experience of executing similar projects in their regions. These grassroots NGOs then worked with the local administration to identify the "cluster of schools" that would benefit most from the interventions. Once the schools were identified, the local community was apprised of the work that would be carried out. With permissions and paperwork in place, these grassroots NGOs executed the project with a defined timeline and a budget. The overall implementation and project management was done by CAF through a combination of regular field visits and methodical reporting.

Representatives of campaign partners visited several of these schools during the implementation phase and apprised the executing NGOs of possibilities and best practices. The phasewise implementation led to several learning goals being captured and translated into action in subsequent phases. Feedback was also sought from a committee of external experts on the implementation.

Results

Effects of power of this partnership were realized in the first season (2011–2012) with transformation of 101 schools across 13 states in India. In its second season (2012–2013), this partnership is aiming to revitalize more than 250 schools.

Key Learnings From Case Study

1. Mantra for organizations to remember: have a long-term vision for innovating.
2. Innovation requires resources, which are limited. Collaborative partnerships are critical for both nonprofits and for-profit organizations. They help both achieve important objectives with shared resources.
3. Think big! Substantive change is possible with collaborative partnerships, change that would not be possible if parties acted alone.

Conclusion

Innovation is often an optional topic for many nonprofit organizations. They focus on their current products and services. However for nonprofits to grow and prosper, they need to learn and apply the concepts and techniques presented in this chapter!

Key Assessment Questions

1. How could my mission be better served with an innovation objective? What innovation initiatives do we have, if any?
2. What attributes do I look for in potential partners?
3. What are the top unmet needs of your customers, consumers, or clients? How do you regularly evaluate these unmet needs?
4. What processes do you use for making innovation choices and related investment decisions?
5. What stage-gate or similar process do you use to run innovation projects? How do you make decisions on whether to stop or continue these innovation projects at significant milestones in these projects?

Notes

1. Wikipedia (2013a).
2. Chesbrough (2003).
3. Wikipedia (2013b).
4. Cooper and Mills (2005).
5. Cooper and Mills (2005).
6. Havarden and Barnard (2010).
7. Unilever. Retrieved from Hindustan Lever. http://www.hul.co.in/sustainable-living/casestudies/Casecategory/Project-Shakti.aspx
8. Embrace. Retrieved from http://embraceglobal.org/
9. Chesbrough (2003).
10. Chesbrough (2003).
11. Tapscott and Williams (2010).

References

Chesbrough, H. (2003). *Open innovation—The new imperative for creating and profiting from technology*. Boston, MA: Harvard Business School Press.

Cooper, R. G., & Mills, M. S. (2005). *Succeeding at new products the P&G way: Work the Innovation Diamond™, Working Paper No. 21, Product Development Institute Inc.*, Ancaster, Ontario, Canada.

Havarden, V., & Barnard, H. (2010). *Danimal in South Africa: Management innovation at the bottom of the pyramid*. Ontario, Canada: Ivey Publishing.

Tapscott, D., & Williams, A. D. (2010). *Wikinomics—How mass collaboration changes everything*. London, UK: Penguin Books Ltd.

Wikipedia. (2013a). *Innovation*. Retrieved from Wikipedia The Free Encyclopedia: http://en.wikipedia.org/wiki/innovation

Wikipedia. (2013b). *Research and development*. Retrieved from Wikipedia The Free Encyclopedia: http://en.wikipedia.org/wiki/research and development

CHAPTER 7

Making Good Decisions Using Data

Laurence J. Laning

Laurence J. Laning, PhD, retired from Procter & Gamble after 29 years in IT. He was the Chief IT Global Architect for P&G in his last 5 years with the company. He is currently the Missions Director at Northminster Presbyterian Church in Cincinnati. He is an adjunct professor in Xavier's University College of Business. He is an active consultant for YourEncore Inc. and Xavier's Leadership Center.

Introduction

This chapter deals with the analyses of both quantitative and qualitative data and its synthesis with human judgment to make good decisions.

Organizations make hundreds of decisions every day. Why is making decisions based on data so important? The opposite of making decisions based on data is making decisions based on what you think is true, or what you think is the current situation, or just simply what the decision maker wants to do. This can lead to very poor outcomes. Data-based decisions mean that you define and collect objective, accurate, and current data (both quantitative and qualitative) that describes what the current situation **actually** is. You allow the data to speak and give you insights as you analyze the data using valid and proven analysis techniques.

People who lead nonprofit and faith-based organizations often do so with great passion for the mission of their organization. It is important to not let this passion drive an organization to make decisions without objective and high-quality data.

Many nonprofit organizations are now being required to measure the impact and overall outcomes of their programs. This chapter provides a starting point on how to analyze both quantitative and qualitative data to measure and document results.

An organization that follows data-based decision making actually empowers its people to make significant contributions. This is done because people at all levels and seniority in the organization know that if they can collect and analyze the data surrounding an issue or a problem, the conclusions they draw and the recommendations they make will be listened to and acted upon. This is a tremendous asset for an organization. Another reason that data-based decision making is good for an organization, is that it levels the playing field in leadership team meetings or even in board meetings. By gaining insight through the analysis of data, it prevents a few opinionated or powerful people from dominating a meeting and imposing their will.

It must be noted that following this principle does not mean that intangible or political factors cannot be considered in making complex decisions. It just means that you need to include objective analysis of the data relevant for a decision and factor this insight into the decision being made.

The purpose of this chapter is as follows:

- Learn why making decisions based on data is so key to an organization.
- How to define and collect high-quality data.
- How to perform quantitative analysis techniques and gain insight from their use.
- See why qualitative data is critical, especially for nonprofit and faith-based organizations.
- How to do data analysis of qualitative data and gain insight from this analysis.
- How to integrate all factors present to make good decisions.

The emphasis of this chapter is on simple and easy-to-use analysis techniques. We present a wide variety of the most commonly used analysis techniques. The references will provide more in-depth treatment of similar and related analysis methods.

Introduction to United Way of Greater Cincinnati

In 2001, United Way of Greater Cincinnati (UWGC) began a journey to change its business model. Despite the strength of the organization and others in the region, many problems in the community were not getting better. It was clear that the organization needed to get beyond funding good programs, working with community partners (i.e., nonprofit human service agencies, schools, government policy makers, businesses, philanthropic groups, and the faith community) to focus on the root causes of problems and change conditions to improve lives of community populations, not just those of individual clients.

The key question for United Way leaders became:

How can we have **maximum impact** on improving our community and peoples' lives? This is the journey to greater **community impact**; more recently it has been termed collective impact.

Defining and Collecting High-Quality Data

The logical question when posed with an important decision to make is, what data do I need or can I get to help us make this decision? It is helpful to distinguish what are called **in-process measures** from **outcome measures**. These two types of measures are best understood in the context of work processes.

Let's consider a work process within an organization (described as follows) to staff projects with the right skilled people to be the project manager. Let's simplify the process to the following steps:

1. A member of your organization comes forward with a request for a project to be done and requests a project manager be assigned to the project.
2. Based on the project and work to be done, a set of skills and experiences needed by the project manager are identified.

3. Your organization then generates a list of candidate project managers. A selected group of managers who know the project area then evaluates the top three to five expert project manager candidates and selects the preferred candidate.

4. Once a candidate is selected, the potential project manager sits down with the group of managers who selected him or her to discuss the role and see if it is a fit. This group then reaches a consensus and the project manager begins their work or the evaluation process begins over to select the project manager.

For this process, some example **in-process** measures are as follows:

- Number of candidate project managers identified with the requested skills.
- Elapsed time in days it takes from the date of initial request until the project is staffed and begun.
- Number of projects requesting a project manager.
- What percentage of project manager candidates accept the role?

For this same process, some example **outcome measures** are as follows:

- Financial measures for completed projects such as
  - total dollars spent;
  - total benefits booked (e.g., return on investment [ROI] or net present value [NPV]).
- Customer satisfaction with the project manager (subjective measure from 1 to 7)
- Was the project delivered on time? How many days late or early was the project completed?

Collecting High-Quality Data

It is preferred if you can collect data from your information systems if the data you want is actually being stored in the computer applications used to run your business. However, sometimes the data you need for a study will require at least some of the data to be collected manually or with

Table 7.1 Check sheet for consumer comments

Type of comment: (Circle one or fillout other)	Date _____ Shift _____
CH–Complaint re: Checking account	Verbatim comments:
SV–Complaint re: Saving account	
LN–Complaint re: Loan	
CO–Complaint for good service	
Other (explain) _____	

special computer programs to collect data that are not normally collected in your systems.

If you are collecting data manually, you will need to define a form or what is sometimes called a check sheet to collect the data you want.[1] Table 7.1 hows a simple check sheet used to collect consumer comments that are received at a call center for a bank. Call centers often use automated systems to track their performance, so it would be likely that consumer comments are already tracked by the call center in their problem tracking system. However, if comments are not tracked, Table 7.1 lays out a simple form used to collect this data. Note that there is one sheet for each consumer comment. Therefore, there is a need to summarize this raw data by shift, by date, by type of comment, and so forth.

Issues that need to be considered are what event/transaction are you collecting and how much data, and exactly what data will be collected? For example, do you want to know the exact time of day when each comment was tracked, or is having consumer comments grouped by 8-hour shifts sufficient level of detail? For the type of comment, do you have a finite list of choices and one "Other" category? Or do you allow people to write in freeform text to explain those comments that do not match one of the choices provided? The form has to be as clear as possible so that it can be consistently used.[2]

A useful concept is to define in writing exactly what you mean by each data element that you are collecting. This written definition is called the **operational definition**. For example, the operational definition of a consumer comment could be: "When a consumer of our products calls our 800 numbers, we will categorize the nature of why they are calling based on the developed standard list of types of consumer comments we typically receive. If a consumer calls with a comment that does not match a predefined type, we record the comment as other and then record the actual words or verbatim of that comment." Now this is not a perfect definition but does reflect the level of precision needed when writing a good operational definition.

It is helpful to consider the types of quality attributes you should strive to achieve as you collect data, either via information systems or manually collected. Common attributes that are helpful are timely, accurate, clear, consistent, and relevant.

Analyzing Quantitative Data

In today's world, most quantitative analytical techniques are automated and provide fast and accurate capabilities. However, it is important to understand the basic intent or approach for an analytical technique that is embedded in the software. In this book, the underlying logic and mechanics for quantitative methods are explained

The techniques included are the following:

- Simple graphs and measures
- Simple statistics, probability, and uncertainty measures (includes confidence intervals)
- Trends and patterns (histograms, Pareto charts)
- Decision analysis.

Simple Graphs and Measures

Often the best thing you can do with quantitative data is to simply graph it and examine it visually to see what the data is telling you. We will look at a few of the very basic types of charts and graphs. Figure 7.1 shows a line chart over time (sometimes called a run chart). Run charts show trends for a process over time. This is useful to see what is happening to sales over time—that is, are things getting better or worse?[3]

These types of simple charts can easily be done using Excel software or many other simple tools.

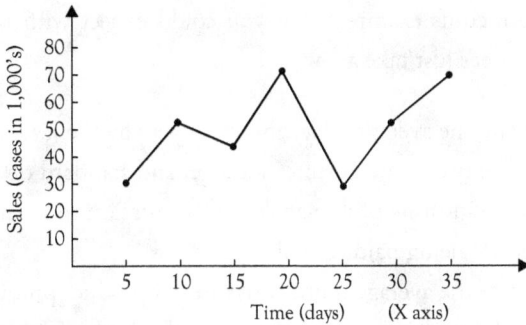

Figure 7.1 Run chart

Simple Statistics, Probability, and Quantifying Uncertainty[4]

The important thing to know about quantitative data is that there is inherent uncertainty and variation in much of the data that we collect and analyze. For example, we may measure the weight of an individual package (e.g., potato chips) coming off a packing line in a sheltered workshop. We may take samples each hour rather than weighing 100% of the packages. For our sample we can calculate the **mean** or **average** weight of a package. This measure of mean is simply adding all the sample observations and dividing by the number of observations in the sample.

Median and **Mode** are two other measures of central location that can be useful. Median is defined as the value in the middle when the data is arranged in ascending order. Mode is defined as the value that occurs with the greatest frequency or most number of times.

Example

Let us look at some common ways that these basic measures are used. If you collect information from your organization's databases, representative kinds of data are[5]

- employee data;
- production records;
- finished product inventory information;
- sales data;
- customer data.

There are numerous examples that you could expect with this kind of information. Let's just take a few:

- Calculate the average salary for employees by the level they are in the company. The mean, range, and standard deviation would be most helpful to analyze this situation to see if people are being paid equitably.
- Calculate the average number of cases of product produced by line by plant and compare these averages to see which lines and plants make the most number of products.
- Calculate the average inventory levels by type of product and by warehouse. This will tell you what product(s) have the most inventory and which warehouses hold the most inventory.
- Calculate sales by product and week to see which products are your top selling products and to see which products vary by week (e.g., seasonality).
- Calculate the average number of customers who buy each product. Also look at the customer's annual sales to see the relative size of your customers.

Uncertainty Measures

We all know that the world is full of uncertainty. Therefore, there is inherent random variability in many of the process data that we collect for analysis. In this section, we talk about the basic measures of uncertainty and how to use this information.

Probability is the numerical measure of the likelihood that an event will occur. Probability ranges from 0 to 1. A probability of 0.50 means that this event is as likely to occur as it will not occur.

Uncertainty means there is variability in what we are measuring, like the package weight mentioned previously. The measures we will work with are **range, variance,** and **standard deviation.** The formulas to calculate these measures are a bit more complex.

- **Range = Largest Value – Smallest Value**
- **Variance = $s^2 = \sum (X - X_i)^2/n - 1$**
- **Standard Deviation = $s = \sqrt{s^2}$**

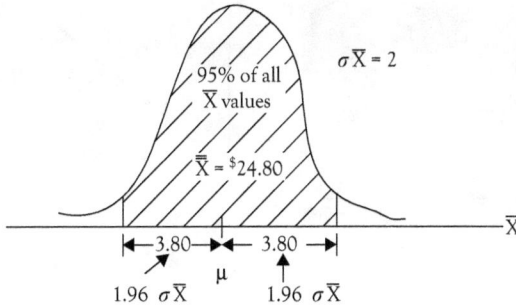

Figure 7.2 Sampling distribution of X (restaurant spending)

Range is a simple measure of how far apart the smallest and largest observations are. Variance is actually a statistical measure that utilizes all the data. That is, the measure is based on the difference of each observation from the mean. The standard deviation is the square root of the variance which makes that measure a smaller number and in the same units as the original data.

One of the most common analyses that combine both means and standard deviations is called a **confidence interval**. Figure 7.2 shows the normal distribution bell-shaped curve for sample means (X). The curve shows approximately two (1.96) standard deviations to the right and left of the sample mean (X). This is the normal variability seen in this sample. Calculating the two end points by using $X \pm 1.96$ s gives you a 95% confidence interval so that the true mean falls within this range.

This type of analysis can be very helpful when the inherent variability for your data is significant. For example, let's look at data from a restaurant that shows the amount of money spent by a customer for dinner. As the owner of the restaurant, you will want to know what the average customer will spend for dinner. You can see in Figure 7.2 that the sample mean is $24.80 with an upper and lower 95% confidence interval of $28.60 to $21.00.

Examining Trends and Patterns

Often, historical quantitative data is used to learn from and to forecast the future. When a data item is collected over time, such as sales by day

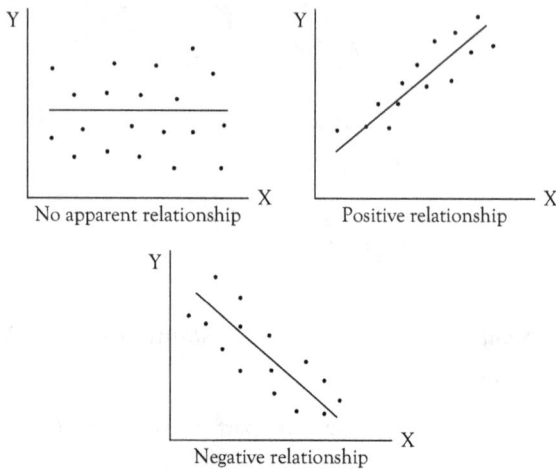

Figure 7.3 Scatter diagrams—types of relationships

or by month for example, it is helpful to examine it to see if there are any underlying trends or seasonal patterns to the data. Figure 7.3 shows a scatter diagram or trend line with three common scenarios: a positive relationship, a negative relationship, and no apparent relationship.

Two other common and very powerful graphical techniques that are used to look at the relationships in the data are **histograms** and **Pareto charts**. (Both these diagrams can easily be produced using Excel as well as other graphic computer programs.)

Histograms are basically bar charts showing the frequency distribution of the variable being collected. Figure 7.4 shows a typical histogram for the number of days for completing IT projects as an example.

The shape of the histogram provides insight as to how the construction time varies. Is it symmetric, that is, is it equally likely to be over and under the mean? In this case, the histogram would tell you that it is more likely to be over the mean. Figure 7.5 illustrates four different shapes that can be detected using histograms.

Pareto charts are also very useful to visualize the relative frequency or size by using a descending bar graph. Figure 7.6 illustrates sales by brand data. Here we arranged the bars with the most frequent or largest bar first and then descending from there. This enables us to examine the brand that sells the most so that we can focus our marketing efforts, for example,

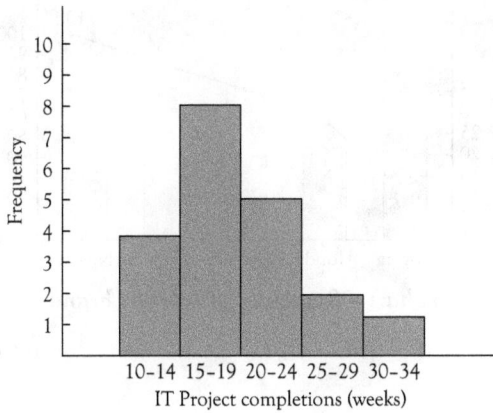

Figure 7.4 Histogram for IT project completion

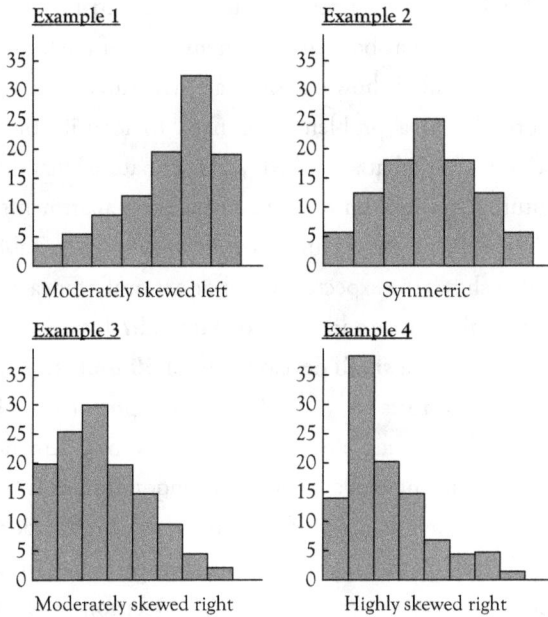

Figure 7.5 Varying levels of histogram skewness

on our largest selling brand. (The Pareto chart is named after Vilfredo Pareto who was an Italian economist.) In this Pareto chart, we have also added the optional cumulative frequency line to show the cumulative frequency as you move from left to right on the chart.

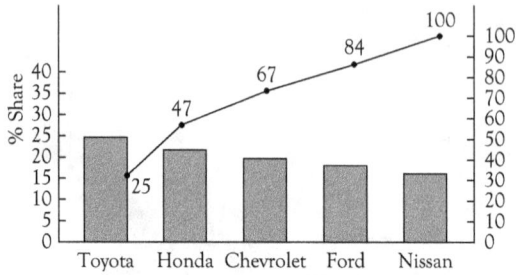

Figure 7.6 Pareto chart—frequency of sales by brand

Decision Analysis

Decision analysis techniques represent ways to make decisions when a decision maker is faced with several alternatives and the future events have uncertainty or risk associated with them. Part of the beauty of decision analysis approaches is how decisions are structured.[6]

When formulating a problem, you need to identify the "decision alternatives," as well as what are called "states of nature" that describe the uncertain future. Let's take an example of building apartments in a new real estate development project in a downtown U.S. city. Table 7.2 is a payoff table that shows the expected payoff or net profit for each combination of a decision alternative and a state of nature. In this case, the decision alternatives are to build a **small** development of **50 units** (d_1), a **medium** development of **100 units** (d_2), or a **large** development with **150 units** (d_3). Two states of nature are identified. They are strong demand for condominiums (s1) or having weak demand for condominiums (s2). Table 7.2 shows the expected payoffs/net profits for those six combinations.

It is often helpful to visually depict this decision situation using what is called a decision tree, as seen in Figure 7.7. Decision trees enable people to decompose problems into sequential steps. Large complex decisions can be formulated by being decomposed into a series of smaller subproblems.

The only thing missing now is getting information on how likely is each state of nature. In other words, what is the probability that there will be strong demand for condominiums in this area? Once we estimate these

Table 7.2 Payoff table for apartments at the banks project in Cincinnati (payoffs in $million)

State of Nature		
Decision alternative	Strong demand (S$_1$)	Weak demand (S$_2$)
Small complex (d$_1$)	11	10
Medium complex (d$_2$)	17	8
Large complex (d$_3$)	23	-6

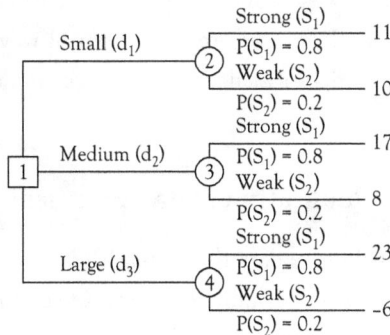

Figure 7.7 *Decision tree for apartments at the Banks project in Cincinnati (payoffs in $million)*

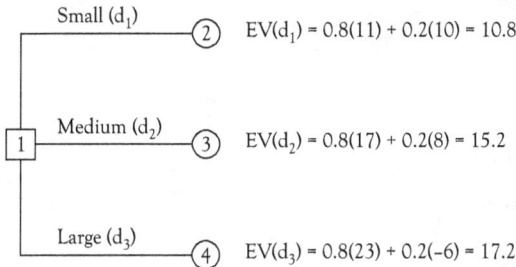

Figure 7.8 *Expected values for the Cincinnati apartment project*

state of nature probabilities, we can calculate what is called the **expected value for each decision alternative**.

You can calculate the expected value using the data in the payoff table in Figure 7.8, and the newly estimated probabilities (0.80 for strong demand and therefore 0.20 for weak demand). Therefore, the expected values are calculated as

$$Ev(d_1) = 0.8(11) + 0.2(10) = 10.8$$
$$Ev(d_2) = 0.8(17) + 0.2(8) = 15.2$$
$$Ev(d_3) = 0.8(23) + 0.2(-6) = 17.2$$

Looking at these expected values, we choose the decision alternative that gives us the largest expected value, which is d3 or building a large complex of 150 units. We can add this expected value to the decision tree as seen in Figure 7.8. This is a compact graphical way to depict all the necessary data involved in calculating the expected value approach for decision analysis.

Qualitative Data Analyses

We use the term qualitative data to distinguish it from quantitative data where the variable takes on a numerical value. Qualitative data can come in many flavors including **categorical data**, textual responses to questions, as well as ideas and other meaningful observations where their value is not a number that has a physical meaning.

The types of analyses used for data collection and analyses discussed are as follows:

- Survey
- Interviews
- Affinity diagrams
- Multivoting

Survey

Survey design is a large and detailed subject. We will cover the very basics in this section so that you are able to consider collecting and using this type of qualitative information. Surveys are useful ways to collect information such as ideas, opinions, levels of satisfaction, and feelings.[7] Surveys can collect information from a wide cross-section of people at a relatively low cost. Especially now with web-based tools to construct and widely distribute surveys online, surveys can be used effectively.

Surveys are often used to create useful sample information to make conclusions about the larger population being observed. Classic surveys are Gallup polls or TV watching surveys to create insight on overall behavior of the population as a whole. Therefore, surveys need to be representative and have a large enough sample size to be worthwhile.

A useful example would be if you inherited a successful radio station: you may want to survey your listeners to see why they listen, what they like about your station, and what they think you could improve.

Some basic tips on useful survey design are as follows:

- Define the objective of the survey and identify what information you plan to collect to achieve this objective.
- Do not use biased wording that can skew your responses.
- Recognize that a low percentage return could be a problem. Less than 25% returned could be biased negatively.
- For a survey, consistently use the same 3- or 5- or 7-point scale for responses.
- You can use multiple-choice questions.
- You can use yes/no and explain questions.
- You can use open-ended questions to explore areas not well understood.

Interviews

Interviews are more intensive, normally done face to face, and can collect more in-depth information.

Interviews are often only as good as the person conducting the interviews. Interviews can be a useful step in talking with key decision makers to understand what key issues they believe need to be looked at when examining a business situation. Structured interviews with key people can collect key information and identify key themes and trends.[8] Detailed design and validation of interviews and how to conduct effective interviews are beyond the scope of this text.

Affinity Diagrams

The affinity diagram is one of the most powerful analysis techniques for grouping large numbers of complex ideas, opinions, and issues that may at first appear unrelated to meaningful groupings that are displayed visually.[9,10] This analysis technique is very useful with groups of people, getting their input and collective knowledge to understand the nature of a problem and to identify key ideas and action items. This technique requires both logical and creative forms of thinking. It depends on effective teamwork that values different perspectives. (This is also known as the KJ Method developed in the 1960s in Japan.) We provide a bit more detail than normal because of the usefulness of the affinity diagram.

Steps to Construct an Affinity Diagram

1. Select the topic or problem statement you want to address. Use a full statement and use neutral terms. Write this sentence on the top of a flip chart or on a large post-it note and put it at the top of the working space on a wall or several flip charts.
2. Explain what brainstorming is and the guidelines you will use. General guidelines normally include the following:
   a. All ideas are valuable. Evaluating or criticizing ideas at this point is not allowed.
   b. Participants can piggyback or build on the ideas of others.
   c. Participants must wait their turn to add new ideas or build on a previous idea.
3. Use brainstorming to generate ideas or issues around the central problem or topic statement. Each person has some private time to generate as many ideas as they can come up with. Each person writes one idea or issue on a post-it note.
4. Each person has their turn where they put up on a wall all their ideas. As they post the ideas on the wall or flip chart, they read the idea and clarify if there are any questions. Each person is not to sell or advocate for their ideas as they post them. An option is to have each person put one idea up and then allow the next person to put up an idea and continue in this "round-robin" fashion until all the ideas from everyone are posted.

5. Note: Typical affinity diagrams have 40–60 items with those having 100–200 ideas not unusual.

6. In silence, have the group sort the idea post-it notes into related groupings. No verbal discussion is allowed. Post-it notes can be moved from one group to another by anyone anytime. This step can take awhile. If you have a large number of people participating, you may want to break them into two or three subgroups and have each subgroup have some dedicated time for grouping—such as each subgroup gets 15 minutes and then they sit down and let the next subgroup to group, and so forth. You continue grouping until all items are in a group or by themselves and no additional moves are being made by anyone. Having an idea all by itself is called a loner or an orphan and they are valid.

7. Now for each grouping, create a HEADER card that describes the overall theme that those ideas or issues are largely about. You must gain consensus of the wording of the header card by the team so that it captures the central idea of that grouping. It is legal to separate groupings of issues into multiple groupings, each with their own header card. Write the header card on a post-it note in a new color and place it above the grouping it summarizes. Ideally you should have between five and ten header cards or groupings.

8. Examine the final groupings and header cards. See if they make sense. Find a way to capture and summarize in writing the work you have done.

9. The next step after an affinity diagram is completed depends on the nature of the team and the problem or issue statement they are working on. For example, if the groupings represent key tasks to accomplish the overall objective, then the groupings could be logical categories of work in a work breakdown structure for managing a complex project. However if the groupings represent ideas on how to solve a major problem, then develop plans for how you would implement each grouping's set of ideas.

10. You should have an overall visual of the groupings and their header cards, as well as a written document listing all the ideas and issues by grouping header. Figure 7.9 illustrates a typical format of an affinity diagram.

What are the roles—and attributes of a contemporary worship leader

* Courtesy of Northminster Presbyterian Church
Cincinnati, Ohio

Public face of the worship service	Organizes contemporary worship service	Personal attributes
Most frequent interactions with worshipers	Plays contemporary christian rock music	Feels called to serve
Represents contemporary services to the rest of the church	Is an outstanding trained musician	Energetic, self-starting, high initiative
Best able to Recruit volunteers	Respects, motivates, and inspires other band members	Leadership
	Selects songs	Works well with others
	Selects musicians	Creative
	Leads prayer	Articulate
	Recruits volunteers	Agile
	Coordinates with pastors	"EDGY"

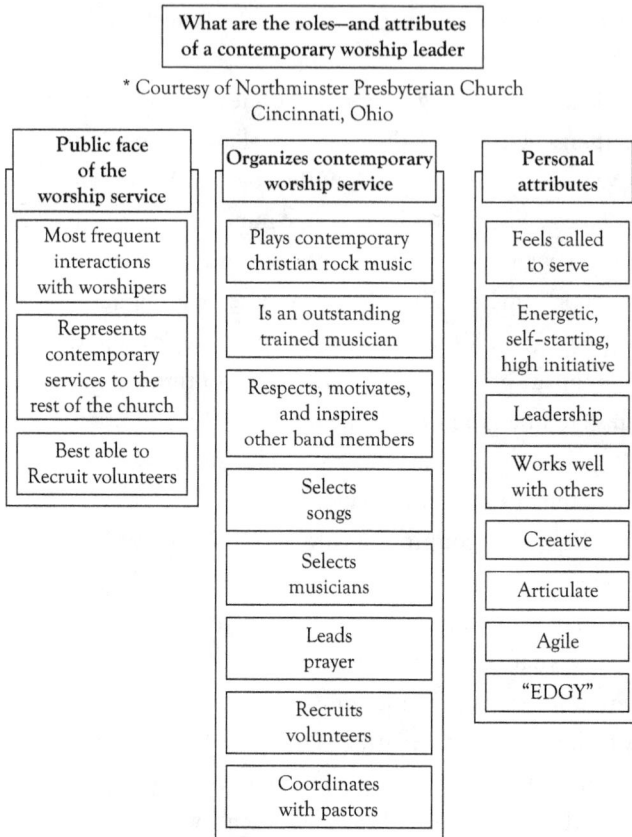

Figure 7.9 Affinity diagram
Source: Courtesy of Northminster Presbyterian Church Cincinnati, Ohio.

Multivoting

Multivoting is a very common technique used in many total quality and group methods. There are several variations to how multivoting is conducted. It is basically asking a group of people to vote on what they think are the most important items based on some criteria that the group understands.

For example, a project team lists 10 major potential risks for their project. The team is then asked to vote on these 10 items based on which risks they believe are the most important to have mitigation plans for. A standard round of multivoting would look like this:

1. Divide the number of total items in half and that becomes the number of votes each person gets. In this case, each person gets five votes.
2. Then you specify the voting rules. One option is to allow people to spend all their votes on one item if they feel that strongly about it. Another option is to restrict voting by stating that you cannot place more than one vote on any item.
3. People would then cast their votes based on the declared voting rules and the votes would be counted and the top item(s) identified.
4. Multiple rounds of voting can be used if you have a large number of items to be voted on. In each round, you start with step 1.

Making good decisions consists of using all the data you have at your disposal, applying selected quantitative and qualitative analysis techniques, and synthesizing those results with the political reality of the situation to make the best call you can.

Making Good Decisions With Data at United Way of Greater Cincinnati

STORY: Prior to 2001, United Way of Greater Cincinnati (UWGC worked to improve lives by mobilizing the financial resources of businesses, individuals, and foundations in support of direct service programs. Despite all the money raised and all the services United Way and others had provided, many problems in the community continued and some grew worse. While the community had provided high-quality child care that improved children's lives, it didn't know what percentage of the children were ready to succeed in kindergarten. While providing programs to help youth build character and skills, a large percentage of them weren't graduating from high school. While many adults received job training, too many did not attain and retain jobs.

To address these issues, United Way saw a need to change its work, to deal with the conditions that created them in the first place. In 2001, United Way began a series of efforts to implement a new model focused on mobilizing diverse resources and partnerships that go beyond the dollars pledged through the annual campaign. The new model, called Community Impact, is represented in Figure 7.10.

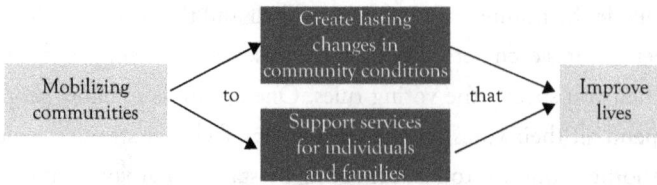

Figure 7.10 Mobilizing communities

Why Develop an Agenda for Community Impact

The basis for development of the *Agenda for Community Impact* can be summarized as a commitment to establishing long-term community goals, determining how we'll measure success, developing and implementing the right multidimensional strategies, and measuring results over time as depicted in Figure 7.9. The *Agenda*

- tracks community trends that relate to the identified community indicators;
- establishes and prioritizes outcomes or goals;
- builds on existing community strengths and assets;
- addresses gaps and redundancies in services;
- identifies multidimensional strategies needed to create community change;
- measures progress and results;
- requires supporting partnerships and collaboration.

To make the change, the Board and leadership of UWGC convened community researchers to develop an environmental scan, combined it with data from United Way of America, and developed a case for change in Cincinnati. This case for change highlighted the key business challenge facing United Way: that key problems were standing in the way of Cincinnati's quality of life, and UWGC could be a leader in achieving greater community impact.

These two trends were clearly supported by data. In Cincinnati Public Schools, the largest urban school district in Hamilton County, 56% of the children were entering kindergarten behind and studies show that most won't catch up. Unemployment and poverty rates were not improving substantially, despite the exponential proliferation of nonprofits in the area over the last three decades.

Beginning with Vision 2010, a new strategic direction approved by its Board of Directors in 2002, United Way used critical community data as follows:

1. Develop a baseline of community indicators issued in 2004 (and every other year after) called *The State of the Community* Report.
2. Engage more than 600 community leaders, volunteers, citizens, community and agency partners in the development and launch of the *Agenda for Community Impact* in 2005.
3. Issue a *Call for Investment* that became the way that United Way invested in community and agency partners to achieve the Agenda's goals. The first three-year funding decisions for 2007–2009 were made in 2006.
4. Partner with other key organizations to initiate important system-change collaboratives such as *Success by 6, Strive and Partners for a Competitive Workforce.*

The Connection of Education, Income, and Health

Research at United Way Worldwide and UWGC confirmed three essential building blocks for a good life—education, income, and health—that are interconnected, with poverty having a profound effect on all three. For example, education is the basis for individual success; it is essential to getting and keeping a job with a livable wage and health benefits. In the Cincinnati region, 28.1% of adults have a bachelor's degree or higher, ranking our region 10th compared to 12 peer regions. Data shows that when an individual's education level rises, lifelong earnings rise with it. And children who have access to health care have better attendance and grades.

The Current Agenda for Community Impact

The *Agenda for Community Impact* has been revised several times in the past 8 years. The current version shows how the insights and data shared

Agenda for Community Impact

United Way
of Greater Cincinnati

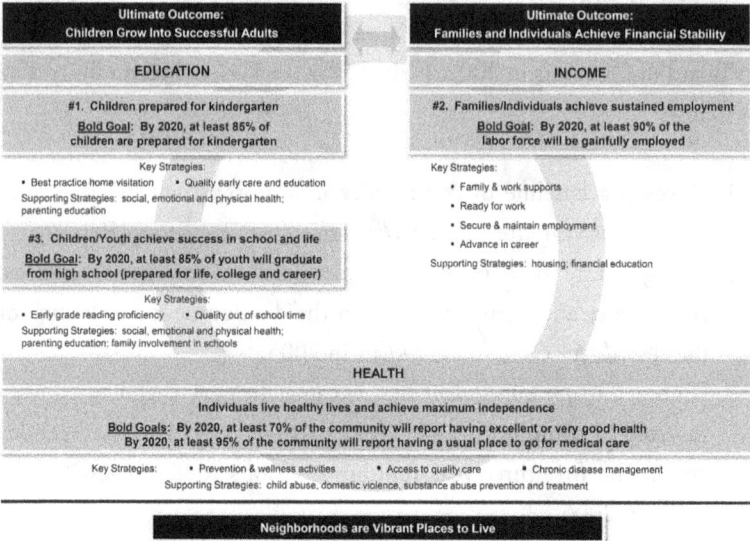

Ultimate Outcome:	Ultimate Outcome:
Children Grow Into Successful Adults	Families and Individuals Achieve Financial Stability

EDUCATION	INCOME

EDUCATION

#1. Children prepared for kindergarten
Bold Goal: By 2020, at least 85% of
children are prepared for kindergarten

Key Strategies:
• Best practice home visitation   • Quality early care and education
Supporting Strategies: social, emotional and physical health;
parenting education

#3. Children/Youth achieve success in school and life
Bold Goal: By 2020, at least 85% of youth will graduate
from high school (prepared for life, college and career)

Key Strategies:
• Early grade reading proficiency   • Quality out of school time
Supporting Strategies: social, emotional and physical health;
parenting education; family involvement in schools

INCOME

#2. Families/Individuals achieve sustained employment
Bold Goal: By 2020, at least 90% of the
labor force will be gainfully employed

Key Strategies:
• Family & work supports
• Ready for work
• Secure & maintain employment
• Advance in career
Supporting Strategies: housing, financial education

HEALTH

Individuals live healthy lives and achieve maximum independence
Bold Goals: By 2020, at least 70% of the community will report having excellent or very good health
By 2020, at least 95% of the community will report having a usual place to go for medical care

Key Strategies: • Prevention & wellness activities   • Access to quality care   • Chronic disease management
Supporting Strategies: child abuse, domestic violence, substance abuse prevention and treatment

Neighborhoods are Vibrant Places to Live

Figure 7.11 Current agenda for community impact

influence the focus and priorities of the Agenda (Figure 7.11). The key components are as follows:

- Ultimate outcomes
- Bold measurable goals
- Key strategies
- Supporting strategies

The *Agenda for Community Impact* is data based and focused on the root causes of poverty in the Cincinnati region. The bold goals are the measures of focus to achieve the following ultimate objectives:

- Education = Children grow into successful adults
- Income = Families and individuals achieve financial stability
- Health = Individuals live healthy lives and achieve maximum independence
- Overall = Neighborhoods are vibrant places to live

Conclusion

This case illustrates that "What Gets Measured Gets Done." While UWGC was a successful United Way and its programs were achieving positive outcomes, it realized that it was not achieving needed improvements in community life. By using objective data, priorities were chosen, an effective *Agenda for Community Impact* was developed and, in collaboration with many community and agency partners, is being executed in the Cincinnati region.

Progress on this agenda is measured and reviewed quarterly and changes made as needed to reach the stated bold goals and other important in-process outcome measures.

Key Learnings

1. The detailed analysis of data pointed the UWGC to a more effective portfolio of projects that deal directly with root causes.
2. The *Agenda for Community Impact* is a business model that drives the work of the entire organization, not just select departments and volunteer committees. Leadership from all departments in the organization had to be involved in the process or success wouldn't have been achieved.
3. Research and data play a much larger role than in former United Way work. It meant creating new partnerships, and recruiting volunteers and staff with different skill sets.
4. It was critical to build in an intentional course of action to educate volunteers and staff on the new business model of community impact as well as the goals of the *Agenda* to garner ownership. Along the way, it was also important to build in buy-in from key stakeholders such as agency partners and their boards.
5. Course corrections were necessary. The "what" (*Agenda for Community Impact*) was developing at the same time as the "how"—the methods in which the investment decision-making process would change. United Way was too quick to describe the proposed "how" and had to dial back its enthusiasm and focus harder on the "what," and embrace the consideration for both direct and systemic solutions.

6. The development of guiding principles kept volunteers and staff focused and moving forward. Guiding the transformation were principles such as "bold but smart" and "impact, alignment, and accountability."

7. Board commitment and leadership was imperative to guiding the transformation to community impact, and staff leadership was critical in developing Board commitment.

Robert C. Reifsnyder, President, United Way of Greater Cincinnati UWGC

Patricia Nagelkirk, Director Community Impact, United Way of Greater CincinnatiUWGC

Key Assessment Questions

1. On a 5-point scale (1 = do not support, 3 = support to some extent, 5 = fully support), to what extent does your organization support the use of data (both quantitative and qualitative) to make important decisions?

2. Identify three to five important processes where you are tracking both in-process measures and outcome measures.

3. What ongoing scorecards, graphs, and so forth do you use regularly to monitor the progress of your business results?

4. What types of uncertainty are central to your organization's core mission? How do you measure and manage/mitigate this uncertainty?

5. What do you forecast as a part of running your organization? What overall trends and patterns do you look for? What forecasting techniques or approaches do you use?

Notes

1. Swanson (1995).
2. Brassard and Ritter (1988).
3. Anderson, Sweeney, and Williams (2006).
4. Anderson et al. (2006).
5. Anderson et al. (2006).
6. Anderson et al. (2006).

7. Swanson (1995).
8. Patel and Riley (2007), pp. 459–474.
9. Swanson (1995).
10. Brassard, Finn, Ginn, and Ritter (2002).

References

Anderson, D. R., Sweeney, D. J., Williams, T. A. (2006). *Modern business statistics* (2nd edn.). Mason, OH, Thomson South-Western.

Brassard, M., Finn, L., Ginn, D., Ritter, D. (2002), *The six sigma memory Jogger II*, Salem, NH: GOAL/QPC.

Brassard, M., & Ritter, D. (1988). *The memory jogger – A pocket guide of tools for continuous improvement.* Methuen, MA, GOAL/QPC.

Kloppenborg, T. J., & Laning, L. J. (2012). *Strategic leadership of portfolio and project management , New York, NY:* Business Expert Press (This chapter draws heavily from this other Business Expert Press Book).

Patel, V. N., Riley, A. W. (2007, October). Linking data to decision making: Applying qualitative data analysis methods and software to identify mechanisms for using outcomes data. *The Journal of Behavioral Health Services & Research, 34*(4), 459–474.

Swanson, R. C. (1995). *The quality improvement handbook.* Delray Beach, FL, St. Lucie Press.

CHAPTER 8

Portfolio Management

Paul R. Kling

Paul Kling, PE, PMP, completed a 30-year Management career with Duke Energy in 2013 focused on enterprise Project Portfolio Management, Process Design, and Business Development. He is currently involved in business consulting, as well as venture capital and nonprofit business development in Cincinnati, Ohio.

Every organization, large or small, exists to accomplish a set of objectives. Whether seeking financial goals, governmental administration, or altruistic social purposes, each organization accomplishes its objectives through the ongoing implementation of the aggregate projects, programs, and initiatives that it selects and ultimately undertakes—its own unique "Portfolio."

The Project Management Institute definition of a Portfolio states:

> *A Portfolio is a collection of components (i.e. projects, programs, subportfolios, and other work such as maintenance and operations) that are grouped together to facilitate the effective management of that work in order to meet strategic business objectives.*[1]

Bringing this universally accepted definition into view, forms the basis of the discussion as it applies to any organization of any type. The often overlooked factor is that the business and organizational environment affecting the Portfolio is dynamic and ever-changing. Organizational priorities and the paths leading to accomplishing objectives through the Portfolio are in a continuous state of flux. Effective Portfolio Management requires the implementation of timely and consistent techniques applicable to any organization.[2]

This chapter will cover how organizational leaders can approach a diverse and dynamic combination of organizational objectives in conjunction with successfully implementing the Portfolio of initiatives needed to accomplish these objectives. It will also present ways in which the true cost and risk of certain initiatives can be better understood. The ability of leadership to understand, communicate, govern, and conduct the implementation of the Portfolio is essential to organizational success. It is a continuous, comprehensive, and interactive process that involves ongoing risk and change management at all levels of the organization.

This chapter is designed to help you better understand and begin mastery of the following areas:

1. Translating strategic organizational objectives into well-communicated Portfolio development factors. You will be able to provide a framework for determining and communicating those initiatives that best serve the organization's most pressing objectives.

2. How individual projects, programs, and initiatives can be selected and ranked to form a Portfolio that represents a balance of organizational priorities. You will be able to use a simple tool to evaluate the value and risk of moving forward or delaying each project.

3. Determining true Portfolio limiting factors and associated risk levels in addition to readily identified funding and resource limitations. You will be able to visualize and quantify the real risk to your organization associated with each project and build a framework for discussion.

4. Identifying the processes and leadership required to support the quality and successful outcome of the Portfolio over the long term. You will be able to pinpoint the critical factors for the success of both individual initiatives and the entire array of projects being undertaken.

5. Governing the Portfolio management process flexibly to account for changing business conditions. Most importantly, you will have a method to support consistent ongoing decision making relative to your organization's most important objectives.

Introduction to Starfire Council

Starfire Council was formed over 20 years ago and focused on creating social opportunities for people with disabilities. Following 20 years of continuous service, Starfire was considered a highly successful and growing organization dedicated to improving the lives of young adults with disabilities in the Greater Cincinnati area.

In the midst of this success, Starfire's Executive Director had an opportunity to review the impact of Starfire on the community it served over this 20-year span and came to the realization that the core products and services that his organization delivered were more part of the overall societal problem, rather than a sustainable long-term solution.

The social isolation and exclusion that Starfire as an organization was intending to change had inadvertently become institutionalized and accepted as part of their ongoing operations. What was once considered intolerable isolation had merely become "tolerable isolation." It became alarmingly clear to the Executive Director that the fundamental Mission and Vision of the organization and the associated Portfolio of initiatives, projects, and programs currently under way had to be steered in a completely new direction. Nearly all of the efforts, investments, resources, projects, programs, tools, and training, and the underlying foundational assumptions of the organization had to be re-examined:[3]

- How does an organizational leader go about making this type of transformation?
- How can all of the initiatives, programs, and projects either under way, or under consideration be re-evaluated against an entirely new set of criteria?
- How can this effort be managed with a level of quality, accountability, and certainty that accounts for the lives, careers, and expectations that will be impacted as a result?

Portfolio Management—A Comprehensive Leadership Approach

Realized or not, every organizational executive is in fact continuously leading the implementation of their Portfolio at all times. Whether significant or seemingly insignificant, each decision, indecision, or unawareness of the need for a decision is a signal to stakeholders and staff members of the organization's priorities relative to accomplishing strategic objectives. The emphasis organizational leaders place on specific initiatives within the Portfolio is a signal watched closely at all levels. It is imperative that leaders understand and can effectively communicate the risks and priorities of all elements of the Portfolio for the organization. Daunting as it may seem, there are simple techniques that can be used to manage an organizational Portfolio to realistically deliver results and recognize risks.

Project and Initiative Analysis

Without new and ongoing projects, programs, and initiatives, any organization would become stagnant and unable to cope with ongoing changes occurring both internally and externally. Here are some examples we will examine:

- Buildings and facilities are aging, outgrown, need to be replaced, repaired, or removed—**A facilities infrastructure project is born.**
- Government regulations change, and an entire staff requires training—**A human resources (HR) training program is undertaken.**
- An opportunity to save significant operating expenses and improve customer service is recognized by developing expanded website capability—**A critical IT project is initiated.**
- An entirely new market can be served by redirecting advertising in the right way—**A strategic marketing initiative is launched.**
- The Board requires community feedback on recent program changes—**An extensive survey study commences.**
- A neighboring organization with a similar client base and mission is ceasing operations and a potential combination with your organization has been offered—**A comprehensive organizational merger is contemplated.**

In each of these examples, the opportunities presented by the choice to move forward need to be weighed against the cost and risk of deploying various limited resources to successfully achieve objectives. With each new opportunity, a "Yes," "No," or "Wait" decision is made. But, what are the true opportunities, true costs, and true risks? What are the potential "costs" to the organization besides impact to capital and operational budgets? What are the real consequences to the organization (in any potential decision scenario) beyond the factors associated with a singular project, program, or initiative considered in isolation versus consideration in the context of all efforts under way? The answer is found in a Portfolio Management methodology.

A Simple Model to Enable Evaluation

As a demonstration, taking the six hypothetical initiatives and placing them in a commonly used weighted scoring model (see Figure 8.1) is an example of a fundamental element of the Portfolio Management process. Beware... this type of spreadsheet itself appears simple, but the level of executive and organizational discussion required to accurately and representatively construct it is not. Simply identifying and representing all potential and ongoing initiatives can be a large task for executives and staff alone. Putting all relevant Portfolio information in one place, at one time, in a standardized format for evaluation is an essential first step. Many sophisticated, computer based, yet user friendly, Portfolio analysis tools are available on the market today at very reasonable costs.[4]

Key Learning: Utilizing a Portfolio evaluation tool as an executive-level, decision-support focal point is the central element of Portfolio Management.

Leadership Task List

- Create a process in your organization to establish a complete Portfolio review at least annually prior to final budgeting decisions.
- Conduct a search to obtain a computer-based Portfolio analysis tool that fits your organization's needs.

Simplified Value/Risk Project Portfolio Evaluation Model

Scoring:
1 = Lowest Impact
10 = Highest Impact

Project Description	Planning Year Project Costs ($000s)	Project Value — Strategic Areas and Relative Weighting					Weighted Value Score	Project Deferral Risk — Strategic Areas and Relative Weighting					Weighted Risk Score	Combined Weighted Risk Score	Initially Selected Projects
		Operating Cost Reduction 30%	Staff Retention 30%	Client Base Expansion 20%	Staff Core Skills Expansion 10%	Impact on Federal Funding Grant 10%		Operating Cost Reduction 30%	Staff Retention 30%	Client Base Expansion 20%	Core Skills Expansion 10%	Federal Funding Grant 10%			
Buildings and Facilities Project	$ 55.00	7	7	2	7	2	5.50	9	9	2	2	2	6.20	11.70	☆
Training Program	$ 80.00	3	8	2	8	6	5.10	2	3	5	8	9	4.20	9.30	
Website IT Project	$ 164.00	8	4	8	5	8	6.50	4	8	8	5	5	6.20	12.70	☆
Marketing Initiative	$ 30.00	2	4	9	6	5	4.70	2	4	8	4	5	4.30	9.00	
Community Feedback Study	$ 169.00	2	2	8	5	7	4.00	1	3	6	5	9	3.80	7.80	
Merger Analysis	$ 80.00	2	1	9	9	6	4.20	7	5	10	9	5	7.00	11.20	☆
Planning Year Budget Limit	$ 300.00														
Selected Project Spend Forecast	$ 299.00														

Under budget, but... Opportunities missed?

What are the risks of deferral?

Figure 8.1 Simplified value/risk project portfolio evaluation model

- Assign a high-level staff member (and team) to oversee the gathering, formatting, and recording of the information.
- Be prepared to keep meticulous records of the consensus assumptions underlying the numbers in the chart as well as the strategic scoring weighting factors in place at the time of analysis.
- Prepare to review the ongoing accuracy of the underlying assumptions at least semiannually and perhaps quarterly. This includes data for initiatives that were chosen and also those that were deferred.

Opportunities—Projects That Create Organizational "Value"

Opportunities associated with initiatives are measured by the extent to which they move the goals of the organization forward. We will refer to the extent to which an initiative accomplishes this as "Project Value." As calculated in the chart, a project's value creation capability is derived from the weight of the strategic goals assigned by the organization at that particular time. And, of course, these can change. In the example in the chart, the "Website IT Project" had the highest value at 6.50 based on the value criteria in place within the chart. Value analysis creates the order of those initiatives that bring the most strategic value, given the factors considered important at that time.[5]

Note the five strategic factors being weighted by this hypothetical organization for value in the example. Also note that they are identical to the risk factors shown in the chart that will be considered in the next step:

- Organization cost reduction
- Staff retention
- Client base expansion
- Staff core skills expansion
- Impact on federal funding grants

Key Learning: Project Value analysis determines which initiatives most positively impact the balance of weighted organizational goals. (Project Risk analysis determines when those initiatives should be undertaken and should be based on the same set of weighted strategic goals.)

Leadership Task List:

- Create a "library" of recognized potential projects proposed throughout the organization and have them routed to a central group for conforming to a standard evaluation format based on expected strategic evaluation goals.
- Regularly re-evaluate previously approved and ongoing initiatives in the Portfolio to ensure that they continue to create strategic value and deserve ongoing allocation of limited resources.

Analyzing Limited Resources

Traditionally, project approvals are treated as investment decisions weighing the capital required to implement a particular project versus the anticipated return of capital from that isolated project (ROI, Payback, and NPV are common evaluation measures). The dollars needed to complete projects are typically drawn from a limited source, which then invokes prioritization of objectives and estimates of project success. In almost every organization, available capital resources are limited.

There are however many limited resources and consequential impacts, in addition to capital, that create risks for initiatives within the organization's Portfolio. And, of course, these can change significantly over the duration of an initiative's implementation and create unforeseen issues within the Portfolio. Here are a few categories and specifics to consider.[6]

Human Resources and Discretionary Effort—Obvious, but easy to ignore. The skilled HR needed to complete important projects normally have many other tasks and obligations. Make sure the limits of all project responsibilities down to the individual level are well understood (and a contingency plan is in place).

Time—Always balanced against cost and quality elements of a project. If either quality or cost is considered a fixed, non-negotiable factor, time (basically taking longer to complete the project) becomes a balancing element. If time is instead the fixed parameter, there may be quality or cost consequences to be considered for mitigation under adverse or unforeseen implementation conditions.

Skills and Experience—Do the key project participants have the skills, experience, and behavioral capabilities to carry out the effort for the duration? At what point and under what conditions might skill and experience limitations be reached?

Family Life Balance/Key Individual Capacity—Do not take this item for granted. Make sure key personnel are chosen wisely, and that there is a backup plan in place. Individual endurance limits and personal priorities will create limits on initiatives going forward.

Adverse Consequence Absorption—What are the limits of the organization to absorb change induced by projects in the Portfolio (i.e., relocating staff or offices)? Consider how this will affect other projects in the Portfolio.

Sustained Organizational Commitment—Can all the initiatives in the Portfolio run the full distance? Are there limits to any stakeholder's ability to take on the challenges or stay the course? A few of these to consider include Board of Directors, Investors and Donors, Leadership Staff, Key Suppliers, and Community Groups

Key Learning—Resource limitations stretch far beyond available capital into many other factors. These limitations ultimately create risks to the Portfolio as various dynamic factors and assumptions change, and cost, quality, and time inevitably need to be balanced as a result.

Leadership Task List:

- Before undertaking a project and Portfolio risk analysis, make sure the definitions of Portfolio success are well understood in terms of time, cost, and quality.
- Ensure that a comprehensive review and discussion of limiting factors has occurred for each project within the Portfolio, and for the Portfolio as a whole.

Analyzing Implementation Risk Versus Deferral Risk

Following the Value Analysis and Limitation Assessments described previously, an analysis of risk needs to occur. Risk should be considered within three specific and distinct areas.

1. The risk of undertaking and then not completing one or more projects in the Portfolio at the level of quality required, in the time frame needed, and for the cost that was expected.
2. The risk that when completed, regardless of the cost, timing, or quality, the Portfolio will not deliver the full strategic value intended.
3. The risk to the organization associated with decisions to defer or forego potential projects within the Portfolio that have inherent strategic value.

Definition of Risk

Basically, risk is the probability that an undesirable consequence will occur. Shown as an equation, it looks like this:

$$\text{Risk} = \text{Probability} \times \text{Consequences}.$$

When shown as a simple four-quadrant chart where probability and consequences can be plotted and compared, it can look like that in Figure 8.2.[7]

Now, let's go back to the three categories of risk that were numbered previously. In the first two of the three areas, risk is the probability of an undesirable or intolerable situation occurring during or after the implementation of the Portfolio (including unintended collateral impacts). The key point from a Portfolio Management standpoint is that the first two risk areas need to be well understood for the purpose of implementation,

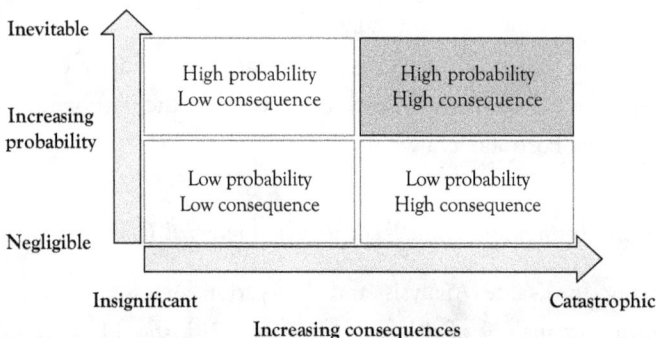

Figure 8.2 Risk analysis grid of probability and consequence

but the associated risks are dealt with as a part of the implementation by the Portfolio and Project Managers with risk mitigation methods and contingency planning. They are accepted hazards of the initiatives when they are approved to go forward.

The real effort from an organizational leadership standpoint involves decision making relative to the risk of deferring or relinquishing initiatives with important strategic value. Using the Portfolio analysis laid out in the example chart, the risks of deferral are associated with five strategic objectives matching those used in the value analysis. In this hypothetical case, deferring the "Merger Analysis" carries with it the highest strategic risk of 7.00. When the risk scores in the chart analysis are considered in conjunction with the value scores (additive in this example), only the top three of the six initiatives would be undertaken while staying within budget limits.

Is This the Correct Decision?

It is at this point, that the most important strategic leadership conversations an organization can conduct actually need to take place. The extensive discussion of Portfolio risk at the organization's executive leadership level is the best way for the organization to understand its own risk tolerance and the relative priority of specific strategic objectives. The decisions that follow show the entire organization where executive leadership places priorities.

Topics for Consideration*: In this very simplified example, what are the potential consequences of the three initiatives that are not selected (deferred— Training Program, Marketing Initiative, and Board's Community Feedback Survey)?*

- *Which stakeholder groups are impacted?*
- *How might the deferred initiatives affect the ability to implement those projects that were selected to move forward?*
- *How important might other limiting factors besides budget (skills, personnel availability, Board tolerance, and so forth) be to the leadership decisions to be made?*

Key Learning: Separate risks associated with initiative implementation from risks associated with initiative deferral. Allow Project Managers to handle implementation risks, while ensuring executive staff discusses deferral risk.

Leadership Task List

- Prepare to facilitate the discussion involving the risk of deferral of high-value projects and initiatives.
- Understand the limiting factors associated with each project and the risks that are consequently inferred.
- Note that the Portfolio analysis discussions at this level should occur at least once in each budgeting cycle and whenever changes to strategic direction occur. Executive-level responsibility for assignments associated with this process needs to be in place to support this critical function.
- Properly communicating the outcome of the executive Portfolio decisions to the organization is a critical piece of the process.

Ongoing Evaluations

A common mistake made by organizations is the assumption that the substantial effort needed to conduct a Portfolio analysis should occur only once per budget year. In fact, once the processes to conduct the analysis are in place, this type of evaluation becomes much more standardized and routine. In many organizations, brief quarterly reviews of the entire Portfolio are appropriate. A quick review of key points is given as follows.[8]

- Involve the organization's executive team in the evaluation of any strategic changes in objectives and their impact on the Portfolio.
- Establish processes and functions that support evaluation of the ongoing Portfolio in terms of new projects to be added.
- To ensure that the Portfolio analysis process receives appropriate attention, assign ownership of the process at the executive level.
- Purposefully and proactively communicate the decisions that were made and the known opportunities, risks, and implications to all levels of the organization.

- Solicit feedback from all levels of the organization regarding limiting factors and associated risks and incorporate this organizational knowledge into the Portfolio analysis process.

Portfolio Management at Starfire Council

The fact that Starfire needed to re-evaluate its strategic direction revealed itself in a simple chart that was originally created by Jack Pealer, an advocate for societal inclusion in the early 1990s, at about the same time Starfire was formed. The chart was the result of a survey indicating the categories of people that a person with disabilities would normally contact in their lives and is shown as Figure 8.3.

What was learned from the chart indicated that 20 years after the original chart was prepared, after thousands of individuals and families participated in the programs Starfire offered, after thousands of volunteers caringly offered their time, and the organization was considered highly successful by all other measures, a new survey indicated "no significant difference" in the numbers or categories comprising the people involved in the lives of those with disabilities. By this measure, the multiple projects and programs that had been undertaken and were currently under

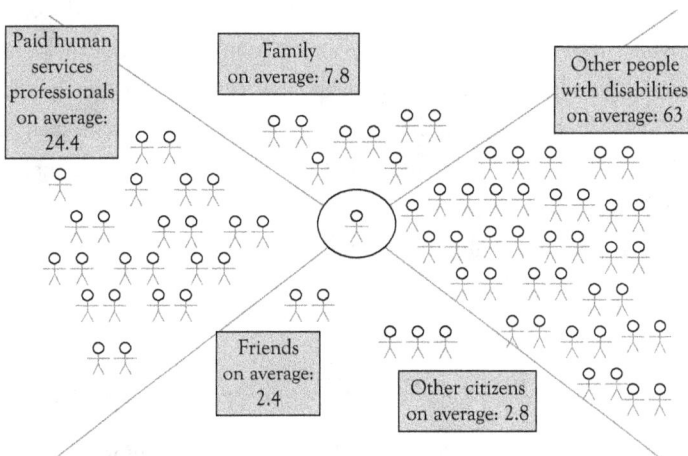

Figure 8.3 Jack Pealer chart—who is in the life of a person with disabilities?

way were not meeting the organization's core objectives of inclusion of people with disabilities.

It became quite clear to the Executive Director that the fundamental Mission and Vision of the organization and the associated Portfolio of initiatives, projects, and programs then under way had to be steered in a completely new strategic direction. Nearly all of the resources, initiatives, projects, programs, facilities, and the underlying foundational assumptions of the Starfire organization had to be re-examined and redirected.

How Starfire Made the Changes to Their Strategy

Starfire's Executive Director had to first convince all key stakeholders of the value in comprehensively re-evaluating the organization's strategies to match the new Mission and Vision. The more onerous problem was that no one immediately knew what the new strategies should be. An enormous societal dilemma was being addressed by Starfire. The strategies would need to be tried and tested along with ongoing evaluation of impacts to the Portfolio. Uncertain limits would be revealed and tested bringing about uncharted areas of risk. Significant ongoing Board-level involvement would be required along with new processes to solicit and incorporate critical feedback from staff and stakeholders.

Numerous communication sessions ultimately brought logic, clarity, and Board-level support. A framework of change was created in the organization, and newly developed strategies were tentatively rolled out. The focus was no longer about mechanically bringing a small percentage of isolated people with disabilities from the entire region to Starfire, but on creating a sustainable social structure within communities to foster natural inclusion of people with disabilities. Starfire would change from proving a tangible social service at their facility to facilitating tangible social change throughout the region.

Risks Evaluated, Recognized, and Communicated at All Levels

Multiple new areas and levels of risk, relative to the new Portfolio of initiatives, had to be now evaluated going forward. At one level, analysis and feedback showed that the new strategies would not match the career ambitions, experience, or skill sets of many staff members. This set up new limits relative to staff capability and availability. Several staff members soon left Starfire for similar organizations still offering familiar services.

Starfire's Executive Director headed an effort to saturate stakeholders, staff, clients, and their family members (who avidly supported the organization's previous strategies) with information establishing the certainty of specific aspects of the strategies going forward. Also communicated in a clear way was the uncertainty of the timing and the many hurdles that would be faced along the way. This communication took place at all levels of the organization and emphasized the impact on ongoing Board-level decisions as well as daily operational and staffing decisions. Focused discussions regarding changes in strategy and projects were held with key stakeholder groups—donors, volunteers, clients, and their family members. The communication began over 3 years ago and is ongoing as the pervasive changes continue to unfold.

Central to the communication function was openness to learning and feedback from all stakeholder areas and a plan to incorporate what was learned into the organization's unfolding strategies. In fact, facilitating this specific type of "learning discussion" in the community would itself become a fundamental core competency and service product of the new Starfire as an organization going forward.

Shifting Priorities and the Reconstruction of the Portfolio

Starfire's Portfolio analysis showed that projects such as planned upgrades to Starfire's headquarters were no longer evaluated as a top priority under the new strategies, but initiatives such as finding locations to conduct community meetings were a main concern. The same analysis showed that Starfire University would still continue to be a centerpiece of the organization but in a new context, one that supported sustainable social strategies in the community rather than being a top tier goal for just a few individuals.

The changes to the Mission and Vision and ultimately to the organization's strategic objectives recreated the evaluation criteria by which ongoing and new efforts were being judged. A thorough, comprehensive, and fully communicated approach to the changes that would eventually alter lives and careers is enabling Starfire to successfully "learn" its way along an uncertain path to a promising future.

The basic concepts fundamental to Portfolio Management outlined in this chapter continue to be at the center of Starfire's efforts to manage the transition of their organization going forward.

Key Learnings From the Starfire Case

The Starfire case points out, in a very real way, how the basic concepts of Portfolio Management can be applied to a significant strategy change for an organization. These same principals can be readily applied to organizations undergoing little or no changes to strategic goals. Establishing the Portfolio Management process ensures that the projects and initiatives under way match strategic intent and risk tolerance levels, while providing a ready, consistent, and ongoing decision-support tool for management. There are several key benefits and lessons learned that can be readily applied to any organization:

1. Having ongoing familiarity with the process, Starfire's Executive Management can readily adjust the relative importance of specific goals to match the organization's evolving strategic emphasis. The emphasis placed on each strategic area can then be communicated and used as the standard throughout the organization.
   o **Management involvement in understanding, defining, weighting, and then communicating strategic factors to depict the current business environment to those involved in implementation is essential for consistent decision making and effectively achieving objectives.**
2. All potential projects as they are conceived and developed are set up to be evaluated based on a consistent value and risk criteria. The outcome provides Starfire's management and staff members with consistent and well-understood decision-making information applicable to all initiatives in all areas.
   o **Ongoing year-round management of project and initiative selection allows strategy discussions to occur whenever needed**

with updated strategic priorities and consistent decision support available.

3. Ongoing risk analysis is a key part of the overall process. Starfire Management recognized that risks would change as the strategy changed and new resource limitations were identified.

o **Separating the risk of project implementation from risk of project deferral enabled decision making to move forward in spite of the concerns related to unknown factors in each new initiative.**

4. The most significant result of the Portfolio Management process may well be the certainty to which implementation of the Portfolio can be approached. Even in a transition as significant as that Starfire is approaching, high levels of well-communicated management scrutiny leave little doubt about executive support for the plan going forward.

o **The Portfolio Management evaluation process enables management and staff to approach each initiative or project with a high level of confidence and the ability to re-assess and make course corrections readily, if needed.**

Most organizational leaders will not face changes to strategic goals on the scale of Starfire's transition. However, many leaders do face complex arrays of projects and initiatives that may not, at times, align with organizational strategies and emphasis. Deploying limited resources of capital, time, people skills, or Board-level patience to a Portfolio that is not moving the organization in the desired direction can be difficult to recuperate.

Many organizations of all sizes have adopted a Portfolio Management approach to evaluate their unique set of ongoing and incoming projects and initiatives. The key principals to success are recognizing that the effort is an ongoing commitment requiring high-level management oversight, adequate administrative staffing, and strong communication channels within the organization and among key stakeholders. Success at performing Portfolio Management is essential to the long-term success of any organization. Once established as a standard process within the organization, it will become integrated as an essential ongoing business function.[9]

Key Assessment Questions

1. Describe the process your organization currently uses to ensure the alignment of Portfolio projects and initiatives with strategic goals?
2. Which executive-level area of your organization "owns," or do you believe should own, the Portfolio Management process?
3. How are the priorities associated with various potentially conflicting strategic goals and subsequent project decisions communicated throughout your organization?
4. How well understood is Portfolio risk at the executive level in your organization? How is implementation risk differentiated from project deferral risk in the analysis at the executive decision-making level?
5. Describe how a project that is being implemented in your organization might be re-evaluated if changes in strategic direction suddenly occur. How is feedback from staff members and stakeholders included in the analysis?

Notes

1. Project Management Institute (2009).
2. Microsoft Corporation (2008).
3. Vogt (2012, December).
4. Kloppenborg and Laning (2012).
5. UMS Group (2012).
6. Lee Merkhofer Consulting (2012).
7. AIRMIC, Alarm, and IRM: 2010 (2013).
8. PM Solutions (2013).
9 Crawford (2008).

References

AIRMIC, Alarm, & IRM: 2010. (2013). *A structured approach to Enterprise Risk Management (ERM) and the requirements of ISO 31000*. Retrieved April 15, 2013, from http://www.theirm.org/documents/SARM_FINAL.pdf

Crawford, J. K. (2008). *Seven steps to strategy execution—Center for business practices*. Haverstown, PA; PM Solutions.

Kloppenborg, T. J., & Laning, L. J. (2012). *Strategic leadership of portfolio and project management*. New York, NY: Business Expert Press.

Lee Merkhofer Consulting. (2012). *Priority systems*. Retrieved March 9, 2012, from http://www.prioritysystem.com/reasons2c.html

Microsoft Corporation. (2008). *Project portfolio management—Doing the right things right*. Van Haren Publishing.

PM Solutions. (2013). Make the commitment to project portfolio management. Retrieved May 30, 2013, from http://www.pmsolutions.com/white_papers

Project Management Institute. (2009). *A guide to the project management body of knowledge* (PMBOK® Guide), (Chapter 1). Newtown Square, PA: Project Management Institute.

UMS Group. (2012). *The optimizer – An investment prioritization tool*. Retrieved October 15, 2012, from http://www.umsgroup.com

Vogt, T. (2012, December). *Starfire: An inclusive*. Cincinnati, OH: Starfire.

CHAPTER 9

Leveraging Information Technology

Laurence J. Laning

Laurence J. Laning, PhD, Laurence retired from Procter & Gamble after 29 years in IT. He was the Chief IT global architect for P&G in his last 5 years with the company. He is currently the Missions Director at Northminster Presbyterian Church in Cincinnati. He is an adjunct professor in Xavier's University College of Business. He is an active consultant for YourEncore Inc. and Xavier's Leadership Center.

Introduction

For many nonprofit organizations, information technology (IT can be a confusing, intimidating, and costly area. The technical jargon, endless acronyms, and IT professionals, consultants, and vendors who speak "geek," can be very frustrating.

Purpose

The purpose of this chapter is listed as follows:

- What are the possible benefits to my organization?
- Acquaint you with the basics of IT so that you have an understanding of what is possible using information/ computer technology
- Why is data management so important?
- Outline practical advice on how and when to use IT consultants
- Give you insight into how best to select and work with software vendors

Literally every organization today depends on IT to operate in some way. As you look to execute projects of all types in your organization to implement change, many of these projects will have significant IT components and applications directly involved.

Information technology can be leveraged significantly to help you achieve your organization's mission. Information technology is a strategic component for significant change and achieving overall cost efficiencies.

In Thomas Friedman's groundbreaking book, *The World is Flat*,[1] he explains how 10 key forces are at work to make the world a level playing field for people in all countries around the world. Eight of the 10 forces have either a direct or an applied use of IT.

It is for these reasons that we have chosen to include a chapter on IT in this book.

Introduction to the Health Collaborative

The Health Collaborative is a nonprofit organization in Cincinnati, Ohio that works together with patients, providers, and payers to create better care, better health, and lower costs for the greater Cincinnati area.

One priority of the Health Collaborative is to help the community achieve better control of Type II diabetes. This case example illustrates how IT and data management coupled with doctors and patients working together using common health goals are improving health care and outcomes for patients who have Type II diabetes.

Key question facing the Health Collaborative leadership:
How do we get physicians and patients working together to improve the health of patients with Type II diabetes?

Possible Benefits From the Use of Information Technology

While it is true that most organizations use IT to run their operation, it is important to identify the tangible and intangible benefits possible from the use of IT.

There are three fundamental value drivers that can be used to describe and quantify potential benefits to an organization:

1. To do something **better** or with improved *quality*
2. To do something *faster* or with greater **speed**
3. To do something **cheaper** or with less *cost*

Quantifying the benefits derived from these value drivers is not always easy. Many financial methods exist to estimate the ROI (return on investment) or the NPV (net present value) for a set of potential benefits.

Not all benefits can be quantified. Sometimes intangible benefits are present and can be very important. Do not ignore intangible benefits. An example of intangible benefits could be "What is it worth to a consumer in Cincinnati to have comparative health outcome data for physician practices so that they can make an informed decision on what physician practice to choose to use for their care?"

Information Technology—A Basic Framework

This chapter provides a basic framework to help you understand what IT is all about. To help keep it simple, the major categories of IT that we include in the basic framework are software, hardware, database technology, and the Internet as shown in Figure 9.1.[2]

Software

The two major types of software are *application software* and *systems software*. An application (often called an "App") is a computer program designed to do a specific set of tasks (e.g., process payroll checks, find a restaurant, pay an invoice, and so forth) or support a set of business processes such as providing resumes and job postings for the recruiting processes in the HR function of a company.

Applications can range from a very specific program for your handheld device (i.e., smart phone or tablet) or personal computer to do very specific things (e.g., find gas stations with the cheapest prices) to enterprise-wide sets of applications that automate hundreds of cross company work processes like electronic medical record systems for hospitals.

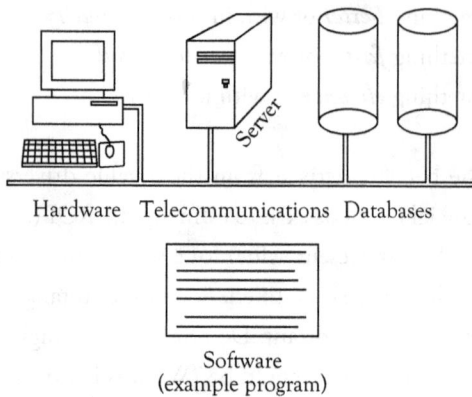

Hardware   Telecommunications   Databases

Software
(example program)

Figure 9.1 Information technologies—four major technologies

Systems software is the class of computer programs that work with the computer hardware to run or execute your application programs. These consist of programs called operating systems that control the hardware components of your computer (processor, main memory, disk storage, and so forth) and have obscure names like Vista or XP for your IBM Windows personal computer or MAC OS X (stands for the Macintosh operating systems version 10) for the Apple MAC computers. Systems software also includes language compilers that enable application programs written in different computer languages (e.g., C, Perl, JAVA, or Python) to execute or run on various types of computer hardware.[3] There are also software programs that provide basic tools that enable the user to use these programs to do meaningful work that can be tailored by the user to do exactly what they need. Examples are word processors and spreadsheet programs.

Hardware

The term hardware refers to the physical equipment that the software runs on.

Hardware can range from small personal digital assistants (PDAs), to personal computers, to midrange computers or servers, to large mainframe computers, all the way up to supercomputers. As computers get larger, they typically get faster and have more storage capacity to run more software and store more data.

It does help to "demystify" what computers do and how they are built. Computers (of any size) have the following generic components:[4]

- *The central processing unit* (CPU) is the "brains" of the computer. The CPU directs and controls the tasks done by the other components and moves and manages the data needed to perform the tasks being done.
- *Input devices* allow data and programs to be input into the computer and converted to a form that the computer can understand.
- *Output devices* take data and information and present it to people in forms that they can understand.
- *Primary storage* is an area that allows the computer to temporarily store data and programs while it is being worked on. It is like intermediate storage for "work in progress."
- *Secondary storage* is the ability of the computer to store large volumes of data over long periods of time for future use and access.
- *Communication devices* enable data and programs to flow across computer networks that link computers together either physically or virtually.

Databases

Databases, as the name implies, are the electronic storage of very large collections of data. Data is a critical asset for most organizations and organizing and storing this key information is an important capability of computer technology.

Database management software (often known as DBMS) allows people to define, and populate databases, and then to analyze, and report on data/information contained in these databases.

Databases can contain many different types of data. Quantitative information and textual descriptions are quite common. But one can also store diagrams, pictures, images, even audio recordings and video clips. Storing many different types of information is becoming common.

Data Management

An important topic closely related to databases is "data management." Think of data management as how you operate and organize to answer the following practical questions about the data you will store in your databases:

1. Specifically, what data elements will you store?
2. Where will you get these data elements? What are your reliable sources?
3. Who or how will you enter this data into your databases and how often?
4. Are the definitions of this data clear and well understood?
5. Who will know if this data is wrong and how to correct it?
6. Who is the person or persons responsible for making changes to what data you will store as your needs change over time?

You will see that data management is a critical aspect of the Health Collaborative/s example case study for this chapter.

BIG Data

There is a new set of technologies emerging in the database technology area called "BIG Data."

Big data refers to new hardware and new database management software (DBMS) that is able to store and process orders of magnitude larger databases than had been feasible or cost-effective to do on a traditional DBMS and computer.

Queries, Business Intelligence, and Data Visualization

One of the most important things to do with data held in databases is to access it, produce meaningful reports, and to analyze the data using a range of sophisticated analytical tools. There is a broad spectrum of ways to access and look at data. The umbrella term of "business intelligence (BI)" is being used to denote many different ways of "examining the interrelationships of presented facts in such a way as to guide actions toward a desired goal."[5] BI is one of the fastest areas of innovation and new developments.

The spectrum of BI tools includes the following major types:

1. *Dashboard*—The ability to publish a formal report online with intuitive VISUAL display of information including dials, gauges, and traffic lights indicating the state of performance.[6]

2. *Drillable Data*—The ability to click on data presented on the screen, with the resulting display being the underlying data, that is, drilling down a level of detail.

3. *Standard Reporting*—Provide preformatted reports whose measure and dimension types are predefined, where user parameters can optionally be provided to select the specific rows for their business need.

4. *Save as Excel*—Microsoft Excel is such a dominantly used tool that any list of BI tools must include EXCEL, either as a tool used directly against the data, or as a common medium for exchange/transport.

5. *Ad Hoc*—End users being able to generate new or modified queries with significant flexibility over content, layout, and calculations.

6. *Analytics*—Application of statistical methods against select data to solve specific questions.

7. *Advanced Visualization*—The ability to display numerous aspects of the data more efficiently by using interactive pictures and charts instead of rows and columns.

8. *Offline*—Offline capabilities imply that even though the user is disconnected from the network, they can still access the data they need and perform whatever reporting/analysis functions they require.

The Internet

Clearly one of the biggest and most impactful uses of computer technology has been the advent of the Internet—often called the World Wide

Web or the Net. It is a network of networks. In fact, the name Internet is short for the term Internetwork. The Internet is basically the ability of computer networks of all types (private, public, universities, business, government, and so forth) around the world to connect with one another, by all using the same transmission protocol (i.e., TCP/IP). This creates a global network of almost unlimited capacity and scope.

Internet 1.0 and 2.0

It is useful to think of the two generations that the Internet has gone through in the past 10 years. The first generation or sometimes called Internet 1.0 was primarily a static compilation of information—like an online library of information. This was a huge breakthrough and allowed information to be shared with billions of people around the world.[7]

As people have used and leveraged the Internet, a new generation of usage of the Internet has emerged called Internet 2.0. While Internet 1.0 was an online library of information, Internet 2.0 is like having a shared canvas where people from around the world can participate in mass collaboration to create a beautiful picture together. This now enables a dramatically different type of use of the Internet. This is the era we are now experiencing as we see thousands of apps being made available over mobile and tablet devices.

Social Media

Social media refers to how people interact with one another by creating, sharing, and exchanging information and ideas in virtual communities and networks. Facebook, LinkedIn, Flickr, and Twitter are examples that come to mind when you think about how people interact with one another these days.

Social media and social websites are not a passing fad. They represent fundamental ways that people all around the world are connecting with one another as they share common interests.

As nonprofit organizations strive to connect with new types of people, it is imperative that you plan how you can appropriately use it to achieve your organization's mission.

New Business Models Enabled by the INTERNET

The classic justification of using computer technology in businesses was to automate transactions (e.g., order management, accounts receivable, and so forth) to reduce the number of people needed to perform these tasks, improve speed, and overall efficiency and accuracy, and primarily to reduce costs. This cost savings business model is still evident in business today, but computer technology is enabling other business benefits such as faster innovation, deeper insight into data, and the ability to do things virtually versus physically.

As described briefly in the Internet section, the Web has evolved from a static source of information like a newspaper or a library (i.e., Internet 1.0), to a shared canvas where the contributions made by one party can be enhanced and built upon by others (i.e., Internet 2.0). In their book *Wikinomics, How Mass Collaboration Changes Everything*, Don Tapscott and Anthony D. Williams explain how business models can be created to leverage this new world of Internet 2.0 in dramatic new ways.[8]

Dealing With IT Consultants

Many ssmall- and medium-size organizations have very little if any IT expertise on staff. When important IT decisions need to be made or when key IT projects arise that need to be executed well, then the use of carefully selected IT consultants could be very helpful and cost-effective.

Why Use an IT Consultant?

The primary reasons organizations hire IT consultants are as follows:[9]

1. You are making a major software purchase selection and you don't believe you have adequate expertise in that area. For example, you might be purchasing supply chain software for the first time and really don't know the supply chain market place, what software vendors are good for organizations of your size and business model.

2. Information technology is becoming more important for your organization and you lack IT technical expertise on your staff. For example, you might be a medium- to large-size church and you want to put up a new website that serves the needs of your members and people searching for a church.

3. You may have a major IT project coming up that you need to implement with excellence and you don't want to hire a permanent IT staff to do this project. For example, you may be a major health care company with several hospitals, some of which you have recently acquired. And you have chosen to implement a major new hospital information system for all your hospitals and you need to hire IT consultants who can provide the staff to run and manage the projects to implement these systems over the next 2 years.

Types of IT Consultants

There are different types of firms that exist in the IT consulting industry.[10]

Professional service firms that have large professional staffs, can do most types of IT work, and normally are fairly expensive. These can be firms like one of the big accounting firms like Deloitte & Touche or a technical firm such as IBM Global Services:

- Staffing firms that primarily provide incremental IT professionals to join your staff temporarily to do very specific projects or tasks
- Typically smaller, independent consultants that typically specialize in very specific areas
- Professionals (often semiretired) who work for a fee or pro bono through companies (e.g., YourEncore) to do projects in their fields of expertise on a part-time as needed basis

And there are hybrid IT consulting firms of all shapes and sizes. Much like choosing a software vendor, be very clear what you want and how to evaluate and compare alternative consulting firms. Word of mouth referrals and checking references are critical when choosing an IT consulting firm you can trust and work with effectively.

Fixed Versus Variable Priced Consulting Engagements

Most IT consulting firms can do work either at an hourly rate, or for a fixed price for a specific project. There are pros and cons for each type of project. Fixed price contracts have the advantage of you knowing what you are paying up front, but have the downside of needing to carefully manage scope of the work being done because any change in the work will require additional costs. Hourly rate types of engagements are good when you don't know the total scope yet and you need the expertise to explore and scope out the work.

Dealing With Software Vendors

A basic principle that many organizations have adopted is to buy versus build their own software. This allows you to be a customer of a carefully selected, high-quality vendor versus being in the business of developing and supporting your own software by using resources on your staff. Buying software is typically much less costly (when looking at the total costs) and more effective in giving you software that has new capabilities added to it in a timely fashion.

However, it is important to understand some basic facts on how software vendors operate and how best to deal with them. I will deal primarily with application software vendors (vs. software vendors who write systems software like operating systems or programming languages, and so forth) since that is what most organizations care about the most.

Selecting Software Packages

When evaluating potential application software packages, it is important to do this well because once you have made an investment in a software vendor and their products, the cost and time to switch choices is very large and not easily done (although it can be done). Typically people look at a short list of market leading vendors for the application area they are most interested in. The factors I suggest people consider are as follows:[11]

- "Have to have" major functionality features—the things the software MUST do

- "Nice to have" features that are not required but could be very helpful
- Does this package comply with the important standards in this application area?
- Total cost of ownership—purchase costs, maintenance costs, training costs, operating costs
- Strength of vendor factors:
  - Is this a thought leading vendor? Will they improve their product regularly?
  - Will this vendor be in business for the long term?
  - What is this vendor's track record regarding new releases, quality, and stability of their products?
  - What do the current customers of this vendor think about this vendor and how they operate?
  - Can you work with and trust this vendor?
  - Does the vendor operate in all the geographies you need?
  - Other factors?

Software as a Service (SaaS)

A recent innovation that enables organizations to use software on an as needed basis without expensive software licenses is software as a service (SaaS).

An important tactical decision that you will need to make is whether your organization will own (lease or buy) its own computer hardware and software, or you will buy services from a company that provides "software as a service." In the SaaS scenario, the company providing the service owns the hardware and relevant software licenses and provides you the ability to interact with their hardware and software to use the application software you need when you need it. An early example of a SaaS offering that is broadly used is a customer relationship management (CRM) application called SALESFORCE.COM.[3,4]

Cloud Computing

A concept that has emerged and has gained a lot of publicity is "cloud computing." It is actually a very technical area, but in simple terms cloud computing is the ability to run an application (whether you own the application or lease the application as in SaaS) on a network of computers (most often the Internet) that you do not own. The network of computers is referred to as "the cloud." The vendor who offers cloud computing, enables you to pay for running your application(s) on a "pay as you go" basis—like a utility would. In fact, some experts also call this overall concept "utility computing."

There are many advantages and disadvantages to SaaS and cloud computing. Some of the basics are as follows.

Advantages

- You do not need to own your own application software licenses and hardware, so it can be much less expensive. The utility-based pricing leverages the economies of scale across many users.
- You receive high-quality application software written by experts who regularly provide new versions of the software with new features provided. You do not have to have expert programmers on your staff to write and maintain these applications.

Disadvantages

- One size does not fit all. You will be running applications that are written for all and will not be customized for the way you run your business. You may have to make changes to your work processes to run commercial application software.
- You do not own the software or hardware, so you will not be able to make any changes. Only the vendor providing these services can make changes.
- People who have highly secure data and application needs, often prefer to store this data and applications on hardware and software they own and control for security reasons.

Software Sales Representatives

As stated before, software sales can be very lucrative and as such is normally staffed by aggressive sales people who are driven to meet customer needs by selling products and services. It is not unusual that these positions face a turnover often. Therefore when trying to get accurate information about current or potential future products, it is helpful NOT to rely solely on your sales representative. You will need to find a way to talk with the vendor's product development leadership via a customer user group or special working sessions that you ask for.[12]

Software Versions (Major and Minor Releases, Release Cycles, Compatibility)

On a regular basis (e.g., every 6 months or annually) good software vendors will issue a new software release for a version upgrade on their existing products. There are two basic types of version upgrades:

- **Minor software release**—An increase in version number of a decimal point such as moving from release 3.0 to release 3.1 would be a minor release. Minor releases focus primarily on fixing known and reported problems with the existing software version as well as introducing enhancements that extend existing capabilities but do not usually introduce entire new areas of functionality.
- **Major software release**—Typically denoted by an increase in version with the whole number increasing such as moving from release 3.2 to 4.0, for example. Major releases are significant new products and represent significant new functionality that is being asked for by the customers of this product. Major releases will also include fixes to known product problems, but that is not the primary intent of a major release.

One important factor to understand and ask about is whether a new software release is technically compatible with the previous versions. You definitely want new releases to be compatible. Major new releases are where the most risk exists around this issue of compatibility. If a new release is NOT compatible with previous releases, you may have to rewrite any unique customizations you have made to make this work with the new software version.

Upgrades can be free or be priced separately or be included in your annual software maintenance contract. In some instances, it may be smart to SKIP a version upgrade if the cost is significant and the additional capability being added is of little or no interest.

Customer User Groups

Application software vendors most often have a customer user group organization that is established by the software vendor to provide a way for current customers to network with one another and learn from each other's experiences. To be clear, it is a marketing-oriented activity as well as a way for customers to input their future needs to the vendor for consideration in being addressed in a future release of the software.

I strongly encourage organizations that have made a commitment to an application software vendor to become active in that vendor's customer user group! In fact, I would also encourage prospective customers to attend a customer user group meeting BEFORE they make a purchase commitment so that they can get input from current customers, and to see how the vendor operates and what their impression is of how this vendor works with their customers. This will be very useful information to consider when evaluating possible vendor choices.

Contracts

It is beyond the scope of this book to go into great detail how to negotiate and establish contractual relationships with application software vendors. But from years of experience when dealing with application software vendors, there are a few basic points that will prove to be very helpful to understand.

1. Software companies have high margins and their marketing people are normally very aggressive and willing to deal, especially near the end of their (the vendors) fiscal year! Do not be bashful in asking for special accommodations.
2. It is imperative you to get your strategic purchasing manager (if you have one) involved in contract discussions as early as possible. They

are professionals in this area and can save you much money and time. IF you do not have such a resource on your staff, this is an area where a consultant specializing in software selection and contracts could be a very wise choice.

3. A common practice in the software industry is to have your annual maintenance fee be a fixed percentage (e.g., 10%) of the purchase cost. So if the software cost you $50,000, the annual maintenance fee could be $5,000 per year. Make sure you understand these clauses. Annual maintenance for software normally includes new software releases, providing support for the product, and reporting and fixing problems. Some training may also be included.

Leveraging Information Technology at the Health Collaborative

Recall the key question facing the leaders of the Health Collaborative "How do we get physicians and patients working together to improve the health of patients with Type II diabetes?"

In 2008, the Health Collaborative and several other health care providers in Cincinnati were awarded a grant by the Robert Wood Johnson Foundation to focus on improving health care in Cincinnati in an effort known as Aligning Forces For Quality (AF4Q). The community selected Type II diabetes as a focus area because of the epidemic spread of diabetes in the United States, the significant co-morbidities (e.g., heart problems, vision problems, neuropathy), the number of people impacted, the fact that Type II diabetes is preventable and manageable, and the significant costs involved.

The Physician Leadership Group of the Health Collaborative and AF4Q adopted the health goals for living well with diabetes established by the National Quality Forum as the standards that would be universally applied to patients in Cincinnati. These goals became known as the "D5 goals." They are as follows:

1. Keep your blood pressure under 140/90 mmHg.
2. Keep bad cholesterol (LDL) under 100 mg/dl.
3. Keep blood sugar (A1C) less than 8%.

4. Be tobacco-free.

5. Take aspirin daily as recommended.

It was agreed by the health providers working with the Health Collaborative that a single measure would be publicly reported as the primary goal for managing Type II diabetes in a health care practice. This single measure was the percentage (%) of Type II diabetic patients who met ALL five of the health goals. Data is also captured and reported for the percentage of patients who meet each goal individually.

This data is then publicly reported on a website developed by the Health Collaborative called YourHealthMatters (www.yourhealthmatters. org). This website was developed using a third-party systems provider to do the technical work. The Health Collaborative did a great deal of consumer/patient research to understand what information would be most helpful to patients and how they would best like the data presented.

Having these common health goals for Type II diabetes is very powerful. It enables patients and physicians to have common goals that they can strive to achieve. It also creates a common language or vocabulary to use to discuss patient care. Physicians like having this objective and important data describing their practice because it establishes a measurable baseline that they can then use to focus on improving.

This data has been collected and reported since 2009 (a pilot year) through 2013, with an increasing number of physicians participating each year. Figure 9.2 shows the trend of the number of physicians/providers providing data, going from 83 providers in 2009 to over 550 providers in 2013. Figure 9.3 shows the number of patients receiving care in these provider practices over that same time period.

Results

In 2009, the overall score for the Cincinnati Regional average was 9%, which means that 9 out of 100 Type II diabetes patients met all five health goals. In 2010, that measure went up to 28% and in 2011 this overall measure went up to 30%.

An illustrative example of how these measures can be used to drive improvement in health care is the West Chester practice of TriHealth

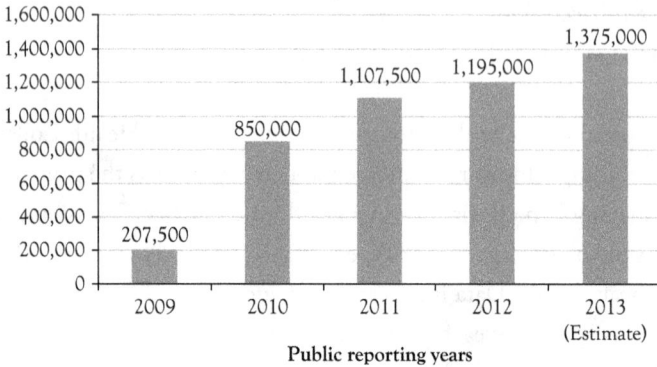

Figure 9.2 Estimated number of patients receiving care in public reporting practices

Physicians Group. In 2010, this practice reported a respectable 28% overall measure that was right in line with the community average for percentage of patients in good control of their Type II diabetes. Average wasn't good enough for this group. Their practice manager, Mary Jo Drohan, took the challenge personally. She became focused on running database reports several times a week to see which patients needed attention. Patients in good control were celebrated with certificates. Those who were struggling with their diabetes goals got extra attention such as nutrition counseling or fitness support. "Every patient is different and the secret is determining what they need and getting them the

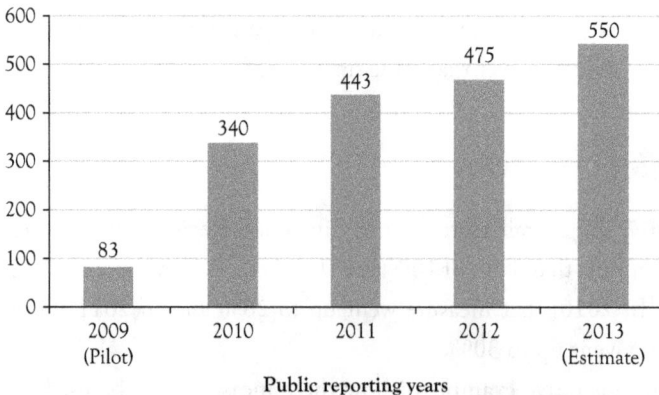

Figure 9.3 Number of providers publicly reporting diabetes data

resources," said Drohan. In 2011, this practice reported a dramatic 48% overall measure, which was the highest improvement rate of any reporting practice. "Patient care is what it's all about and focusing on that changes outcomes," said Drohan.

What It Takes to Do This

It is important to look behind the scenes and really understand what it takes to pull something like this off. In the information systems world, key components of the Health Collaborative's work on diabetes consist of the following:

- A physician's portal that enables doctor's offices to enter in the data and request database reports of this data.
- Both manual and automated data interfaces to move patient's and practice data from current systems into the Health Collaborative's database.
- An extensive website (i.e., www.YourHealthMatters.org) that publicly reports the data on these health goals and produces comparative reports for the public.
- Data standards that are developed/adopted and used consistently by physicians and patients.
- Providing training for physician's offices how to use the physician's portal to enter data and run reports.
- Conducting auditing of the collected data to make sure it is accurate and reported consistently over time.
- Produce helpful tools that patients can use such as the patient checklist shown in Table 9.1 to help patients prepare for an upcoming doctor visit.

What's Next?

The Health Collaborative will continue to focus on improving health care for Type II diabetes patients in addition to reporting on cardiovascular disease, colon cancer screening rates, and hospital ratings. They are also examining options for adding additional disease states of conditions using

Table 9.1 A diabetes checklist for your doctor visit

*Your*HealthMatters

A Diabetes Checklist For Your Doctor Visit

The following chart lists the medical tests and exams that should be part of your regular office visits. It includes why each test is given, what the results should be and how often the test is typically needed. Use this checklist as a tool to communicate with your doctor and to make sure you are receiving recommended care for your diabetes.

Medical Test/ Examination	Why the Test is Given	Goals for Living Well With Diabetes*	MY TEST RESULTS	MY GOALS	How Often the Test is Typically Needed
☐ Blood Sugar (A1C)	To evaluate how well your diabetes treatment plan is working as it measures the average of all blood sugars over 2-3 months	Below 8%			Every 3-6 months
☐ Blood Pressure	Determines if medication is needed to control blood pressure and reduce risks of high blood pressure to the heart, eyes, kidneys and nerves	Less than 140/90mmHg			Every doctor visit
☐ Cholesterol Control (LDL-Bad Cholesterol)	Determines if medication is needed to lower cholesterol and reduce the risk of heart attack and stroke	LDL is less than 100 mg/dL			Once a year
☐ Kidney Function Test (Urine Test)	Determines if medication is needed to prevent kidney damage or kidney failure that could lead to dialysis (treatment that replaces kidney function)	Less than 30 mg/24 hours			Once a year
☐ Referral for a Comprehensive Dilated Eye Exam	Determines if there is diabetes-related damage to the eyes	Normal Eye Exam with no evidence of diabetic retinopathy			Once a year
☐ Foot Exam	Identifies high risk foot conditions and determines if loss of feeling exists in the feet that may lead to injury or infection	Normal protective sensation or feeling			Every doctor visit
☐ Smoking Status and Stop Smoking Advice	Because smoking increases the rate at which complications from diabetes will occur	Stop smoking			Review at every doctor visit
☐ Take aspirin daily as recommended	Aspirin reduces the ability of blood to clot and may decrease the chance of heart attack and stroke in some patients that are at increased risk related to diabetes, personal medical and family history	You and your doctor can decide if this is right for you			Review at every doctor visit

* Your doctor may recommend lower numbers for your individual A1C and blood pressure

a similar system of collecting and reporting data. Also in September 2013 the Health Collaborative will begin publicly reporting data on patient experience with their physicians using a nationally recognized standard for measuring patient experience.

Key Learnings

Some key learnings from this example are as follows:

1. Having doctors and patients working together using objective data and common goals is very powerful in terms of improving health care.
2. You must use widely accepted data definitions and measures to secure participation, enable effective analysis, and comparison of health care data.
3. Public reporting of data is an effective motivator for physician practices to improve health care.
4. Information system components are essential (e.g., patient facing websites, data interfaces, physician and patient reports) to make this type of data collection and reporting consistent and sustainable over time.

5. Automated interfaces with other health care systems (e.g., EPIC) are especially important in making data acquisition reasonable in terms of effort and costs.

Laura Randall
Director of Communications
The Health Collaborative
Cincinnati, Ohio

Conclusion

The effective use of IT, as described in this chapter, can be critical for a nonprofit organization being successful in achieving its mission and reaching new people and finding new innovative ways to meet emerging needs. If your staff is not competent to assess the potential benefits to use IT in your organization, you need to find some help to do this well. The survival of your organization may depend on this effort.

Key Assessment Questions

1. How strategic is IT in your type of organization? How do you know?
2. Do you buy versus build your software solutions/applications? Why?
3. What is your next strategic IT application project in the next year?
4. Have you evaluated the potential impact of social media applications on the Web for your organization? If not, why not?
5. What categories of data/information are most important for your organization?
6. How do you proactively develop and maintain important relationships with your key IT vendors? If you are not currently working with your vendors, what should you begin doing with which vendor(s) to get started?

Notes

1. Friedman (2005).
2. Turban and Volonino (2011).
3. Cusumano (2010), pp. 27–29.

4. Choudhary (2007), pp. 141–165.
5. Luhn (1958).
6. McFadden (2008).
7. Tapscott and Williams (2008).
8. Tapscott and Williams (2008).
9. Twentyman (2009, April), pp. 30–33.
10. Wikipedia Information Technology Consulting (2011).
11. Damsgaard and Karlsbjerg (2010), pp. 63–71.
12. Yurong, Watson, and Kahm (2010), pp. 113–117.

References

Choudhary, V. (2007). Comparison of software quality under perpetual licensing and software as a service. *Journal of Management Information Systems 24*(2), 141–165.

Cusumano, M. (2010). Technology strategy and management: Cloud Computing and SaaS as new computing platforms. *Communications of the ACM 53*(4), 27–29.

Damsgaard, J., & Karlsbjerg, J. (2010). Seven principles for selecting software packages. *Communications of the ACM 53*(8), 63–71.

Friedman, T. L. (2005). *The world is flat—A brief history of the twenty-first century.* New York, NY: Farrar, Straus, and Giroux.

Kloppenborg, T. J., & Laning, L. J. (2012). *Strategic leadership of portfolio and project management.* New York, NY: Business Expert Press.

Luhn, H. P. (1958). A business intelligence system. *IBM Journal of Research & Development 2*(4).

McFadden, T. P. (2008). *A discussion of business intelligence.* MBA class presentation. Cincinnati, OH: Xavier University.

Tapscott, D., & Williams, A. D. (2008). *Wikinomics—How mass collaboration changes everything* (Expanded ed.). New York, NY: Penguin Group.

Turban, E., & Volonino, L. (2011). *Information technology for management* (8th ed.). Hoboken, NJ: John Wiley & Sons, Inc.

Twentyman, J. (2009, April). *This gun's for hire. SC magazine: For IT security professionals*, pp. 30–33.

Wikipedia. (2011). *Information technology consulting.* Retrieved from Wikipedia The Free Encyclopedia: http://en.wikipedia.org/wiki/information_technology_consulting

Yurong, Y., Watson, E., & Kahn, B. K. (2010). Application service providers: Market and adoption decisions. *Communications of the ACM 53*(7), 113–117.

SECTION 3

Getting Things Done

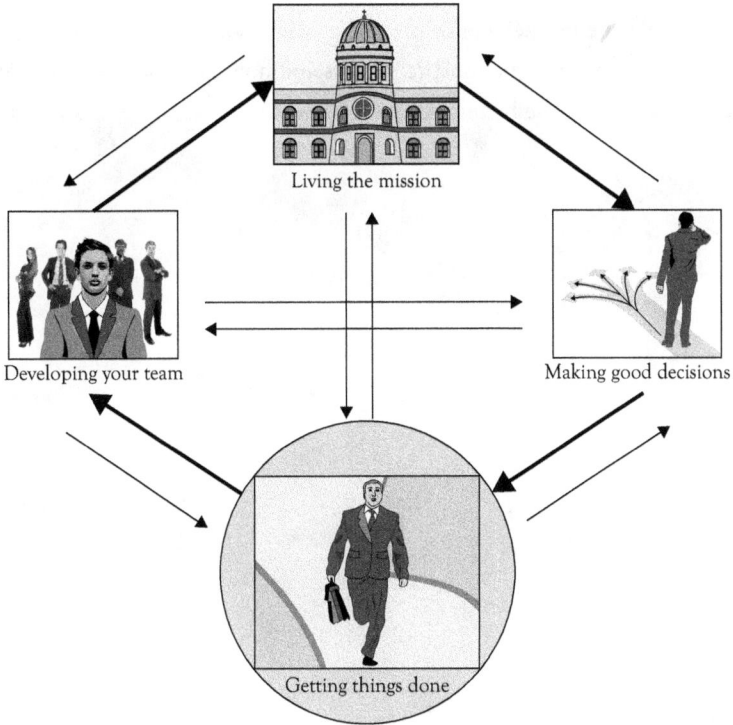

Living the mission

Developing your team

Making good decisions

Getting things done

The Getting Things Done section is a very pragmatic set of chapters that help leaders of nonprofits learn how to plan and execute major changes within an organization as well as how to effectively execute projects to completion. This section is all about doing, with a close eye on the financial realities of what it takes to keep the doors open and be able to pay your people.

The first chapter, Financial Management, is required reading for any nonprofit organization's leadership. It clearly lays out the basics of finance and accounting, how to fund your growth, and how to separate needs from wants. The second chapter, Change Management, discusses how to identify and lead appropriate change in an organization and to understand what things you can control or influence and those factors that are beyond your control. The third chapter, Planning and Managing Projects More Effectively, outlines the fundamentals of how to establish and manage a successful project, including how to allocate the project work and how best to track your progress. The last chapter, Sponsoring Projects, shows what the few key behaviors of a project sponsor are at each project stage that contribute the most to success and how sponsoring, done well, helps you achieve the benefits of your project(s).

CHAPTER 10

Financial Management

Phil Glasgo

Phil Glasgo, PhD, is a finance professor at Xavier University and has been a banker and an Army officer. He is a Presbyterian elder, and has served on the board of the Presbyterian Child Welfare Agency for the past 8 years. Phil has a PhD in finance from Ohio State University.

Introduction

Nonprofits and faith-based organizations are not founded to make profits and please shareholders (however, they do need to satisfy other stakeholders). But arguably good financial management is even more important for them than to for-profit organizations, because they have fewer options when facing a financial need. For-profits can issue additional equity, pledge assets as collateral, or do both to borrow money. Equity isn't possible for nonprofits, and their borrowing potential may be limited either because they have restricted assets or they have few valuable assets to pledge. Hence, the "margin for error" is smaller.

Individuals usually do not choose to work in the not-for-profit world for financial reasons. But as they grow with the organization, it seems more and more of their time is spent on financial issues, and less on what attracted them to the organization in the first place. Some of the board members may be accounting or financial experts, but they usually come from the for-profit world, seem to speak a different language, and want the organization to do things "their way."

The purpose of this chapter is to help readers understand basic financial concepts and ideas that are crucial for their organization. Topics covered include the following:

- Understanding basic financial statements
- Accounting and finance are more different than you think
- The cash conversion cycle (CCC)
- Growth and how to finance it
- Separating needs from wants.

Introduction to Buckhorn Children and Family Services

Buckhorn Children and Family Services (BCFS) presently provides compassionate residential care and treatment of troubled youth and also help for their families on campuses in Eastern Kentucky. During more than 100 years of operation, Buckhorn has provided a variety of services to the Eastern Kentucky area including residential mental health treatment, residential schools, pre-schools, group homes, foster care, and family preservation assistance.

Major expansion of facilities and services during 1985–2000 strained the resources of the organization and led to a number of financial emergencies.

The key question BCFS faced:
Why do we always seem to have a cash crisis when we offer a growing number of programs and services which have revenues exceeding expenses?

Financial Statements

Any nonprofit will have, at a minimum, balance sheets and income statements. These are necessary in order to report the organization's activities and condition to donors, clients served, sponsoring agencies, and sometimes, governmental authorities. The *balance sheet* shows what the organization owns, and how it financed that ownership. It represents the financial history of the organization from its founding until the present.

Typically, the left side of the balance sheet shows items such as cash, accounts receivable (revenue earned but not yet collected), inventory, property, and equipment; these are collectively called the *assets*. The right side of the balance sheet shows how the ownership of these assets was financed, and usually includes accrued wages and taxes, accounts payable (expense incurred but not yet paid), short-term borrowing (notes payable), long-term borrowing, and lease obligations, all of which are called

Table 10.1 Typical balance sheet

Cash	150	Accrued Wages and Taxes	80
Accounts Receivable	600	Accounts Payable	320
Inventory and Other Current Assets	150	Notes Payable	200
Total Current Assets	900	**Total Current Liabilities**	600
Property and Equipment, net	1100	Long-Term Borrowing and Leases	400
Total Assets	2000	**Total Liabilities**	1000
		Net Assets	1000
		Total Liabilities and Net Assets	2000

liabilities (or debt) because they represent money that *must be repaid at some specific future date.* The right-hand side also shows the financing that came from other sources that need not be repaid in the future. In a for-profit firm this financing is called net worth or equity, but in nonprofits this is usually called Surplus, Reserves, or Net Assets. For example, if Total Assets are $2 million and Total Liabilities are $1 million as shown in Table 10.1, then Surplus or Reserves or Net Assets will be $1 million and their debt ratio (the percentage of assets financed by debt) will be 50%.

The *income statement* is a report of the organization's activities for a specific period of time such as the most recent year or the most recent 3 months. It shows the revenues and expenses of the organization over that period of time. A typical income statement is shown in Table 10.2.

Table 10.2 Typical income statement

Program Revenue	1420
Donations	250
Total Revenues	1670
Salary and Benefits	810
Food and Clothing	200
Insurance and Utilities	180
Repairs and Maintenance	250
Depreciation	100
Interest	50
Total Expenses	1590
Addition to Net Assets	80

Not-For-Profit Doesn't Mean No Profit

In the long run, "profits" are necessary for a nonprofit organization to survive; they are just called something else that distinguishes them from the typical for-profit firm's income statement and balance sheet. As noted, Surplus, Reserves, or Net Assets are frequently used on an organization's balance sheet and represent the cumulative excess of revenues over expenses during the organization's *entire lifetime*. Addition to Surplus, addition to Reserves, or addition to Net Assets are typical terms used in the income statement to denote the amount by which revenues exceeded expenses *in the period covered by the income statement*. If revenues exceed expenses by $80,000 during the year, the result will be an $80,000 addition to Net Assets on the firm's balance sheet at the end of the year.

While it seems to be an oxymoron to speak of profits for a nonprofit, they are in fact necessary. If the organization wants to grow over time, then it will need to own new assets. And when old assets are replaced, the cost is likely to be higher due to inflation. If "profits" or an excess never occurs, then the increase in the value of the firm's assets will have to be financed entirely with liabilities, leading to a higher and higher proportion of financing coming from debt. In the short run this is possible, but eventually lenders will refuse to increase the debt limit. In the previous example, if the organization adds $200,000 of new assets but has no addition to reserves, it will have to borrow to finance the purchases, resulting in Total Assets of $2.2 million and borrowing of $1.2 million.[1] This increases the debt ratio from its previous 50% to 54.55%.

The rate at which an organization can successfully grow its assets is directly tied to its profitability. This is called the *sustainable growth rate (SGR)*, and a full explanation is beyond the scope of this chapter. It is approximately the addition to Net Assets for the year divided by the Net Assets on the balance sheet. Thus, in the example, the SGR would be approximately 80/1000 = 8%. An excellent discussion of SGR is available in Higgins.[2]

Accounting Versus Finance—
Similarities and Differences

Successful organizations need both accounting expertise and finance expertise, and they can be quite different. Properly prepared financial statements must conform to rigid accounting rules and standards called Generally Accepted Accounting Principles (GAAP) that are designed to allow comparability across organizations in any given year, and also to allow this year of a firm's operations to be compared to prior years. While nonprofits do not face the scrutiny of their financial statements that a for-profit faces from shareholders, financial analysts, and the IRS, its stakeholders do want to see annual reports on the organization's operations that are similar in nature to those of the for-profit.

The financial function, by contrast, is far more concerned with ensuring that revenues are received in a timely manner, payments are made when ethically required, and that adequate funds are acquired *in advance of need* for major new projects. Those with financial expertise spend far more of their time trying to predict future revenues, expenses, and other cash flows than they do analyzing the past.

A major tool used by financial analysts is the *cash budget*, which literally predicts *cash in and cash out* on a daily or weekly basis. While a cash budget is somewhat similar to financial statements prepared using GAAP principles, there are three major differences and these differences can lead to a firm seeming profitable on an accounting basis but struggling to pay the bills in a timely manner.

Cash budgets are prepared for shorter increments of time than are projected or actual accrual-based accounting statements; larger firms usually prepare daily cash budgets, while smaller firms need to have at least a weekly budget. But the major differences go far beyond the frequency of their preparation. Key differences include the following:

- Cash budgets recognize income *only when received* and expenses *when paid*, whereas accounting statements are required under GAAP to recognize both income and expense when the customer is billed for the goods or service.

- Non-cash items such as depreciation and amortization are essential for accounting statements, but are not included in cash budgets since no actual cash is spent.
- Financial flows such as borrowing money or repaying loans are essential for cash budgets, but show up only indirectly in the balance sheet and not at all in the income statement.

These key differences mean that the actual *cash* the organization has on any day can be far different from what it would seem to be from the accounting statements. This will be demonstrated in the next section, which explains the CCC of the firm. An excellent explanation and example of a cash budget is shown by Helfert.[3]

The Cash Conversion Cycle

A diagram of the CCC for a service-oriented organization is shown in Figure 10.1. Different nonprofits have very different CCCs, and often have greatly different operations from month to month. Organizations heavily dependent on donations, for example, may have revenues heavily concentrated near the end of the calendar year while expenses are incurred evenly during the year.

Buckhorn Children and Family Services receives some of its financial support from donations which are heavily concentrated in December, but

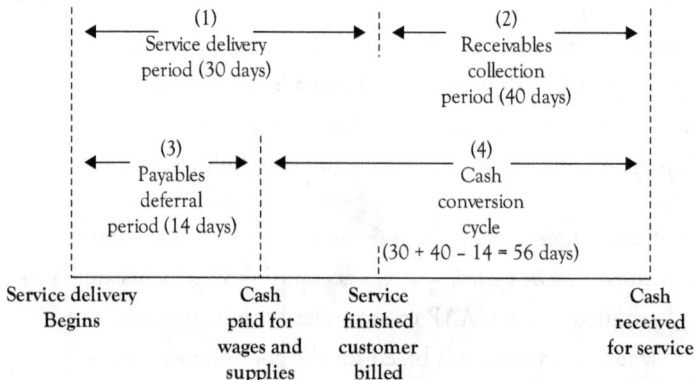

Figure 10.1 *The cash conversion cycle*

most of its revenues come from Medicaid and from Kentucky state child welfare agencies, and the number of children and families served is relatively consistent during the year. Thus, its business cycle is very similar to what is shown in Figure 10.1.

The *operating cycle* of a service-oriented agency begins when it starts to deliver service to a client. Since Buckhorn treats residential patients over a period of many months, the *Service Delivery Period* for one child begins on the first day of the month, and continues for the entire month as the child receives an assortment of services including food, clothing, housing, counseling, education, mental health services, and so forth. At the end of the month (assumed to be 30 days) BCFS bills Medicaid, the appropriate state agency, or both for the services provided.

At that point, the amount owed becomes an Account Receivable on the BCFS books and is shown in Figure 10.1 as the *Receivables Collection Period*. Suppose that the bill is paid 40 days after the agency is billed. The *operating cycle* is thus 30 days for Service Delivery plus 40 days for Receivable Collection, or a total of 70 days. Buckhorn's largest expense is employee payroll, and it pays its employees every 2 weeks. Assume for simplicity that food, utilities, and clothing expenses are also paid in *14* days as well. This is called the *Payables Deferral Period*.

The time from when BCFS pays for wages and other expenses *until it is paid* by Medicaid or Kentucky agencies is called the CCC, and in Figure 10.1 is calculated as 30 days service delivery plus 40 days Receivable Collection minus 14 days Payables Deferral or 56 days.

Don't "Grow Broke"

While the CCC model shown is admittedly quite technical, an understanding of it is absolutely essential for good financial management. Stated in simple English, it shows that the organization *pays out* cash long before it *gets paid* cash from services it provides. Hence, it must plan in advance for how it will finance the CCC. A detailed cash budget that recognizes the lags between collection for services and payment made to employees and other vendors is essential.

The implication of this is almost totally counter-intuitive, and thus requires special emphasis: ***The faster you grow, the greater will be your*** *financial pressure and cash need*. Bankruptcy courts are filled with companies that thought they could sell their way out of a cash crisis. This is roughly the equivalent of trying to put out a fire with gasoline. What these companies ignored was the fact that to sell more, they had to produce more, and when they produced more, they had to pay employees and vendors before they received revenues from their customers, so their cash need increased rather than decreased.

Notice that there was no mention of profitability in the CCC model. It is quite possible that when the organization is finally paid for the service it delivered, the revenue exceeds all of the expenses incurred in delivering the service, and so the accounting statements will show a profitable activity, even after properly recording an interest expense for the cost of borrowing. But since profits aren't cash, the CCC dilemma remains.

In fact, the issues presented by excess growth are even more severe than shown in the CCC model. With any significant growth comes the need for additional fixed assets such as land, buildings, computers, vehicles, and so forth that are not considered in the model. Thus, the organization planning to grow rapidly needs to plan in advance not just for financing the CCC, but for acquiring the funds necessary for the fixed asset growth as well.

Long-Term Needs and Short-Term Needs: How to Finance Them

As discussed previously, it is normal for an organization to need to raise funds to finance the CCC and also to periodically acquire new fixed assets. Careful planning *in advance* is necessary in order to determine what type of financing is appropriate and for how long the funds will be needed. A good cash budget will be an invaluable aid in making this determination.

Short-term needs should normally be financed with short-term borrowing. Short-term borrowing is almost always cheaper, and requires payment only for the days when the money is actually needed. If expenses are quite even during the year but revenues are highly irregular, such as receiving major donations in December, then a short-term line of credit from a financial institution is appropriate, **although a better solution is to make**

donors aware that donations made throughout the year rather than at the end would greatly improve the financial health of the organization.

Fixed assets should always be financed with long-term funding. A for-profit firm can borrow for 3–5 years from a bank, issue longer term bonds (up to 30 years maturity), retain some profits, or issue common stock to acquire such assets. A nonprofit can use all of these except issuing equity, although it is unlikely to be "profitable" enough to finance all long-term assets with annual surpluses or addition to reserves. The nonprofit equivalent (or nearly so) for issuing stock is receiving grants, bequests, or other large one-time gifts.

Before committing to any large asset acquisition, your organization should consider whether any of these alternatives are feasible: can we borrow the money; can we pay it back on the agreed upon terms; do we have major donors who will donate specifically for this purpose? If none of these seem to be likely, the proper decision is to not acquire the asset.

Separate Needs From Wants

Organizations are often guilty of wanting more new assets than they can afford. Constrained by the *SGR* concept, they must prioritize which new asset acquisitions are *crucial* to continue the organizational mission, which ones are *desirable but not critical*, and which ones *could be satisfied by less costly means*. Typical examples include the following:

- We want a new building. We *need* additional space. Remodeling an older building or making better use of existing space may suffice.
- We want new vehicles. We *need* adequate transportation. Used vehicles, ride sharing, or even public transportation may meet the need at a lower cost.
- We want to develop, continue, or expand in-house staff expertise. We *need* the job function performed. Many organizations have discovered that it is more cost-effective to outsource some or all of the following: janitorial services, payroll services, HR services.

- We want to send key employees to conferences and training sessions. We *need* to develop our employees' abilities and skills. Teleconferencing, online educational programs, and other Internet-based services may accomplish the objectives without incurring travel expenses.
- We *want* to start a new program that is an extension of what we presently do. The community has a *need* for this program. Do we have a competitive advantage in offering this program, or might some other agency do it as well or better than we can?

Financial Management at BCFS

Buckhorn Children and Family Services faced many of the issues addressed during a significant period of growth in the 1990s. Growth in excess of the *SGR* and inattention to the CCC in particular led to significant financial problems.

Buckhorn Children and Family Services began early in the 1900s as a missionary effort by a Presbyterian church in New York to serve the educational needs of children in the remote eastern part of Kentucky. It evolved over time to serve many additional needs involving children and families in the area, and by 1985 had developed into a much larger organization providing residential treatment for troubled youth in many locations in Eastern Kentucky, and some in other areas of Kentucky as well. The original New York donor church was no longer involved, but Presbyterian churches throughout Kentucky, Ohio, and Michigan regions were highly supportive. Over the next decade, BCFS also opened group homes for children who had "aged out" of the state-supported residential treatment system, wilderness camps for first-time offenders, video home training for troubled families, and other services to troubled children and their families. They also acquired another similar residential treatment facility in the area (Dessie Scott) when its charismatic founder/CEO retired with no successor available to run the agency independently.

In the late 1980s, Presbyterian church boundaries were redrawn so that Kentucky was no longer in the same church governing region (called a synod) as Ohio and Michigan. This presented a major problem for fund raising, as a large proportion of BCFS's donor base came from these two states. At about the same time, a large church in Columbus, Ohio donated a 300 acre former church campground in Central Ohio to Buckhorn, with the understanding that some of the services BCFS offered in Kentucky would be offered in Ohio as well.

Funding each of the new programs required large expenditures for start-up costs and in most cases, fixed asset acquisition, remodeling, or both. Donated properties throughout the state were sometimes used, but invariably required significant costs to modify them for program usage.

Aggressive development of the Ohio property occurred, at a cost of over 3 million dollars for two homes for residential treatment, remodeling of buildings on the property, plus building homes for key staff who needed to be "on call" at all times. While some of this cost came from large gifts from individuals and churches, over 2 million had to be financed with new debt.

The cumulative effect of the major expansion in Ohio and the large number of new or expanded programs in Kentucky raised almost all of the financial issues discussed. Many new employees were required to staff the new programs. Few, if any of the employees, with the exception of the Chief Financial Officer (CFO), had significant finance and accounting training. Most of the programs showed reasonable accounting profitability, or at least "breakeven," and all employees, including senior management, tended to focus far more on the accounting statements than on cash flow. While the successive CFOs bore the daily brunt of the cash flow shortage that resulted from CCC problems as explained before, they were unable to convince top management that "more" was not always "better." Thus, there was a continuous shortage of cash due to growth beyond any reasonable estimate of sustainable growth, as well as CCC issues.

New employees joined Buckhorn to serve suffering children and families, not to complete paperwork. After working with a troubled child, the social worker was eager to move on to help the next child, rather than document the services rendered and time involved, and record the conclusion of the service so that the appropriate state or federal agency could be billed for the service. Thus, the *Service Delivery Period* was frequently delayed due to failure to file the appropriate paperwork in a timely manner, or the invoice was returned by the paying agency asking for additional information.

As the state and federal agencies experienced financial problems themselves, they tended to delay payment to BCFS for services rendered even after the invoice had been properly submitted, extending the *Receivable Collection Period*. The combination of longer Service Delivery Period and longer Receivable Collection Period forced Buckhorn to itself delay paying some of its vendors in a timely manner in order to avoid a huge increase in the CCC, but understandably incurring the wrath of key vendors, as well as raising serious ethical issues.

Even if BCFS had been managing its CCC well and growing within its *SGR*, the expansion into Ohio would have caused serious problems. The 3 million dollar expenditure represented almost a 30% increase in the assets of the agency, and thus placed huge pressure on the organization to earn significant cash flow from other operations to support the start-up of the new facility and the interest on the long-term debt incurred.

The development of programs and facilities in Ohio was certainly well-intentioned, and honored the desire of donors of the property and financial supporters in Ohio and Michigan. However, a very thorough feasibility analysis of the campus and programs conducted in 2002 revealed that it was virtually impossible to ever avoid losing money on the Ohio campus even after considering the generous donations from Ohio and Michigan supporters, and thus subsidies from Kentucky operations would be needed in perpetuity.

Lessons Learned and Actions Taken

The question posed for BCFS at the beginning of this chapter was
Why do we always seem to have a cash crisis when we offer a growing number of programs and services which have revenues exceeding expenses?

The answer to this question is that the growing number of programs and services was actually causing most of the cash crisis:

1. The lag between delivering service and receiving payment for the service as shown by the CCC model meant that the more new programs they offered, the greater would be the cash need to support these

programs. Their growth rate in assets was far in excess of their *SGR*, meaning that additional borrowing, large donations, or both would be necessary to support the growth.

2. The new programs required new asset purchases to support them. Such long-term asset needs must be anticipated and financed with a combination of long-term debt, profits, and large donations.

3. All employees were given training about the importance of thorough, accurate, and timely completion and submission of reports detailing client services rendered in order to improve the CCC.

4. While a small agency such has BCFS has limited ability to demand payment from state and federal agencies, management worked with other child welfare agencies to lobby for reasonable payment terms and, on rare occasions, asked state and federal legislators to intervene on their behalf when payments were long overdue, thus aiding the CCC.

5. Existing programs were reviewed to determine if they had the potential to generate revenue in excess of costs on an ongoing basis. If the answer was no, then the program was terminated unless it was deemed so "mission critical" that it should be subsidized by other more profitable activities. This decrease in programs offered brought BCFS within its *SGR*.

6. Potential gifts of property and equipment were analyzed carefully to make sure they were worthwhile, especially if conditions were attached to the gift. As a result, several donations were rejected. In addition, a review of past property donations led to the sale of many of them when it was discovered that they were a drain, rather than an addition, to the financial health of the organization. The proceeds from these sales were used to reduce the debt the organization owed to its bankers and bondholders.

7. Existing programs and potential new programs were examined with a critical eye asking "Is this something that we do better than other providers of similar services" (i.e., Do we have a *competitive advantage* in delivering this service)? If the answer was no, then the program was terminated, improved, or never started.

8. A cash budget has been developed for the organization and routinely circulated among the management team and finance and executive committees of the Board of Directors.

In spite of these changes, BCFS continues to face financial pressures as federal and state budgets reduce the amount committed to children's and family services. But it is safe to say that without the changes noted and a growing sense of the importance of good financial management within the organization, they would not have survived.

Conclusion

It is essential for a nonprofit organization to place emphasis on good financial management. The margin for error is smaller for a nonprofit than for a for-profit firm. All employees and stakeholders should be aware of the need to know about basic finance and accounting principles, about the CCC and ways to improve it, and that while some growth is good, too much growth is as bad, if not worse, than no growth at all.

Key Assessment Questions

1. What financial expertise and accounting expertise do you have on your staff and board? Is this sufficient for your organization now and in the future?
2. Do you have a good cash budget? How can you train employees to better understand the significance of the CCC in order to better manage the Service Delivery Period and Accounts Receivable Collection Period and thus receive cash more quickly?
3. Are you growing within your *SGR?* If you are growing too fast, what process will you put in place to control growth?
4. Are you planning *in advance* how to raise the funds to support new programs and asset acquisitions? What combination of borrowing, annual additions to Net Assets, and major donations will you use to fund this growth?
5. Should you "look a gift horse in the mouth" and decline some major gifts with strings attached? What policies do you have in place to analyze such gift offers to determine if they will constrain your organization severely in the future?

Notes

1. This discussion ignores the impact of depreciation, which greatly complicates the discussion without adding much to it. Technically, the $200,000 asset addition shown is after adjusting for depreciation.
2. Higgins (2009), pp. 124–128.
3. Helfert (2003), pp. 184–188.

References

Brealey, R. A., Myers, S. C., & Allen, F. (2011). *Principles of corporate finance* (10th ed.). New York, NY: McGraw-Hill Irwin.

Helfert, E. A. (2003). *Techniques of financial analysis* (11th ed.). New York, NY: McGraw-Hill Irwin.

Higgins, R. C. (2009). *Analysis for financial management* (9th ed.). New York, NY: McGraw-Hill Irwin.

CHAPTER 11

Change Management

Lynda Kilbourne

Lynda Kilbourne (PhD, University of Texas at Austin, 1990) is an Associate Professor of Management at Xavier University. Her teaching specialty is Change Management for undergraduate and graduate students. She researches risk perceptions and safety systems, innovation and change systems, and mentoring. She owns a change consultation firm, Management Troubleshooters.

Introduction

Managers are generally hired into an organization that has existed for some time before they arrived. Often their jobs are to maintain the organization's current operations as they exist—and that may be all they ever need to do, so long as the organization is successful in all ways and the external environment is perfectly stable. Stability allows the organization to become more efficient while producing at consistently higher levels of quality; however, dynamics are likely to exist inside and outside any organization! That means that all managers need appropriate knowledge and methodologies to determine when and how to change either their entire organization or some portions of it or its operations. While that sounds self-evident, even the most successful organizations with the best, most knowledgeable and brightest managers have a great deal of difficulty determining when and how to change their organizations. So, how do managers know when and what to change?

For organizations to remain successful, they must adapt to changes in the external environment as well as maintain efficient and effective internal operations. In this chapter, we present a model to aid managers in implementing an ambidextrous approach, recognizing and adjusting to external opportunities and threats and changing internally to build strengths and eliminate weaknesses. This involves using a change process to recognize a need to change, identifying what to change and how to change it, and making sure that desired effects of a change process have been achieved.

Purpose

This chapter will help the reader to

- understand and be able to use a systems model to relate internal operations, systems, and people to conditions in the external environment: the "statics and dynamics" of organizations;
- understand that appropriate change can be incremental and narrow in scope in an organization, or dramatic and large-scale;
- learn what managers control (managerial variables), as well as what they don't control but to which they must and can respond, and which they may influence;
- identify appropriate interventions for the degree and scope of the change and the managerial variables involved.

Introduction to Xavier University

Xavier University is a private, Jesuit school founded in 1831. Since then, Xavier's dramatic changes[1] include being "spun off" by its original founding organization, becoming coeducational in 1969, and acquiring another private college in 1980. Smaller scale changes include installing central heating and air conditioning and electronic media in classrooms, becoming a largely residential rather than commuter campus, and achieving national recognition academically. A new President was coming into office in 2001, and the university had no major or obvious problems to solve. What should the university do over the first 10-year term of the new President?

How can any leader know what he or she should do at any point in time—especially at the beginning of his or her tenure? The Xavier scenario provides an opportunity to examine the change process, with all the intricacies of implementing it. Furthermore, it affords the opportunity to examine the interplay between the general external environment in which an organization sits and the organization's internal environment. As we will see, the intersection of these two can never result in complete stability, but the instability can be addressed with change activities that can range from quick to yearlong, and from small, incremental to large (quantum), fundamental changes.

A Model of the Change Process

Ensuring that an organization continues to play a meaningful role in society is important for a business organization—it is absolutely mission critical to a not-for-profit or faith-based organization. Changing the organization so that it remains viable in a changing external environment is one of the most difficult and challenging functions of any leadership team. Yet managing change is made even more difficult because most of the "normal operations" of any organization are set up to pursue "business as usual"—not to recognize the need to change, and not to change in major ways. This means that we need to recognize the likely sources of a need to change and create processes—even specific jobs or assigned duties—to observe those needs.

Systems theory has been recognized for years as a valuable approach to strategic management. Thinking about an organization as a series of interconnected and interdependent subsystems, like those of a human body, can give leaders the appropriate perspective on how every job, process, and structure they use must align, or "fit" together. Its greater value is probably in focusing leaders on the need to realize this alignment of the entire organization within its external environment. The fate of the dinosaurs is a vivid image of an organism that was NOT aligned appropriately with its external environment. Perhaps their internal systems were misaligned to cope with shifts in the external environment. We can only theorize at this point.

Figure 11.1 shows that an organization takes elements from the external environment, puts those elements together to transform them, and

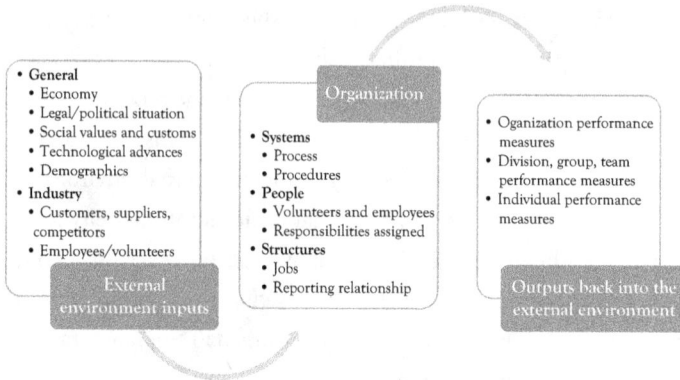

- **General**
  - Economy
  - Legal/political situation
  - Social values and customs
  - Technological advances
  - Demographics
- **Industry**
  - Customers, suppliers, competitors
  - Employees/volunteers

External environment inputs

Organization

- **Systems**
  - Process
  - Procedures
- **People**
  - Volunteers and employees
  - Responsibilities assigned
- **Structures**
  - Jobs
  - Reporting relationship

- Organization performance measures
- Division, group, team performance measures
- Individual performance measures

Outputs back into the external environment

Figure 11.1 A model of the organization with its external environment

puts the results of the transformation back into the external environment. To the degree that all the internal systems are designed and implemented with internal consistency and appropriately for the external environment, any measure of performance would show success. To the degree that the internal elements are not appropriate for the external environment, or are not internally consistent (misaligned), the measures of organizational performance would show less success. One problem is noticing when an organization would be doing better, even though it is "successful" according to the goals that have been set. This suggests that goals could be inappropriately calibrated.

The Xavier case illustrates that the onset of a new administration is an opportune moment to consider where an organization should be going from its current position. As indicated in the chapter on Financial Management, an obvious change is to grow—but leaders have to examine growth opportunities as one external environmental possibility among many others. A munificent external environment allows growth, even rapid growth; however, there can also be significant threats that arise in the external environment. Neither can be ignored by the wise management team, because leaders need to make changes in their organizations to deal with all the external situations. The Xavier case shows that, given appropriate strategic action, what might be considered a threat in the external environment can actually provide an opportunity for an organization. Such is the case for many not-for-profit organizations. Identifying one opportunity that leads to the creation of an organization does not remove the need to scan the external environment for continual shifts that could lead to growth, rejuvenation, or downsizing.

Issues can arise within the organization that also require the management team to modify the organization in various ways. Within the organization, internal needs are likely to be observed by failure to achieve departmental goals, or by individual job performance lower than desired or expected—or by individuals who find new ways to perform old tasks. These are the issues that are most easily recognized by managers in any organization, because performance reviews or departmental reports are designed to capture them fairly quickly. As a result, they are the issues that lead an organization to change most often. These are also the changes that are typically modifications to what is already being done, representing incremental change. In the case of Xavier, the changes to programs were internally driven.

Incremental Versus Quantum Change

The fundamental change management model illustrates what leaders control: all those elements within the organization that they can design and redesign—change—as needed. Managers must create internal systems to achieve the goals, to determine how the organization is progressing against current goals and targets, and to sense shifts in the general external environment that could be threats or opportunities, depending upon the capabilities of the internal systems. To the extent that the measurement tools are sensitive enough and adequately timed, and that the external shifts are more moderate and captured, smaller, incremental change will be possible. So long as the incremental changes are managed to maintain internal consistency, over time, change will be effective.

When larger change occurs in the external environment, larger scale, dramatic change would become necessary. To the degree that top leadership is adequately engaged with the external environment, they might anticipate the shifts and enable "first mover" change to become industry leaders—or even "game changers" like Wal-Mart in the consumer products industry. A nonprofit example is the Vineyard Church development, whose founder saw a shift in the general environment away from attendance at churches with more rigid rituals and ceremonies. As the social values were changing in the United States, the founder of this church and church movement recognized a gap that a different kind of church could fill. Leaders also have the opportunity to influence external elements. Where the external environment is especially hostile, leaders can create liaison roles to share information across the organization's boundary, use the political process to try to manage change, or create networks with other organizations to adapt on a broader scale than making internal adjustments.

If we think of these changes as being on a scale from small to quantum, the example of Xavier's change prior to 2001 includes both large-scale and small-scale. The larger-scale changes, like acquisition of another private college, edge toward the quantum end of the scale. If the future holds even greater advances in Internet capability, and if those changes are accompanied by changes in social values that shift most people away from attending any university in person, VERY large-scale change would be the result. Students could be anywhere, and so could all employees. Campuses would no longer be necessary. Would there be basketball teams? Would alumni ever want to aggregate anywhere? This would be the educational equivalent of a meteor to the dinosaurs—unless universities prepared internally for such an event by anticipating it.

What Leaders Control and What They Don't

Leaders cannot control the external environment. Knowledge is power, however. If leaders know what is going on in the external environment and how well things are going internally, they gain control by knowing when they need to make changes. Therefore, designing, implementing, and using data from measurement systems are critical for giving leaders control—ergo, the name "control systems" for systems that collect performance data. When a good measurement system is in place, managers can identify when there is a gap between what they wanted or expected and the results that were achieved with internal systems. Such a "performance gap" is a problem to be solved by, generally, incremental change methods. When a good external environmental assessment process is in place, and a large difference from the previous state is sensed, a large-scale strategic level change would be warranted. The gap is closed by changing whichever managerial variables (all those variables listed in the Organization box of Figure 11.1) are not appropriately designed or aligned. All of the elements internal to the organization are the variables that managers control: the systems, the jobs, the capabilities of the employees and volunteers, and the structures that connect all the jobs.

The case of the dinosaurs might seem a bit extreme, but an analogy can be found in modern organizational life: the World Trade Center attacks would have caused a similar fate for airline companies had their leaders not examined how their internal systems needed to change to "fit" the new reality of a very hostile external environment. The airline example may also seem extreme. Indeed, those types of frame-breaking, quantum changes foisted upon organizations by the external environment are rare—thank goodness!

Because middle and line managers have processes for identifying the need to adjust what is being done, less dramatic, incremental changes occur around us all the time. The problem is that, because they are incremental movements in things we already address, we are unlikely to notice that the organization as a whole is becoming unaligned. Like the chassis of a car whose front and rear wheels are out of alignment, the organizational "car" can be crabbing down the highway of organizational life. Sometimes, the organization can travel along being fairly successful, so its leaders never adjust appropriately. Such behavior causes unrealized potential. With the unaligned car, fuel efficiency suffers; the driver has to steer to adjust for pull from the outside, causing fatigue in the driver; and ultimately, a blow-out of an unevenly worn tire can cause the car to overturn with catastrophic results. Analogous effects can accrue in the unaligned organization.

To be successful, what the organization does overall, as the values it holds, the mission and goals it seeks to achieve, must be appropriate given the conditions in the external environment. However, to be successful takes more than just having the right purpose. Leaders also have to put into place the right systems and process, the correct structures and controls, and the right people doing the right jobs and tasks. Each of these different components at all levels of the organization must be designed to fit together—to be internally consistent. This may sound simple, but it becomes really complex to ensure over time that this consistency remains

Table 11.1 Relationship of sources of change to internal roles and scope of resultant change

Source of impetus to change	Likely recognition of need to change	Scope of change needed
External Environmental Shifts	Top Management	Quantum, Macro-level Changes
Internal Shifts	Group Managers Line Managers Employees/Volunteers	Group, Division, Team Changes Individual Job/Employee Incremental, Micro-level Changes

in place. Incremental change can occur because of the focus of work that goes on at different levels and in different sections or departments of any organization. However, such incremental change may occur with little thought about how it will affect other parts of the organization, whether at the same level or across different levels of the organization. The causes for the changes are also different. This is illustrated in Table 11.1.

Steps in the Change Process

For either case, a leader needs to follow a series of steps. First, the manager should determine why the change has occurred. If the cause can be identified by gathering and analyzing data related to the functioning of theoretically related variables, a manager is able to target change interventions to save time, money, and other resources to make changes that have a higher probability of improving outcomes rapidly. Second, the manager must select and implement the appropriate intervention. For changes that can be made more slowly, involving more stakeholders will generate greater acceptance of the need to change and the process for change. During intervention, managers need to monitor to be sure the intervention is being implemented appropriately and that everyone is participating as necessary. Third, the manager must assess the results of the change intervention to determine that it has had the intended results. Obviously, this sets up a continuous improvement cycle if such a system is permanently part of the internal management process. For external environmental changes, the implementation is likely to affect all systems, jobs, and processes, so such changes will take longer, but such change interventions would be needed less often.

Unless the external environment is remaining stable, it is diffi-cult for everything inside the organization to remain the same over time, particularly over long periods of time. In the shorter term, the organization can have some periods of stasis—the "static" part of its existence. Over the longer term, however, leaders need to expect the world outside the boundaries of their organization is changing, and they must change the organization to remain viable—the "dynamics" of organizational life.

Selection of Appropriate Interventions

There are two fundamental issues in selecting a method of intervention: how fast does a change need to happen, and what needs to be changed. To build support and create readiness for a change, moving more slowly can have great advantages. So, when should a change be made more quickly? If something dramatically bad has happened, like the attacks on the World Trade Center, or if the consequences of delaying intervention would be dire, as with a patient in cardiac arrest, quick action is neces-sary. In acting quickly, however, leaders lose the perspective of analysis and deliberation, and they lose the opportunity to gain valuable perspec-tives and insights of other employees and volunteers. They also lose the opportunity to build support. A compromise in a dire situation is to act quickly with a stop-gap measure, and then implement careful data gath-ering and analysis.

Tools to Use for All Types of Change

There are four primary sets of variables that can be changed by managers in any organization: the processes, the employees, the strategic elements, and the technology and structures. Each of these relates to and affects all the others, so alignment should always be the goal. Changing one element of one of these necessitates appropriate modification to the oth-ers. To choose the appropriate intervention, leaders must first recognize that an opportunity or threat exists, collect and analyze data to determine which variables under their control need to be changed, and then choose the appropriate intervention. Each of the four sets is listed in Table 11.2

Table 11.2 Types of interventions to use for specific issues

Types of strategic decisions/issues	Types of strategic interventions
Products, services, markets	Environmental scanning
Strategy selection	SWOT, Five Forces Analysis, strategic planning
Organizational values and culture	Search conference
Functioning	Organization design
Types of process decisions/issues	**Types of process interventions**
Communication	Process consultation
Decision making	Third-party intervention
Problem solving	Counseling
Interpersonal interactions	Team building
Types of human resource management decisions/issues	**Types of human resource management interventions**
Attracting, selecting, retaining employees Attracting, selecting, retaining volunteers	Performance management
Goal setting, performance assessment, rewards leadership	Management by objectives training and development job design
Types of technology and structure decisions/issues	**Types of technology and structure interventions**
Division of labor	Job design
Coordination between departments and divisions	Structure and restructuring
Production of goods, services, or both	Technology interventions
Design of work	Job characteristics model application

with the decisions/issues in the left-hand column, and appropriate inter-ventions to use to address them in the right-hand column.

Once the intervention is implemented, additional data collection and analysis have to occur, first while the implementation is in process to ensure that everyone who is supposed to be involved is doing what they are supposed to be doing, and then at the end to be sure that the desired effect has been achieved. Of course, if the result of assessment at either point is negative, additional interventions need to be identified and implemented.

Leadership Change Implementation

Keeping members motivated to make both major and minor changes is a real challenge to all leaders—resistance is one of the great challenges to implement change.[2] Because many not-for-profit organizations have fewer staff, these dynamic interactions can present somewhat different challenges. For example, many not-for-profits have few(er) regular employees and large numbers of volunteers. The volunteers may come and go, so they may not have the same expectation of stability that the regular employees have. The regular employees may even feel that the transient volunteers cause change that is unnecessary. Alternatively, longer-term volunteers, like longer term employees, may feel it is unfair to ask for changes because they feel a "psychological contract" is being violated, and that their contributions are being discredited or devalued, that the organization to which they volunteered, or the mission they volunteered to serve, no longer exists, or both. Leaders can minimize this negative reaction through the use of choice and involvement in the change process, as illustrated in the Xavier example.

For all change processes, generating and maintaining enthusiasm is essential for success, particularly for large-scale change that can take years to complete. Especially for change implementation that takes place over a long period of time, leaders should plan to implement the changes with a project management approach. This allows a timeline to be established, wherein interim completion points can be identified to acknowledge achievement along the way. These opportunities to celebrate short-term, smaller wins and recognize the efforts of all members to achieve a greater good become essential to maintaining morale, building esprit de corps, and sustaining momentum for changes that involve very large organizations and will require years to complete fully.[3]

Leading Change Implementation at Xavier University

In 2000, a new President had just taken over the reins of Xavier University. Michael Graham, SJ, had served in various roles at Xavier before becoming its 34th President, so he knew the institution well. Still, the idea of leading Xavier University into its future gave him pause: What should he do during his tenure as President?[4]

When President Graham took over, the university was doing well. A number of internal problems it had faced had been solved by Graham's predecessor, President Hoff. Now, however, the university did not seem to have any major problems, so a large-scale change in the university was not needed—incremental change would have been appropriate. But this juncture provided an opportunity for reflection on what the university's strengths and opportunities were, or could be. President Graham employed some strategic organizational change techniques to gather insights of Xavier's stakeholders (faculty, administrators, students, alumni, trustees) and found that a majority wanted some incremental improvements to facilities and processes, but also a way to be a "better university" and more interactive with the city around the university, Cincinnati—one of the Jesuit values to be men and women for others.

As it happened, the City of Cincinnati was facing a crisis. The city had some major race-based trouble that culminated in riots just as Mike Graham was going through his inauguration. President Graham worked through one of Xavier's already established functional department to open the university to a conversation about the riots. The session ran to 2 hours of "raw, visceral comments," said President Graham, and left him with a choice: for the university to do something that mattered or to do business as usual. The end result was a modification of the university's goals and strategies at a macro level with structural changes to implement the focus: the creation of the Eigel Center for Community-Engaged Learning and programs of study to support the new focus. Incremental adjustments followed with individual grants and projects. The center has spawned numerous projects that have facilitated the growth of community relations as well as learning experiences for students and faculty.

Ten years out from his 2001 inauguration as Xavier's President, Mike Graham was pondering the next decade of his leadership. The external environment was moving, and President Graham again had to consider what the future would be for Xavier. This time, Xavier also had a new Chief Academic Officer and Provost, Scott Chadwick, PhD, who was very aware of the more subtle changes that had been occurring in the general external environment. Provost Chadwick had already undertaken internal changes to the Academic Affairs Division to align Xavier's academic offerings with changes in the economy, socio cultural values and needs, political issues, and technological advancements. The two men together, along with the CFO, Beth Amyott, began a series of forums to engage all the stakeholders of the university in another search process to decide what we should do. The process has become somewhat permanent, as the leadership has recognized the perpetual motion of the general external environment and the changing capabilities of the internal elements of the institution. The dynamics of the environment mean that wise leaders will not expect any specific program, policy, or process to remain permanently useful—except a process to learn as an organization. Recognizing the value of voice of organization members is a virtue in successful long-lived organizations. This example from Xavier University illustrates how leaders can facilitate adaptation and change by establishing a process to discover what is changing around them.

Summary

For an organization to remain a viable, successful entity over a very long period of time, leaders must recognize that change must take place. This chapter has identified a process and methods that leaders can use to recognize the larger problems and opportunities, to determine what kind of change is needed to solve the problems or take advantage of the opportunities, to determine the scale of change required, and to determine the appropriate change techniques to use. Small scale change can occur as a part of normal day- to- day operations, so long as periodic checks are made to ensure that internal consistency is maintained over the organization as a whole. Where large-scale change is required, the change implementation is best done as a project. How to lead and manage a change project can be understood using material in the next chapter, Planning and Managing Projects More Effectively.

Key Assessment Questions

1. Do our clients or customers complain about something we do or do not do?
2. Do our clients or customers compliment us or our employees or volunteers for the things we do?

3. Do we have goals for performance and internal measurement systems to ensure we are achieving our goals? If so, do these systems show we are being successful, or that we could improve?
4. Can we isolate problems in performance to specific individuals, to specific departments or units, or to the entire organization?
5. Do we have difficulty retaining our volunteers or employees?

Notes

1. Fortin (2006).
2. Cummings and Worley (2009).
3. Cummings and Worley (2009).
4. Graham (2013).

References

Cameron, E., & Green, M. (2012). *Making sense of change management: A complete guide to the models, tools, and techniques of organizational change* (3rd ed.). London: KoganPage.

Cummings, T. G., & Worley, C. G. (2008). *Organization development and change* (9th ed.). Mason, OH: South-Western Publishing Co.

Cummings, T. G., & Worley, C. G. (2009). *Organization development and change* (9th ed.). Mason, OH: Cengage Learning.

Fortin, R. (2006). *To see great wonders: A history of Xavier University, 1831–2006.* Chicago, IL: University of Chicago Press.

Graham, M. (2013). *Conversation with the author.*

Jick, T. D., & Peiperl, M. A. (2011). *Managing change: Cases and concepts* (3rd ed.). New York, NY; McGraw-Hill Irwin

CHAPTER 12

Planning and Managing Projects More Effectively

Kathryn N. Wells and
Timothy J. Kloppenborg

Kathryn N. Wells, CAPM, MEd, is a bilingual educator and author with international project management training experience. She is a Certified Associate in Project Management (CAPM®) and has written questions and answers for project management text books. She currently lives in Columbia, South Carolina.

Timothy J. Kloppenborg is a Professor Emeritus from Xavier University. He has published books on leadership and project management. Tim is a Certified Project Management Professional (PMP˚). He has worked with over 150 volunteer organizations, directly and through supervising student projects. He has hands-on and consulting experience in six continents.

Introduction

In Chapter 11, you learned about the critical role of change management. But once the need for change has been established, how does an organization actually go about implementing it? The answer to that question is through projects. Many other situations such as starting or expanding a mission, fund-raising efforts, and grant applications (or proposals) can be effectively planned and managed as projects. Projects tend to be the primary method for implementing many organizational objectives.[1]

Purpose

The purpose of this chapter is to define projects, illustrate why project management is both useful and necessary, and demonstrate how to manage a project, using relevant examples. By the end of this chapter, you will be able to initiate projects within your own organization, break each project into manageable parts, assign responsibility for various deliverables, and report progress.

Before we go any farther, take a look at one example of a nonprofit organization that has become adept at project management.

Introduction to Mercy Neighborhood Ministries

Mercy Neighborhood Ministries (MNM) in Cincinnati, Ohio, has a dual mission of helping senior citizens maintain independence, and helping disadvantaged adults enter the workforce. Created by the merger of three existing agencies with a combined history of 55 years, MNM's many ministries have long provided adult work-readiness training and senior services. To enhance its 20-year home care aide service, MNM started a small home care aide training (HCAT) program and within 2 months the Council on Aging (COA) asked if MNM would assume responsibility for COA's regional HCAT program? MNM decided to assume responsibility for this large program. It would be a massive project.

Focus Questions

1. Once an organization has decided upon a project and assigned a project manager, how does it go about planning and carrying out the project?
2. What are some of the necessary components of a Project Management Plan, and how is each created?

Initiating a Project

Perhaps you were able to relate to some part of MNM's experience. Most projects begin either because something is not currently working as well as desired or because of a desire for something entirely new. In both cases, managers need to recognize the current situation, determine the desired outcome, and then figure out the needed actions, resources, and stakeholders while taking into account risks and possible environmental changes. Effective project management merges the skills and insight needed to bring desired changes to fruition.

In Chapter 2, you learned about developing an organizational mission. It is imperative to have a firm understanding of your organization's mission in order to choose projects that will successfully move your organization in a direction congruent with its values, beliefs, and vision. You will learn more about choosing projects in the following chapter, which deals with sponsoring projects. For now, let's assume you already have a project in mind. Where do you begin?

The first step will be a meeting to initiate the project. Each project will have a *sponsor*. Whether the sponsor is a member of the organization's senior management or an external client, she is the person interested in getting the project done. During this first meeting, the sponsor will meet with the project manager and the project team to develop a common understanding of what the project entails and to formally commit to the project by signing a *charter*. A charter is a document that serves as an informal contract between the sponsor and the project team and authorizes the project manager to proceed with the project. Charter lengths vary greatly depending on the size and scope of a project.

Scope Overview

At the very minimum, a charter should include a scope overview, a business case, and signatures of all vested parties. The scope overview is simply a description of what the project entails and—equally important—what the project does *not* entail. By agreeing on the parameters of the project early on, a project manager can guard against differing expectations and *scope creep*, "adding features and functionality without addressing the effects of time, costs, resources, or without customer approval."[2] As you can imagine, scope creep can wreak havoc on a project manager's ability to deliver a satisfactory project on time and within budget.

Business Case

If the scope overview can be thought of as the "what" of a project, the business case constitutes the "why." In other words, why does the organization need this particular project to be completed? The answer could be to comply with legal or governmental specifications, increase revenue, enhance a product, and so forth. Collectively, the business case and scope overview make a succinct, easily understood "elevator pitch." In other words, they give you a pithy way to tell others about your project and why it is needed.

Milestone Schedule With Acceptance Criteria

A charter also includes a milestone schedule with acceptance criteria. The milestone schedule divides the project into a few (generally 3 to 6) manageable chunks, with deliverables and estimated dates for the completion of each. A deliverable is "any unique and verifiable product, result, or capability to perform a service."[3] The milestone schedule provides a way to ensure that the project overall is on track in terms of both quality and schedule. Since each deliverable must meet approval in order for the project to move on to the next step, it is important to decide in advance *what* the acceptance criteria are and *who* will determine if the deliverables meet said criteria.

Here are six useful steps in constructing a milestone schedule. Keep in mind that the milestone schedule does not have to be terribly detailed because this is only an initial assessment of how long the project team thinks the various project steps will take.

1. List the current situation that requires the project in the first row of the milestone column.

2. After agreeing on the starting point, jump to the desired conclusion. Tell what a successful project completion would look like and put that in the last row of the milestone schedule.

3. Determine what the acceptance criteria are for the final project deliverables and who will judge them.

4. Return to the milestone column and agree on a few points during the project at which progress needs to be verified.

5. As you did with the final results in step 2, determine what successful completion of each "milestone" will look like and who will judge each.

6. Lastly, give an estimated date of completion for each milestone. Be realistic and try to space out the steps so that milestones are generally at least 1 week but no more than a couple of months apart.[4]

Risks

It is also helpful to brainstorm what could go wrong and what you will do to reduce the chance of each risk event, reduce the impact if a risk event happens, or both. Most charters will assign a person to be responsible for each risk. Larger, more complicated projects will often have more involved charters, but the components described here are helpful even for small projects.

Stakeholders

Stakeholders are people who have an interest in a project. They can be internal or external to the organization and may favor or oppose the project.[5] By taking time to assess your stakeholders, you can often gain supporters of your project and work to mitigate concerns of your opponents. On a large project with many stakeholders, it will become necessary to prioritize your stakeholders. Whose needs or wants *must* be met for your project to be successful? Something else to consider is how you will contact or update your stakeholders (if necessary) and who will be responsible for doing so. An example project charter for a health care agency training project is shown in Figure 12.1.

Scope Overview

This project will develop and implement a computerized training module to prepare staff to ensure continued patient flow, care, and safety in the event of unexpected system downtime.

Business Case

The current downtime procedure is not universally used on all shifts, nor do all employees know it. The result is patient safety, quality of care, and efficiency are at risk if an unexpected downtime event happens.

Milestone Schedule with Acceptance Criteria

Milestone	Date	Judge	Acceptance Criteria
Currently: process not known nor used universally	3-31		
Evaluate current process	4-21	Department manager	Comprehensive
Build training module	5-19	Training manager	All objectives met
Roll out training module	6-16	Department manager	100% staff trained
Future: universal knowledge and use of process	7-14	Executive director	100% use of process

Risks

Risk	Risk Owner	Contingency Plan
No staff buy-in	Bill (project manager)	Mandatory training
Varying opinions on process	Jill (department manager)	Facilitate meetings
Too costly	Ron (finance rep)	Identify budget needs early

Stakeholders

Primary Stakeholders	Interests in Project
Department head	Patient care continuation
Clerical head	Accurate records
Work team	Patient care, understand responsibilities

Other Stakeholders	
Patients and families	Good care, privacy
Other departments	Accurate orders

Figure 12.1 Project charter for system downtime training project

Planning a Project

Once a sponsor has reached agreement on the project charter with the project manager and team, detailed planning begins. This planning often starts with developing a communication plan so that all stakeholder concerns are addressed and project progress is communicated appropriately. Simultaneously the project team usually starts to outline all of the deliverables that will be created, including all interim and partial items. They often put these in a document called a work breakdown structure (WBS) that forms the outline of all of the detailed "whats" of the project. Figure 12.2 continues the training project example with a WBS.

Project Schedule

Creating a project schedule will help you determine which activities need to be done, in what order, and by whom. It will also factor in necessary resources, including cash flow.

"Recognizing that project schedules are limited by logical order, activity duration, resource availability, imposed dates, and cash flow restrictions, creating a realistic schedule is an iterative process."[6] This

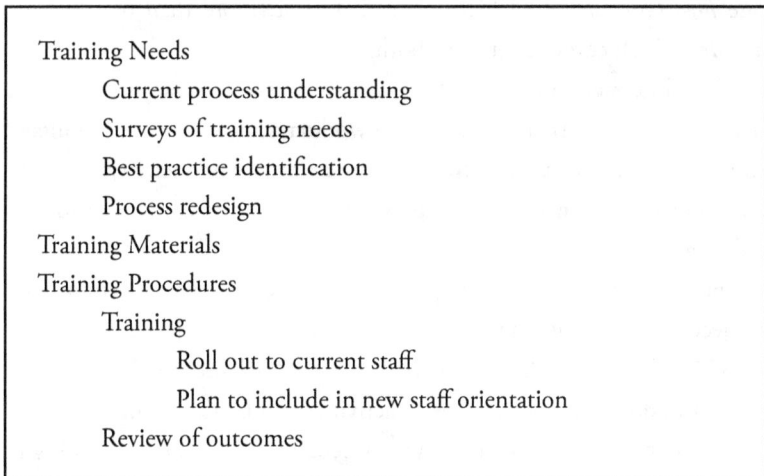

Training Needs
        Current process understanding
        Surveys of training needs
        Best practice identification
        Process redesign
Training Materials
Training Procedures
        Training
                Roll out to current staff
                Plan to include in new staff orientation
        Review of outcomes

Figure 12.2 Work breakdown structure for system downtime training project

means that our planning gets more detailed as we continue because we learn more and, inevitably, changes or unexpected events come up. Rather than be wedded to a no-longer-relevant schedule, project teams need to have the ability to adapt to events and circumstances as they arise.

The first step in developing the project schedule is to define all the work that needs to be done. Earlier we talked about deliverables, which are the output of a project or milestone. Now work backwards to determine *what needs to be done* to come up with those deliverables. Come up with as many specific activities as you can, and put each one on a separate sticky note. While you may still identify more activities during later steps in the planning process, you will risk throwing your schedule off track if you have to add activities after the planning has concluded and the schedule has been approved.

After identifying as many activities as possible, the next step is to sequence them. Which activities must be done before or after others? For example, if your project involves building a house, the frame needs to be in place before the drywall can go up. On a wall or large table, arrange the sticky notes in chronological order. It is possible that several of the activities can begin at once or that several depend on one or two prior activities to begin. It is perfectly okay for an activity to have more than one *predecessor activity* which comes before it, more than one *successor activity*, which comes after it, or both.

The third step in creating the project schedule is to estimate the time needed for each activity. You can use workdays, hours, or other units of time as long as you are consistent. Estimate each work activity individually, and refer when possible to past similar activities completed to provide reasonable time estimates.

Finally, based on your three previous steps, you need to determine your project's *critical path*. The critical path comprises the series of consecutive activities that create the longest path through the project. For example, if I am re-doing my home, several activities can be done simultaneously (or at any point), but I absolutely *must* repair the floor before sanding it, and sand it before refinishing it. So, regardless of how quickly or in what order all other tasks can be accomplished, it would be impossible for my

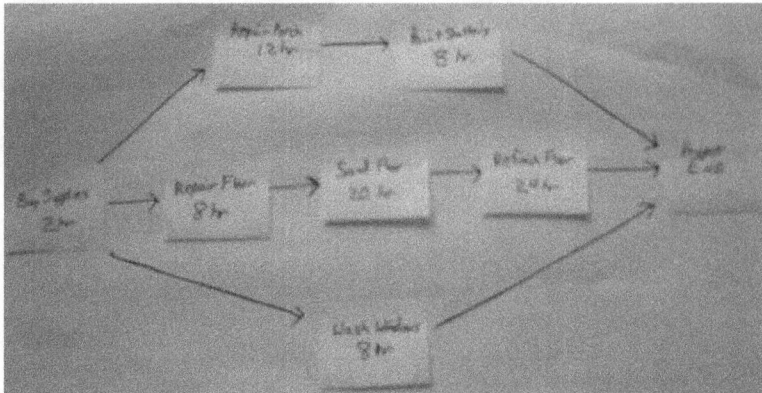

Figure 12.3 Project schedule for house repair project

project's duration to be less than the sum of time it takes for those activities. Figure 12.3 shows the schedule for a house repair project.

Human Resources

Now that we know the project activities and their relative order, it is time to assign our human resources. As you read in the introductory chapter, for a nonprofit organization, that could mean a number of volunteers in addition to employees. Your first step will be to estimate "the types and quantities of resources required to perform each scheduled activity."[7] How many people will you need? What, if any, specific skill sets are needed?

The answers to these questions will help you develop your *Staffing Management Plan.* Begin by identifying potential resources and comparing that to the estimated resources needed. If you have gaps in either the number or skill set of people available, you may need to look elsewhere (other departments, divisions, your volunteer base, or perhaps beyond the organization itself). Once you have a good idea of who you'd like to be a part of the project, you will need to determine their availability and secure their commitment. Find out now whether the team members you want are already committed to other projects, have vacation time coming up, or are unavailable for any other reason. A good project manager may have to negotiate in order to assemble a strong project team.

Table 12.1 Responsible, accountable, consult, inform (RACI) chart for house repair project

Activity	Juan	Alan
Buy supplies	A	C
Repair porch	A	I
Paint shutters	A	I
Repair floor	I	A
Sand floor	I	A
Refinish floor	I	A
Wash windows	A	I

Next, assign a resource to each activity. You can use a simple chart to assign all necessary work and identify any overused (or underused) people. One of the most common assignment charts is called a Responsible, Accountable, Consult, Inform (RACI) chart in which one or more people may have responsibility (R) for doing the work, only one person is accountable for each activity (A), and one or more people may need to be consulted (C) or informed (I). Only once responsibilities have been assigned and any resource overloads have been resolved, the final schedule—including actual work dates— should be approved. Table 12.1 continues the house repair project with a RACI Chart.

Executing a Project

Once the project has been fully planned, the team can move on to the executing phase of the project. This is when the majority of the "hands-on" work is performed. Be sure to check progress often against the project schedule and responsibility matrix. Communication among all project team members and with key stakeholders is vital and can help to head off or mitigate conflict. On many projects a variety of changes may be considered. Remember, most changes require more time and money, so be sure to assess any impacts of a proposed change and ensure that your sponsor, key stakeholders, or both are willing to accept a later delivery, provide more resources to pay for the change, or both.

Closing a Project

When a project is completed, meaning the final deliverables have been approved, there are still some things to be done. For one, *celebrate!* In all seriousness, it is extremely important for your project team to celebrate any success. Chances are, the project team will be disbanded to other projects or activities, so this is the last time to come together as a group and discuss how far you've come. In the same vein, what lessons did the team learn? These should be documented for reference by future project teams or others within the organization. If we can learn from those before us and pass on our hard-earned knowledge to those who come after us, we will collectively save much time and frustration. There may be people to be reassigned, and users of the project deliverables to be supported.

The next chapter will talk more about the various roles executives play in regard to projects. Remember, it is through projects that an organization can put its vision and mission statement into action. The most successful projects will be the ones in which everyone—from executive sponsor to core team member—is engaged and invested in the project's outcomes.

Planning and Managing Effective Projects at MNM

After 4 years, MNM had settled into its new reality as a merger of three agencies. Its home care service employed 25 aides, who cared for 150 elderly clients living in several Cincinnati neighborhoods.

To meet expanding needs, the agency had received approval from the area COA to begin a small HCAT program. Primary candidates for HCAT were economically disadvantaged women who lacked a high school diploma or General Educational Development (GED) credential, but had an aptitude for an entry-level job in health care.

The New Project

Within 2 months of launching this initiative, Executive Director Sue Kathman received a phone call from COA's Executive Director, who asked: Would MNM be willing to assume responsibility for COA's regional HCAT, which it had successfully run for 10 years? That program provided aides for home care agencies across four Southwestern Ohio counties. If MNM could not take over the program, COA would have to close it down in October, due to budgetary changes in Ohio state funding.

As Kathman hung up the phone, she felt an exhilarating enthusiasm to take on the project. "It was immediately clear that this was in line with our mission and 20-year history of senior and home care services," she says. "It also advanced MNM's reputation and increasing experience in preparing disadvantaged adults for employment."

Initiating the Project

But then a thorough assessment immediately showed several obstacles and challenges too.

To make the decision whether to take on this program and to simultaneously put in place the structures for success, Kathman assembled a project management team, including herself, as "sponsor" and project manager, Mary Lou Wolf, MNM program director of home care, other agency staff for specific tasks, and volunteers from the Board's client services committee. She promptly informed the MNM Board that the project was under consideration.

What must be done for MNM to assume responsibility for regional HCAT? Many factors needed to be resolved.

The first factor was easy: the project was clearly consistent with MNM's mission. Other factors would be more difficult: finding space for training, securing staff, identifying best practices and a viable program format, resolving several legal considerations, and establishing student recruitment. The overriding factor, though, was identifying and securing funding, since the new program would increase agency annual expenses by 20%.

Stakeholders

Primary stakeholders for the new program included many of the people MNM had helped for years, but now over a wider geographic area.

These included seniors needing home care, as well as individuals—mostly women—who were seeking to enter the health care workforce.

Other ongoing stakeholders were the health care facilities, education institutions, and community-based organizations that were partners in the Greater Cincinnati Health Careers Collaborative, where MNM was a long-time active member.

A somewhat new group of stakeholders included the many home care agencies, mostly for-profit, which would employ the program's graduates, and could become more active community partners supporting the program, of which they were primary beneficiaries.

Finally, funders were critical. These included MNM's current corps of loyal donors, but also new companies, foundations, individuals, and community organizations.

Planning the Project

Because of the short 5-month time frame, all factors had to be addressed at once. Shortly after the May phone call, Kathman met with the COA Executive Director and her management team. By June, conversations had begun with potential funders. While agency support staff and committee volunteers helped enormously, most of the direct work was accomplished through the long hours put in by Kathman and Wolf.

Space was located and rented in a church office building near MNM. Some equipment needed for training, such as beds, was transferred from COA, and the Department of Nursing at Xavier University donated a number of practice mannequins. Other equipment would be purchased.

For HCAT's principal staff, both the COA program coordinator and assistant agreed to move to MNM. Current MNM home care staff would assist with instruction.

The HCAT program adopted COA's format with additional best practices. A 3-week session would be conducted monthly with a maximum of 16 students per session, which would include a graduation ceremony with family and friends attending.

On the front end of the program, a student recruitment process included formal applications, candidate interviews, and acceptance. Research showed a high degree of interest in the program, and targeted communication promoted recruitment.

To fund the start-up, MNM gained increased funding from a federal grant in which the agency already participated. Even though MNM is not a UW agency, UW funding already allocated to COA for HCAT could be continued through third-party management of the grant by another current UW agency. Other funding was also identified through private foundation grants and from some of the area's private home care providers.

With all of the start-up factors identified and ready to be implemented, Kathman took the staff's detailed proposal to the MNM Board of Directors in July and received unanimous approval.

Over the next 2 months, contracts were signed, start-up funding was secured, approval of the program's transfer from COA was secured from the Ohio Department of Aging, and the legal copyrights to COA training materials were secured. On October 1, responsibility for regional HCAT transferred from the COA to a new home at MNM. And that same month, MNM conducted COA's previously scheduled class with 16 students.

Lessons Learned

In undertaking HCAT, MNM learned four valuable lessons:

1. A strong, existing network of professional colleagues and partner organizations greatly helps achieve project success.
2. In dealing with an already existing program, what may seem like a unified package, may in fact involve complex stakeholder relationships that can be a challenge to modify and restructure in the new environment.
3. In a project with tight deadlines and a small team, key personnel can be stretched to their limits with negative consequences for both the individuals and the organization.
4. In a project where there is a "high degree" of interest from potential participants, an agency must carefully determine that adequate administrative resources are in place to accommodate that volume of interest.

Summary

Projects are temporary in nature and are the means through which an organization realizes its vision and fulfills its mission. When undertaking a project it is important to know who the stakeholders are, and what the various stakeholders' hopes and expectations are for the project. The charter is the document that authorizes a project manager to begin work on a project. Once the charter is signed by all necessary parties, a good deal of work goes into planning the project. This includes planning for deliverables, work activities, human resources, and budget. Project closing is a time for reflection on lessons learned and goals (hopefully) realized. In the next chapter, you will get a better idea for how to choose projects that will best benefit your organization.

Key Assessment Questions

1. Do you use charters to effectively initiate projects? If so, what components are included and are they really effective at reaching high-level agreements between the sponsor, project manager, and team?
2. How do you identify, prioritize, engage, and communicate effectively with all of your project stakeholders?
3. Do you outline the deliverables your project team will create in a WBS (including partial and interim deliverables) and use that as a basis for planning?
4. How do you create project schedules including worker assignments and how accurately do these schedules predict your actual project completion?
5. Do you formally close your projects with lessons learned, celebration, and an effective transition to the users of your project deliverables?

Notes

1. Kloppenborg (2012).
2. Project Management Institute (2013).
3. Project Management Institute (2013).
4. Kloppenborg (2012).

5. Kloppenborg (2012).
6. Kloppenborg (2012).
7. Project Management Institute (2013).

References

Kloppenborg, T. J. (2012). *Contemporary project management* (2nd ed.). Mason, OH: Southwestern Cengage Learning.

Kloppenborg, T. J., & Laning, L. J. (2012). *Strategic leadership of portfolio and project management.* New York, NY: Business Expert Press.

Project Management Institute. (2013). *A guide to the project management body of knowledge (PMBOK® Guide)* (5th ed.). Newtown Square, PA: Project Management Institute.

CHAPTER 13

Sponsoring Projects

Timothy J. Kloppenborg

Timothy J. Kloppenborg is a Professor Emeritus from Xavier University. He has published books on leadership and project management. Tim is a Certified Project Management Professional (PMP®). He has worked with over 150 volunteer organizations, directly and through supervising student projects. He has hands-on and consulting experience in six continents.

Introduction

Many times a leader wants the results of a project because they will be used in her part of the organization or they will be delivered to an important client. This executive often serves as the project sponsor by championing the project and by providing resources and guidance that will enable a project manager to successfully plan and implement the necessary work. This chapter deals with the behaviors a busy executive sponsor can use to leverage her time while a project manager and team develop and deliver project results.

Purpose

The purpose of this chapter is to help you

- determine the duties, motivations, and challenges of the sponsor's role; and
- determine the high value activities you can engage in as a sponsor at each stage in the project life cycle.

Introduction to Redwood Rehabilitation

Redwood Rehabilitation guides children and adults with severe and multiple disabilities to achieve independence and reach their highest potential throughout their lives. Redwood annually guides 700 people with severe disabilities through 24 educational, therapeutic, vocational, and health care programs. Collaborating services provide a continuum of care and intervention that promotes development at each age level from early childhood through adulthood.

To manage reporting requirements, Redwood uses paper-based records, general-purpose software, and home-grown database systems. A strategic evaluation identified the need for an EMR system to enhance service quality through increased efficiency of documentation practices.

The key question Redwood leaders faced is

How can the CEO leverage her time in an effort to increase the success of this project? This is the classic sponsorship question and the subject of this chapter.

Project Sponsors

One way to understand the role of a sponsor is to envision the sponsor and project manager as a team. The sponsor is generally a high ranking executive or manager with significant knowledge and influence. The project manager is generally a lower level manager or individual contributor who is at the center of most project communications and activities, but does not enjoy significant position power. The most essential lesson concerning the partnership of sponsor and project manager is that the values they each bring to the project are complementary but distinct: one person should not attempt to do both jobs no matter how short the organization may be on resources!

A global source is the *PMBOK® Guide,* which is the official body of knowledge of project management published by the dominant project management professional group, Project Management Institute. The *PMBOK® Guide* lists several responsibilities of the sponsor:

- Promote the project.
- Serve as a spokesperson to higher management.

- Gather support and promote benefits for the project.
- Lead the project through the initiation process.
- Play a significant role in developing the initial charter and scope.
- Serve as an escalation for issues beyond the project manager's control.
- Authorize changes.
- Conduct phase-end reviews.
- Make go/no-go decisions.
- Ensure a smooth transfer of project deliverables.[1]

The sponsor has also been described as "a senior executive … who serves as a mentor, catalyst, motivator, barrier buster, boundary manager, and … change leader. Being a project sponsor is to be involved from project initiation to the end."[2]

Sponsor Responsibilities by Project Stage

To fully understand these responsibilities and the timing of each, we now review important sponsor behaviors overall and at each stage in the project life cycle as depicted in Figure 13.1.

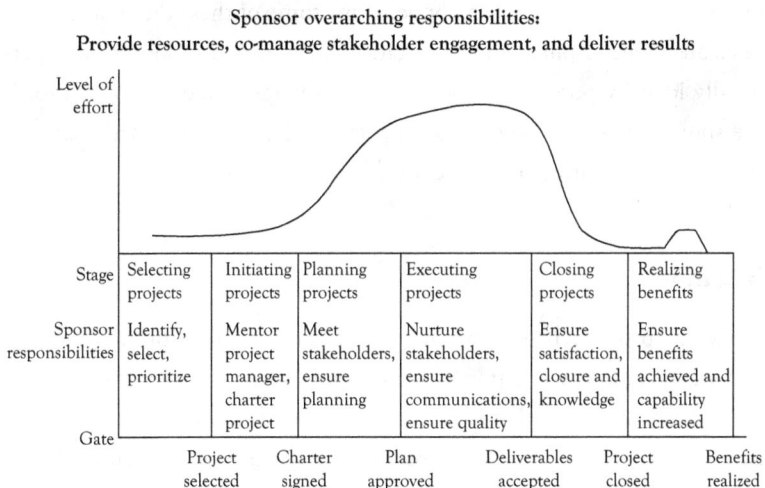

Sponsor overarching responsibilities:
Provide resources, co-manage stakeholder engagement, and deliver results

Stage	Selecting projects	Initiating projects	Planning projects	Executing projects	Closing projects	Realizing benefits
Sponsor responsibilities	Identify, select, prioritize	Mentor project manager, charter project	Meet stakeholders, ensure planning	Nurture stakeholders, ensure communications, ensure quality	Ensure satisfaction, closure and knowledge	Ensure benefits achieved and capability increased
Gate	Project selected	Charter signed	Plan approved	Deliverables accepted	Project closed	Benefits realized

Figure 13.1 Sponsor responsibilities by project stage

Overarching Responsibilities

A sponsor needs to provide the necessary resources to a project and is responsible for delivering results. The project manager is also responsible for delivering results, but the sponsor cannot wash her hands of this and demand that the project manager perform unilaterally. The sponsor is the link between senior management and the project team. The sponsor is also the link between the client and the project team. Serving as these links, the sponsor provides resources and delivers results throughout the project life. This may include help behind the scenes, obtaining resources and removing road blocks as well as visible participation in meetings where the sponsor announces decisions regarding resources and listens to progress reports as a means of emphasizing the need to deliver planned results. We will now discuss the two or three specific types of behaviors sponsors can use at each project stage to help ensure project success.

Selecting Stage

Selecting projects starts whenever any person has an idea and ends when projects are selected for inclusion in the organization's work portfolio. Selecting projects includes **identifying, selecting, and prioritizing** a portfolio of projects that will, hopefully best help the organization meet its goals. The sponsor personally performs some of these duties and helps to create an atmosphere and expectation for others. The sponsor can personally identify potential projects and encourage others to do so also. If the sponsor is part of the leadership team, she generally participates in selecting and prioritizing projects.

Initiating Stage

Initiating projects begins when projects are selected for inclusion in the organization's work portfolio and ends when a project is officially launched by a charter that is signed by the sponsor, project manager, and core team members. The first essential sponsor behavior when initiating a project is to select and mentor the project manager. The other essential behavior is to charter the project.

The project manager may not directly report to the sponsor—so the traditional supervisor–employee relationship may not exist. In many smaller organizations, there may only be one available person who has the experience necessary to be project manager. In larger organizations, many thoughts might come into play:

- How critical and how complex is the project?
- Is this project a good assignment to help someone gain experience?
- Is the sponsor well-seasoned and capable of mentoring a rooky project manager?
- Will there be proven individuals who can be assigned to the project who can help mentor an inexperienced project manager?
- What specific project demands suggest a particular person is assigned as project manager?
- Is there an individual with untapped talent if the sponsor looks widely enough?
- If the sponsor is highly interested in the project but inexperienced in sponsoring projects, is a very experienced project manager available who can "manage up?"

Part of mentoring a project manager is informal and part can be accomplished through a chartering process. The informal part includes helping the project manager develop necessary people skills. Project manager responsibilities are described in Chapter 12.

Some project managers are selected based upon demonstrated technical success. Those people might or might not become effective project managers, but the sponsor can greatly increase the probability of success by helping them deal effectively with the broad range of stakeholders most projects have. The sponsor can role-model some of these skills and can create situations where the project manager is the focal point of the project and the sponsor is in a supporting role.

The sponsor also needs to continually reinforce how the project fits in the big picture of organizational goals. While this will be described tersely in the charter, continuing to reinforce this connection in many different ways informally will help most project managers as they, in turn, need to communicate project goals and needs with many other people.

The sponsor also needs to define project manager performance expectations. Part of this is accomplished through goals identified in the charter and then detailed more specifically later in project planning documents. Part of it, however, should be understood between the sponsor and the project manager. A sponsor/project manager partnership flourishes with a great deal of informal dialogue—especially early in the project. As the project manager proves more worthy of sponsor trust, the conversations can be less often and less detailed.

One of the most important project management documents is the charter. The charter is a high-level project pre planning document. The sponsor makes chartering easier if she starts the process by providing her understanding very briefly of what the project might deliver and why the project is important to the organization. If she has any other firm convictions (such as an approach to use or something to include), it is also helpful to share that with the project manager and team. Sponsors will often provide this information either in one page or less of written suggestions, by attending the first part of a chartering meeting to speak with the project manager and team, or both. Once the project manager and team have constructed the charter's first draft, they will bring it to the sponsor for an interactive discussion that will ideally end in a mutual understanding and agreement of what the project will entail and commitment to make it happen.

Planning Stage

The planning stage begins with a signed charter that signifies high-level agreement by the sponsor, project manager, and core team and ends with acceptance of the detailed project plans by all stakeholders. Much of the detailed work in this stage is performed by the project manager, core team, subject matter experts, and other project stakeholders. The sponsor has two specific responsibilities during this stage. First is to look outward, understand who all of the stakeholders are, and to establish effective communication channels and working relationships with them. The other responsibility is to look inward to ensure the project is planned in the detail required. The planning and executing stages of projects often overlap or occur in a repetitive fashion with some planning, then some doing, and so forth.

Stakeholders are identified in the project charter, but as more detailed planning takes place, it is common to both uncover more stakeholders and more detailed understanding of their wants and needs. Stakeholders can be for or against the project. Sponsors want to reduce the influence of those who oppose and capitalize upon the enthusiasm of those who are for a project. Stakeholders can have an interest in the project process (they may be inconvenienced or they may need to provide resources) or in the project deliverables (their work may be changed by the project results). Just as the business case includes both logical and emotional reasons for undertaking the project, stakeholders have both logical and emotional desires that need to be understood. Some stakeholders are critical to the project in that they can shut it down if displeased while others have less power. Sponsors are responsible to ensure that all the work of identifying, understanding, and prioritizing stakeholders is accomplished and in as transparent fashion as practical. The sponsor creates the environment in which effective communication can occur between the project team and the stakeholders so that stakeholder input can be incorporated into project plans. The sponsor will personally communicate with more influential stakeholders and ensure that the project manager and team communicate effectively with the other stakeholders.

The other sponsor responsibility during the planning stage is to ensure that all necessary planning is performed. The sponsor will not personally do much of this—but needs to understand the depth of planning that makes sense for the project. A sponsor should have the team spend $100 in planning effort to save $1,000 in project cost, but not the other way around. Both high-level and detailed project planning techniques exist for each of the following:

- Scope (work breakdown structure)
- Communications (communication matrix, meeting management tools)

- Change (issues log, change request form)
- Schedule (network diagram, bar chart)
- People (responsibility matrix, individual and team assessment, resource loaded schedule)
- Cost (budget, supporting detail)
- Risk (risk identification, risk analysis, risk response plan)
- Reporting (project kickoff, progress report)

Executing Stage

The executing stage begins when project clients and key stakeholders approve the detailed project plan and ends when the primary project client formally accepts the main project deliverables. In reality, in many projects, the line between creating the plan and satisfying requirements is not so clean. Sometimes substantial work begins before the full plan is approved. Sometimes results of early work need to be understood before later work can be planned. Sometimes a decision is made to use rolling wave planning—that is, to plan a first little wave of work and complete that portion while planning the next wave. The extreme case of this, called agile project management, is becoming more popular especially with software development projects. In this section, we focus on the sponsor responsibilities that occur when the project team is satisfying the agreed upon requirements. The three necessary sponsor behaviors at this time are to build upon the stakeholder relationships that were started during planning (or before), ensure effective communications occur, and ensure the quality of the project processes and results.

One role of the sponsor is to champion the project. This includes reminding both the project team and many stakeholders why the project is needed. Sponsors personally focus on key stakeholders through individual communication, relationship building, and ensuring expectations are met. Sponsors deal with internal stakeholders by managing organizational politics, formally and informally updating the executive team on project progress, and authorizing execution of project activities. Sponsors also remember for whom the project deliverables are being created to serve. They ensure clients and users of the project deliverables remain involved as the project progresses and are updated on progress.

Communications need to occur among the project team and with other stakeholders. One of the most effective things a sponsor can do to aid communications is to visibly empower the project manager. A project manager with little power is like a weak coordinator who people only pay attention to when they want something. Sponsors can work with the project manager behind the scenes to develop communication strategies for specific people and situations. In public, showing confidence in the project manager and making it clear that the project manager speaks for the sponsor, encourages many people to deal directly with the project manager thereby saving precious time both for the sponsor and for the project schedule.

It is also critically important to have open communication between the project team and sponsor. There are situations when a team member would like to give the sponsor direct feedback and this should be encouraged. Effective sponsors actively listen to team members both individually and as a team. Sponsors sometimes need to re-focus teams when a project has drifted.

Sponsors also communicate with other key stakeholders such as donors and influential community members. One way is by supporting the project vision, helping people to progressively understand better what the project entails and why it is critical. Sponsors encourage input and actively listen to all stakeholders, both individually and in groups. There is a delicate balancing act here. On the one hand, the project manager needs to be the primary focal point of communication. On the other hand, when people know you are available to them, few will abuse the privilege and some of the sensitive issues that are brought to your attention will prevent problems.[3]

One major purpose of effective communications is to ensure progress. Several sponsor behaviors that help to ensure progress are as follows:

- Resolve conflicts when escalated.
- Remove obstacles to project progress.
- Defend the project's priority.
- Communicate issues effectively with key stakeholders.

Sponsors should also provide leadership for quality in four areas: ethics, decision making, risk management, and quality control. Ethics leadership includes continually role modeling and reminding people of the ethical standards that need to be used and then ensuring that they are used. Sponsors also strive to ensure all disputes are resolved fairly. Since many people work hard on most projects, it often seems fair to celebrate small wins. People see justice and feel respected when receiving small rewards not just for going through the motions, but for delivering results.

Sponsors make some decisions and create the environment in which other decisions are made. Decisions often have a major impact on quality. Sponsors need to understand what resistance exists to particular decisions. Much of this understanding comes from the project manager, but sponsors need to keep their own channels of communication open to be aware of resistance. Whether the sponsor or project manager makes the decision, sponsors need to insist that consistent criteria and adequate information are used in the decision-making process. Most projects have schedule pressure, so decisions often need to be made with less than full information. Sponsors work with project managers to determine when enough information is available to make the decision.

Sponsors also need to insist that a change management system is used. For most projects, many potential changes need to be considered. An effective change management system requires that each potential change be proposed with any impact described. Any impact resulting from approved changes needs to be included in the current project plan and any unapproved change should not be slipped in by someone who did not take no for an answer. Change request forms should be as simple as possible and make the approval decision transparent. Wise sponsors who have empowered their project managers let those project managers make most of the decisions with only controversial and major decisions being bumped up to the sponsor. A simple change request form is displayed in Figure 13.2.

Another aspect of quality leadership is how risks are managed. Risk identification, assessment, and resolution planning are started at a high level during the initiating stage and becomes more detailed during the planning stage. This needs to continue during the executing stage as new risks will appear with changing circumstances. Sponsors do not need to do much of this personally, but they need to make sure it happens. One good way is to have a member of the project core team assigned as the

Date requested:
Description of change:

Why needed:

Impact on schedule:
Impact on budget:
Impact on quality:
Other impacts:
Approved by:
Project manager   Date   or   Sponsor   Date

_____   _____

Figure 13.2 Change request form

owner of each major risk. The risk owner should understand the predictors of the risk event. For example, a weather report predicting storms tomorrow is a likely predictor that it will rain. As the sponsor, it makes sense to ask for updates on major risks at progress meetings. The updates can include not only the predictors, but also the avoidance and mitigation strategies the project team plans to use.

Traditional quality control is also part of quality leadership. Sponsors do not need to be too involved in details—mostly just ensure these activities are completed. One specific action sponsors should insist on is root cause analysis. Demand to know, with data, why something happened and how the process is being changed so that it will not happen again. This is not blaming individuals—it is improving the system. The other specific action sponsors require here is when a problem occurs, timely corrective action should follow. It is not enough to acknowledge a mistake—it is also important to rectify it quickly.

The sponsor's final part of quality leadership is to secure client approval of the project deliverables. This final approval generally requires a demonstration to convince the key stakeholders that the project deliverables meet their needs. In many projects, the client wants use of the deliverables before they are complete. When this happens, the client and the project manager jointly develop and agree upon a "punch list" of items that still need to be finished. If the list is small, the client may accept the deliverables subject to the project team finishing the listed items during the closing stage. If the list is long or has important items on it, the client will probably not accept the deliverables yet and the project will remain in the executing stage.

Closing Stage

The closing stage begins when the client formally accepts the major project deliverables—with or without a punch list of minor items remaining to be completed. This stage ends when all of the project objectives are met; stakeholders are satisfied with the project results; and resources are successfully transitioned. Alternatively, if the project was unsuccessful, it is terminated. In either event, part of the ending point is capturing knowledge for sharing with future projects.

Successfully transitioning project results begins with ensuring they meet the needs of key stakeholders. While this was started when the client formally accepted the deliverables, it often needs more attention as there was probably a "punch list" to be completed. Also, with many stakeholders on typical projects, it is still likely some are not happy. Understanding their needs and frustrations can help make a smoother transition. Not understanding their frustrations can lead to lack of user commitment and unsuccessful termination as described next. Successful sponsors have their project managers and teams document that all project objectives were accomplished, perhaps, with a checklist that is then archived. Then the project team develops a transition plan to help the customers successfully use the project results. This plan may include documentation, instruction, and mentoring.

The sponsor also wants to be sure project resources are successfully transitioned. Some of this is administrative with budgets and physical items being accounted for. Some is taking care of the project manager and team. Evaluations need to be conducted with sponsor-generated input supplied for people's performance reports. Appropriate reassignments, promotions, bonuses, and celebrations may be in order. Smart sponsors understand that if they take care of their project managers and team members, it will be much easier to recruit and lead on future projects.

A troubled project should be cancelled as soon as it is obvious that it cannot deliver the needed benefits. Also, a project that is creating deliverables that are no longer needed or are no longer a top priority should be terminated as soon as this determination is made. This cancellation could happen during an earlier stage when knowledge gained during chartering or planning shows the project is impractical. It could occur during the executing stage when problems are occurring. Regardless of when it starts to become apparent that the project cannot succeed or is no longer needed, the sponsor should be one of the first people to question its viability. While the sponsor appropriately champions the project while it has a chance, once the sponsor determines it has no chance, it is time to act as an executive of the organization and decide not to throw good money after bad.

If the project is terminated because the organization's priorities have changed, the sponsor needs to ensure that the project manager and everyone working on the project are protected. It is both unethical and impractical to punish people for things beyond their control. However, if the project is cancelled because of failure to do proper work, there may be appropriate repercussions and the sponsor needs to be in the center of those decisions.

Sponsors realize that they need to capture lessons from work experiences and use those lessons to improve future projects. Lessons on a large project are often captured at the end of each life cycle stage or at the accomplishment of key milestones. Lessons on short, small projects may be captured just at the end. Lessons can be captured from both the project team and from other stakeholders. At any rate, sponsors need to insist that lessons are captured, categorized, stored, shared, and then used appropriately in future projects.

Once lessons learned are captured, they should be categorized. Organizations find that having a few categories is better than none or many. Examples of potential categories include scope, schedule, cost, quality, stakeholder management, team management, communications, vendors, leadership, and operations.

After lessons are categorized, they need to be stored and distributed. Companies may use shared drives, wikis, databases, or other means. The key is to make this simple to both input lessons into and acquire lessons from the system.

Perhaps the most essential sponsor responsibility with lessons learned is to insist they are used to change behavior. One easy way for sponsors to do this is to never sign a charter for a new project nor authorize the next phase of an existing project, until the project manager and team describe at least one or two new lessons they have discovered in the lessons learned repository and discuss how they will improve based upon those lessons.

Realizing Benefits Stage

The realizing benefits stage occurs weeks or months after the project is complete. The idea is to assess how well the end users of the project deliverables are able to use them. Were the benefits that were promised during project selection delivered? Has capability improved because of the project deliverables and has capability improved because of utilizing lessons learned from the project process?

The primary reason projects are undertaken is that someone needs deliverables they can use in performing their work. A sponsor should insist that an evaluation take place after the users have been using the project results for a period of time. The exact questions may be context specific, but essentially the users should answer questions such as the following:

- Were the original proposed benefits achieved?
- Were the project deliverables worth the time and effort of development?
- Are the users able to use the project deliverables as intended?
- Are the users "selling" the project results to other stakeholders?

Capability improvements can be assessed for both the user and the organization performing the project. It can be measured both at the organizational level and at the project team member level. Typical questions might include the following:

- Would the users like to work with the same project team again?
- How could the project results have been more useful?
- How could the project results have been more sustainable?
- How has the user's capacity increased through use of project deliverables?

- Are project team members more loyal to the parent organization?
- How have project team members improved their capabilities?
- What organizational learning has occurred?

Sponsoring Redwood's Project

Redwood launched a multifaceted, yearlong strategic evaluation to determine direction for the future. As part of the evaluation, key stakeholders—including staff—identified barriers to achieving agreed upon vision statements.

The Barrier

A key barrier to "quality services" was the patchwork of processes and tools used to collect data from intake through outcomes reporting and billing. The tools and methods simply did not support efficient recording, storing, tracking, summarizing, using, sharing, and accessing of information. This circumstance was highly discouraging to staff.

Selecting the Project

When investigating solutions to service-documentation barriers, the Program Council determined that a comprehensive EMR system would simplify data collection processes, streamline workflow, and provide instant access to well-organized information to support the delivery of quality services. They recommended an EMR initiative for inclusion in the Strategic Plan.

In reflecting on the various projects proposed for the Strategic Plan, the CEO specifically focused on recommendations that would strengthen Redwood's reputation for high-quality, outcomes-focused programs, while optimizing high business productivity, staff morale, and consistent funding. The CEO felt that use of an EMR system would contribute meaningfully to each of these desired outcomes; therefore, she wrote the project into the 3-year Strategic Plan. It was approved by the board in July that year.

Because the CEO did not have the time or the expertise to lead the project from research through implementation, she assumed the role of project sponsor and made the commitment to provide resources and guidance to support the success of others. Work began immediately.

Initiating the Project

To procure relevant intellectual resources, the CEO asked a member of the Medical Advisory Committee to lead an ad hoc EMR Committee to explore the scope of the project from a program perspective; and shortly thereafter, she invited the Technology Committee to collaborate. Through these groups, the project benefited from the expertise of professionals from Redwood, Pediatrics Associates, Beckfield College, Children's Hospital, St. Elizabeth Medical Center, Pediatric Care, Cincinnati Bell, C-Forward Information Technologies, and Xavier University (College of Business).

As project sponsor, the CEO actively participated in the meetings of each committee, but assigned the IT Coordinator to lead product research. She identified three potential products, reviewed product descriptions, scheduled webinar training, confirmed which products met Redwood's policy/regulatory requirements, and conducted a reference survey. After analyzing this information, the committees selected an EMR product in December of the following year.

The next thing needed was money. Utilizing the information researched in the previous 6 months, the CEO developed grant proposals that described the need, project description, methodology, goals, measurable objectives, timetable, and evaluation plans. She and the Chief Development Officer raised nearly $100,000 from charitable foundations and individual donors by the end of 2013 to cover start-up costs for the project.

While fund-raising was under way, the CEO convened an internal EMR Staging Committee to plan for installation, data migration, and customization of screens and reports. She assigned the clinical director and IT Coordinator to co-chair the committee. While the CEO did not serve on the committee beyond the initial meeting, she regularly tracked progress through review of meeting minutes and discussions with the chairs. Within 6 months, the committee analyzed data flow, determined communication requirements, streamlined processes, and standardized documents.

Planning and Executing the Project

The EMR Project Manager (IT Coordinator) alerted the vendor of Redwood's readiness to sign a contract. The project kickoff meeting provided the opportunity for the vendor and Redwood to establish the project framework and to agree upon project roles and the execution strategy as defined in a project charter. This led to a negotiation between the Technology Committee, project sponsor (CEO), and the vendor, relevant to project timelines. The project implementation start date was set for March.

The biggest barrier faced at that point was how to give the Project Manager (IT Coordinator) and Project Team Leader (Clinical Director) enough time to manage project tasks. To meet this need, the CEO authorized hiring of a part-time IT employee and established an IT Triage Plan to funnel daily technology repair needs through an assigned IT Triage Expert.

It wasn't as easy to free up project time for the clinical director. The CEO timed the onboarding of an HR Manager close to the project start date to relieve the clinical director of some HR tasks. The CEO moved a few other responsibilities from the clinical director to herself, and asked staff to follow set communication practices to minimize disruption of project work. Probably most helpful was increased delegation to direct reports.

As project sponsor, the CEO regularly reviewed project status/timelines with key project leaders. At the same time, she shared relevant information with key stakeholders—especially staff and board members—to reinforce the strategic alignment of the project with Redwood's strategic goals, to maintain excitement about the project, and to recognize the project team.

At the printing of this book, the EMR Project was still under way. Redwood is confident that through effective project sponsorship and management the organization will realize an optimal return on its investment of time, money, and other resources, as measured by sustainable improvements in data collection, data access, and data measurement for all services provided at Redwood.

Lessons Learned

1. In large projects, one key executive needs to step forward and lead—this is the sponsor.

2. The sponsor needs to continually reinforce how the project supports the strategic plan.
3. The sponsor needs to provide resources for the project—often including securing external grants.
4. The sponsor needs to mentor and encourage the project manager and team much of the time, but take charge sometimes to keep making progress.

Summary

Sponsors must focus their limited time on a few key behaviors at each stage in a project life, such as mentoring the project manager and chartering the project during the initiating stage and meeting key stakeholders and ensuring the project manager and team perform adequate planning in the planning stage (see Figure 13.1 for a full listing). They partner with and mentor a project manager and personally provide resources, guidance, championship of the project, and key stakeholder engagement. This shared responsibility with the project manager greatly enhances the chance of project success.

Key Assessment Questions

1. How many of your projects have a formally assigned sponsor?
2. How are sponsors selected and trained in your company?
3. What is the overall job description for sponsors' sweeping responsibilities?
4. What are the most critical few sponsor responsibilities in your nonprofit?
5. What do sponsors do during each project stage of your projects?

Notes

1. Project Management Institute (2013).
2. Englund and Bucero (2006).
3. Cockerell (2008).

References

Cockerell, L. (2008). *Creating magic: 10 common sense leadership strategies from a life at Disney*. New York, NY: Doubleday.

Englund, R. L., & Bucero, A. (2006). *Project sponsorship: Achieving management commitment for project success*. San Francisco, CA: Jossey-Bass.

Kloppenborg, T. J, Manolis, C., & Tesch, D. (2009). Successful sponsor behaviors during project initiation: an empirical investigation. *Journal of Managerial Issues 21*(1), 140–159.

Kloppenborg, T. J., Tesch, D., & Manolis, C. (2011). Investigation of the sponsor's role in project planning. *Management Research Review 34*(4), 400–416.

Kloppenborg, T. J. (2012). *Contemporary project management* (2nd ed.). Mason, OH: Southwestern Cengage Learning.

Kloppenborg, T. J., & Laning, L. J. (2012). *Strategic leadership of portfolio and project management*. New York, NY: Business Expert Press.

Project Management Institute. (2013). *A guide to the project management body of knowledge (PMBOK® Guide)* (5th ed.). Newtown Square, PA: Project Management Institute.

SECTION 4

Developing Your Team

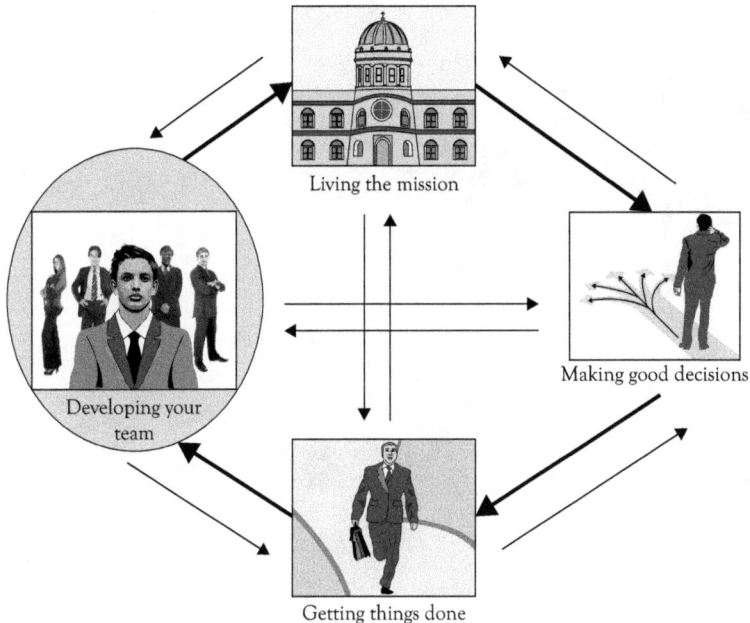

Living the mission

Making good decisions

Developing your team

Getting things done

Developing your team begins with acquiring and developing individuals and fostering the teamwork that will help your organization succeed. This can be greatly enhanced by utilizing diverse perspectives such as those from many of the tangential leadership schools of thought that provide innovative approaches.

The first chapter in this section, Creating Value through Human Resources, describes how HR activities can support strategic alignment, be measured accurately, and effectively deliver HR activities from selection to succession. The second chapter, Total Quality: Integrating Customer, Employee, and Process Voices, challenges us to capitalize not only upon understanding employees but on their interactions with their environments, suppliers, and clients. The third chapter, A Strengths-Based

Approach to Managing Your People, describes how we can lead with a goal of helping our workers develop and use their most vital talents and be more productive and happier in the process. The final chapter, Creating a Sense of Employee Ownership: Lessons from Worker-Owned Cooperatives, helps us understand how transparency and sense of ownership can lead to better decisions, more passion for work, and enhanced organizational performance.

CHAPTER 14

Creating Value Through Human Resources

Tamara L. Giluk and Shari Mickey-Boggs

Tamara L. Giluk is an Assistant Professor at Xavier University. She holds a PhD in HR and Organizational Behavior from the University of Iowa. She has 10 years of HR experience in the retail, hospitality, and pharmaceutical industries and is a certified Senior Professional in Human Resources.

Shari Mickey-Boggs is the Senior Associate Vice President for Human Resources and Chief Human Resources Officer at Xavier University. She has 20 years of HR experience in retail, health care, government, and academia. Mickey-Boggs has a BA from The Ohio State University and an MBA from Franklin University.

Introduction

An organization does not exist without the people it comprises, and its success lies in the hands of its people. The competition for talent, that is, the ability to attract and retain employee talent that can execute strategy, is a key organizational challenge. Effective human resource management (HRM) helps organizations rise to this challenge. It creates an environment in which employees can do their best work, contributing to achievement of the organization's mission and strategic objectives while also respecting the dignity of employees as human beings. In this chapter, we discuss key elements of an effective human resource (HR) strategy.

Purpose

The purpose of this chapter is to help you

- understand the importance of strategic alignment whereby HR activities support achievement of the organization's mission, vision, and strategic objectives;
- describe the three types of metrics an organization can use to assess its HR function;
- describe key principles to effectively deliver the HR activities of selection, onboarding, performance, development and reward, and succession.

Introduction to Xavier University

We illustrate the principles discussed with an exemplar nonprofit organization. Xavier University is one of 28 Catholic, Jesuit universities in the United States. Consistently ranked as one of the top 10 universities in the Midwest by U.S. News and World Report, Xavier is located in Cincinnati, Ohio. The student body includes 7,000 undergraduate and graduate students, and the workforce includes approximately 1,000 full-time continuing faculty and staff.

Two key questions to consider and answer in this chapter are as follows:

- How does HR help achieve the outcomes needed for a thriving 21st century nonprofit entity?
- How does HR prepare the workforce for change and uncertainty in an increasingly global and competitive landscape?

Strategic Alignment

Strategic alignment requires that all HRM activities support achievement of the organization's mission, vision, and strategic objectives.[1] This requires, firstly, that HR professionals have an in-depth understanding of these aspects of the organization. A criticism of some HR professionals is that they have expert HR knowledge, but do not understand their organization's broader operations. Various strategies can increase HR professionals' knowledge in this area, including meeting with different departments during their operational meetings, serving on cross-functional or strategic planning teams, getting mentor(s), and reading relevant journals.

Alignment is also critical within the HR system. Every function within HR affects and is affected by others. For example, a poor recruiting, selection system, or both may result in new employees who do not possess the necessary knowledge, skills, or abilities to do their jobs; thus, additional training will be required for these employees to be productive. HR activities must work in concert to support one another as well as the organization's mission and strategic objectives.

Strategic alignment is a collaborative process. Involving other employees—both inside and outside the HR function—and key stakeholders is vital when developing programs, policies, or systems. Soliciting input allows HR to incorporate various perspectives (e.g., with respect to function, organizational level, work experience, diverse demographics) in the design process, generally resulting in a higher quality outcome. In addition, to manage change effectively, involve individuals within the organization who occupy key roles, are highly respected by others, or are able to drive change through leadership and empowering others.[2] Such individuals can ensure support for, effective transition to, and long-term success of new programs, policies, or systems.

In 2005, Xavier embarked upon a strategic plan in which "Develop the People of Xavier" was a key focus. Xavier's President considered two fundamental questions based upon where the university was headed: (1) whether HR was reporting to the right area to ensure the organization's focus; and (2) whether the right leader was in place to transform the HR function into one that could support transformational change through both strategic planning and operational excellence. Xavier decided to change the reporting structure so that HR would report to the Administrative Vice President within the President's Office, and to create an Associate Vice President for HR and to seek an external candidate.

Upon hiring the new leader, the Office of Human Resources, through a series of open discussion forums called Conversation Cafés, solicited input from Xavier employees to determine the competencies needed for

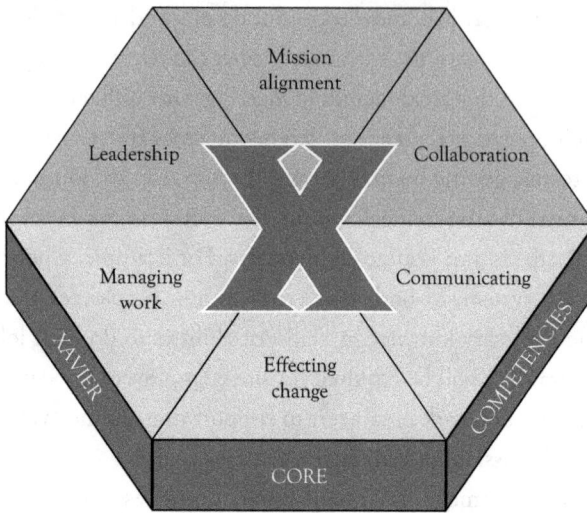

Figure 14.1 Xavier core competency model
Source: Copyright Xavier University 2013, used by permission

Xavier now and into the future. All feedback was organized and themed yielding six core competencies (illustrated in Figure 14.1), for which two signature developmental programs were built. The *Leadership Academy* is a cohort program accommodating 10–12 high performers each year designed to expose participants to 21st century higher education challenges and innovations along with leadership assessments to allow participants to reflect upon themselves as leaders. The *Manager/Leader Program* is a foundational program, designed for 185 managers of people consisting of 10 sessions covering all aspects of management from budget, purchasing, performance management, communication, and compliance.

Key steps:

- Know what your organization's strategy is.
- Ensure your HR structure and strategy align with where the organization needs to go.
- Solicit input from key stakeholders and employees in the development of programs, policies, or systems.

Metrics

Organizations must assess the HR function to ensure it meets the needs of the organization, its employees, and volunteers (although volunteers are often managed by areas other than HR). This is particularly important for nonprofit organizations; given their limited staff and resources, nonprofits need to ensure they are investing them wisely for maximum impact on the organization and its stakeholders. An organization chooses metrics, or measures, to assess HRM processes or practices. Metrics can be categorized into three types, assessing efficiency, effectiveness, or impact of the HR function (see Table 14.1).[3]

Leaders should choose metrics that are both important to the organization and feasible to track. Many organizations focus on efficiency metrics because this type of data is generally easy to collect; however, they fail to illustrate the strategic value of HR to the organization.

There are, however, some essential cautions regarding HR metrics.[4] Remember that metrics are a means to an end. Not everything that can be measured should be measured. Rather, the value of metrics is whether individuals within your organization use them to make different and better decisions that positively impact organizational effectiveness. In addition,

Table 14.1 Metrics to assess the HR function

Metric Type	Key Question	Example Measures	Value of Measurement
Efficiency	What is the relationship between the resources HR uses and the programs and practices it creates?	Cost-per-hire, time-to-fill (open positions), training costs	Foundation for HR credibility
Effectiveness	What is the relationship between HR programs and their effect on those who receive them?	Learning from training, motivation from rewards, test validity	Evidence of program-level results
Impact	What is the relationship between the effects of HR programs and key elements of organizational success?	Organizational impact (e.g., increased efficiency or effectiveness in serving clients) of high versus low performance in jobs	A view of where program results have their greatest effect

the organization's external environment, strategy, and internal processes may change over time; useful HR metrics will change as well. Some metrics may no longer be relevant, while new metrics may need to be created.

Metrics is a weaker but emerging area of focus for Xavier University. Turnover data (effectiveness metric) is calculated for all employees and monitored for trends.

Two key metrics are used for the *Leadership Academy* development program: satisfaction and quality ratings per session (to some extent an effectiveness metric, though true effectiveness metrics would demonstrate whether managers gained needed skills), and retention of cohort participants over time (effectiveness metric). Such metrics allow for necessary improvements and help ensure retention of high-performing employees.

Two key metrics used for the *Manager/Leader Program* include attendance and certification upon completion of all 10 programs (efficiency metric), and overall managerial effectiveness ratings by employees through a climate study (effectiveness metric). This data reported to the appropriate Vice President enables recognition by leaders of managers investing in their development and assessment of managers' effectiveness and future leadership potential.

Key steps:

- Know what information would be important for your leadership.
- Design your metrics and keep it simple.
- Obtain leadership agreement/buy-in on how you are collecting the data.
- Track progress and make appropriate program or personnel adjustments based on results.

HR Activities

Organizations must deliver effective HR activities from employee entry into and exit from the organization. We discuss the key HR activities of selection, onboarding, performance management, development and reward, and succession.

Selection

The goal of selection is to evaluate applicants and identify the best candidate(s) for jobs in a process that is efficient, effective, legal, and ethical. Selection is an essential process to get right. Without the appropriate talent, the organization cannot achieve its strategic objectives; other HR activities—such as performance management, development, and reward—can enhance motivation and performance of employees, but cannot compensate for inadequate talent.

Designing an effective selection process requires understanding the criteria on which you will assess and select candidates. Jobs within the organization should be analyzed to understand their tasks and responsibilities as well as the knowledge, skills, abilities, and other characteristics individuals need to perform those jobs successfully. The criterion of "fit," or whether candidates' values and personality align with the organization, should also be evaluated. Given the significance of mission in the nonprofit arena, fit with mission is critical. Once selection criteria have been determined, the organization should implement a standardized selection process, that is, a process applied consistently to applicants. There are many methods to assess applicants, including applications/resumes, interviews, testing (e.g., assessing applicants' intelligence, personality, integrity), and work samples. A combination of methods will often provide the most information about how an applicant will perform on the job if hired.

The most common selection method used in organizations is the interview.[5] Both managers and applicants often enjoy a more casual, get-to-know-you conversation rather than a formal interview. However, a structured interview, which consists of standardized questions designed to assess the selection criteria, is more effective for predicting performance. Behavioral-based interviewing, in which the questions prompt candidates to describe how they have handled a situation in the past, is recommended. Often these questions target general competencies such as teamwork or communication. Candidate responses to questions are generally rated according to standardized rating criteria. All managers and employees involved in the selection process should be trained as to how to behave in accordance with legal guidelines (e.g., laws prohibiting discrimination based on race, sex, age). Organizations should consult with HR and legal experts to ensure the selection process is efficient, effective, legal, and ethical.

Bear in mind that selection is a two-way process; the organization and the candidate are evaluating one another. Organizations should create a compelling value proposition and communicate this to candidates—why should they want to work for your organization? Communication is also important. Candidates should be informed what the selection process looks like and how long it is expected to take. When the organization has decided against candidates, it should inform them of this decision in a timely and professional manner. Candidates will speak to others about their experience; they also may be volunteers with or donors to your organization. It is in the organization's best interest to maintain goodwill with all candidates.

Xavier's compliance in this arena is driven by policies and procedures in place. The university utilizes an in-house tool, the "hiring resource guide," to house tips and tools for hiring managers and search committees. All persons supporting a search are required to review the guide with special emphasis on legal compliance and selection best practices, such as sample behavioral-based interview questions (see Table 14.2) and mission information to share with candidates.

Table 14.2 *Sample "effecting change" competency-based questions*

Effecting change	1. Have you ever had to introduce a policy change to your work group? How did you do it?
	2. Have you ever met resistance when implementing a new idea or policy to a work group? How did you deal with it? What happened?
	3. Tell me about a time when you made members of your department comfortable when dealing with conditions which had a lot of feelings involved in them.
	4. In situations at work, we often must compromise in order to get things done. Tell us about a time that you were able to remain flexible and open-minded to others' ideas in order to bring about necessary results for your organization.
	5. Many times, getting results requires a full understanding of the organizational culture. Describe a time when your understanding of the organization helped you to deliver on a particular goal or objective.
	6. Describe the methodology or approach you used to lead change in a prior role. What was the result?
	7. Give us an example of a situation when your timing, environmental awareness, and knowledge of how groups work enhanced your ability to generate a change.
	8. Change within an organization is guided by networks and relationships. Describe a time for us when you were able to impact a particular change initiative in your organization using your interpersonal skills.

Source: Copyright Xavier University 2013, used by permission

The area of selection is also an appropriate place to make use of effective technology should your budget allow for an online application system. Xavier uses a firm specializing in mid-size organizations, and has rolled out a career portal and associated website. This system supports compliance, enables a stronger employer brand, supports sustainability in that all applications and materials are housed electronically, and allows search committee members easy access to applicant pools.

Key points:

- Know what you are hiring for; basic requirements (e.g., education, experience, specialized skills) as well as behaviors/competencies critical for success.
- Include persons of diverse backgrounds on your selection team and train all parties in legal dos and don'ts.
- Create standard interview guides, yet allow opportunity for candidates to ask questions (to reinforce a two-way process).
- Provide candidates takeaway materials on your organization, particularly communicating why they should work for your company.

Onboarding

Onboarding is a comprehensive orientation process that helps employees successfully transition into the organization, ensuring they feel welcomed and prepared to be effective in their new role. Research and conventional wisdom indicate that the first 90 days in a new job are critical. An effective onboarding process helps new employees to maximize these 90 days, and has been shown to increase job satisfaction and performance as well as reduce undesirable turnover.[6] Successful onboarding programs consist of four components, referred to as the "Four C's": Compliance, Clarification, Culture, and Connection (illustrated in Figure 14.2).[7]

Compliance is the most basic component and consists of helping new employees understand company policies, relevant laws, and necessary

Four C's of successful onboarding			
Compliance	Clarification	Culture	Connection

Figure 14.2 The components of successful onboarding

administrative paperwork. A robust onboarding program goes beyond compliance, however, to help new employees understand their jobs and performance expectations (Clarification); understand the company history, traditions, values, and norms (Culture); and facilitate effective working relationships with colleagues and one's supervisor (Connection). The ideal result is employees who are clear on what is expected of them in their role, confident in their ability to achieve expectations, socially integrated within the organization, and able to successfully navigate the organization's culture.

Strong onboarding programs tend to be explicitly planned. Organizations will want to consider how to best sequence the components (e.g., a full day of orientation focused on laws and policies may be overwhelming), during what activities it may be beneficial to group new employees together (e.g., new employees may enjoy learning about the organization's mission and values together, while specific role expectations are best communicated on an individual basis), and who needs to be involved (e.g., the key stakeholders new employees should meet early on will differ for each employee). In addition, managers should monitor employees' experience over time, particularly during the first year, to ensure they are transitioning successfully.

Xavier has multiple strategies that support employee onboarding. As part of the *Companion Program*, every new hire is assigned a current employee from outside their immediate work area, who can take new employees to lunch, discuss the informal culture, and facilitate network connections within the organization. In addition, an orientation is conducted monthly to acquaint new employees with the mission, policies and procedures, benefits, and key communication mechanisms, as well as create a community of "newbies" to associate with. Further, executive leaders are encouraged to integrate their own ideas into a structured onboarding process where each new leader meets individually with current leadership, holds a variety of listening sessions with faculty and staff members, meets with appropriate external parties, and participates in a welcoming reception held to foster community.

Additional university-wide onboarding programs are mission driven, specifically *Manresa* and *AFMIX*. *Manresa* provides an overview of Xavier mission and identity. Veteran faculty and staff share aspects of tradition followed by stimulating dialogue and reflection. *AFMIX* is a 2-year educational process that provides a comprehensive understanding of Ignatian vision and heritage through readings, dialogue, presentations, reflection, and spiritual exercises. New in 2012 was the *Mission for Mentoring Program for Senior Administrators* pairing a new hire with a current mission-conscious senior leader.

Key steps:

- Prepare for a person's first day—what plan do you have in place to jump-start the employee's experience with your organization?
- Tailor your onboarding to your mission, vision, and values.
- Find ways to introduce employees to others in the organization ensuring relationships and networks begin early.
- Use checklist (see excerpt in Table 14.3) to organize and ensure all bases are covered.

Performance

Effective performance management entails both enabling and evaluating performance. Figure 14.3 shows a typical performance management process.[8]

Managers must first ensure employees know what is expected of them. The job analyses conducted prior to selection result in position descriptions that provide an overview of a position's tasks and responsibilities. Managers may set specific performance goals related to these tasks and

Table 14.3 Xavier sample onboarding checklist

Informal welcome to campus	
Meet new employee on arrival and make appropriate introductions	Immediate supervisor/new office staff
Tour work area and identify key places (restroom/coat room…)	
Discuss work schedule, workplace flexibility, time reporting, absence from work policy, overtime (if applicable), pay cycles, probationary period	
Explain building access	
Provide campus map	
Take new employee to human resources (HR) for paperwork processing	
Consult HR correspondence for orientation dates to plan for time	
Review and discuss supervisor questions for consideration	Supervisor/new employee
Establish check in meeting schedule	
Establish performance expectations	
Calendar of expectations—academic day, commencement, board events, and so forth	
Discuss performance appraisal process	
Formal welcome to campus	
The President's office or Divisional Leader's office will ensure there are receptions, as appropriate	President's office, Divisional Leader's office, University Relations
President/individual meeting	
Welcomes, shares expectations, initial goals, communicates perceptions of the current state, and highlights competencies that may be most critical for success	

Source: Copyright Xavier University 2013, used by permission

responsibilities. Such goals should cascade from the organization's goals and objectives. To enable employees to achieve the goals, managers must also ensure that employees have the tools, resources, and skills needed to do their jobs. Employees may need equipment, funding, human capital resources, or additional training or coaching in order to meet performance goals.

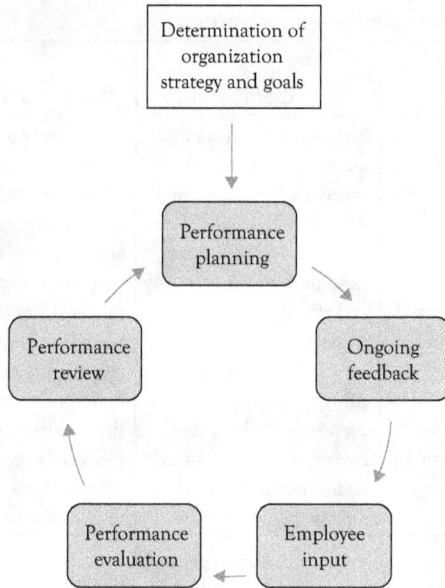

Figure 14.3 A typical performance management process

Managers must evaluate the degree to which employees are performing their jobs effectively. Organizations generally have a system for formal performance evaluation. In most organizations, performance is formally evaluated on an annual basis. However, managers should give ongoing performance feedback to employees to give employees reinforcement to continue what they are doing well and an opportunity to make improvements where needed. It is important to evaluate employees' performance results (*what* is achieved); however, most organizations also will want to evaluate employees' behaviors (*how* results are achieved) to ensure they reflect organizational values (e.g., integrity, teamwork). Additionally, employees should be partners throughout this process; managers should solicit employees' input when establishing performance goals as well as during performance conversations.

Xavier embarked on a 3-year performance management redesign initiative in 2010. Key elements included cascading goals from the top, individual goal setting on objectives and behaviors, conducting performance planning meetings, giving and receiving feedback, and evaluating and rewarding employees. Performance was viewed as a one-time event,

Table 14.4 Xavier performance rating scale

1 = Need for development	2 = Competent	3 = Exemplary
Performance does not meet many job requirements on a consistent basis. Critical goals require more than usual supervisor follow-up and direction. Results and contributions are below those of a fully trained competent employee. Action on performance improvement areas is required.	Performance consistently meets and sometimes exceeds job requirements. All critical goals are achieved and behaviors exhibited are valued and effective. Over the review period, employee has made the expected contributions to the department. Consistently met expectations for the performance of duties and responsibilities identified.	Performance and demonstrated expertise is consistently at a superior level. Employee achieves outstanding results and models effective behaviors that are an inspiration to others. Over the review period, employee has consistently made exceptional or unique contributions to the department. Regularly exceeded expectations for the performance of duties and responsibilities identified.

Source: Copyright Xavier University 2013, used by permission

the annual review with one's manager. In an effort to become a high-performing organization, Xavier set out to transform the culture.

A new performance management life cycle was established. Activities developed to support the change included a new process and review form, a new rating scale (illustrated in Table 14.4), just-in-time training delivered through webinars, and a manager toolkit. Additional critical components for Xavier included identifying and defining values and rating on competencies (the "how") combined with the review of job duties and established annual goals (the "what").

Key steps:

- Set individual goals in a way that helps employees see their connection to the organization's purpose and strategy.
- Provide effective tools for managers that reinforce setting and regularly discussing expectations and performance feedback; this includes the use of position descriptions.
- Define a process for performance management and hold managers accountable.

- Link rewards to performance—show a direct connection between employees' rating and their rewards, including pay (e.g., base salary increase).

Development and Reward

Development and reward programs aid in attracting, motivating, and retaining employees. Development refers to efforts to help employees grow and to prepare for future roles in the organization.[9] Development can occur through formal education, assessment, job experiences, and interpersonal relationships.[10] Figure 14.4 provides examples of each approach.

Growth and development are not synonymous with movement up an organizational hierarchy. Organizations should think broadly about development such that even those employees who stay in the same position continue to grow and feel challenged in their work. Also, many managers associate development most closely with formal education; indeed, this is the most frequently used employee development practice.[11] However, an effective development and career management system uses a combination of development approaches.

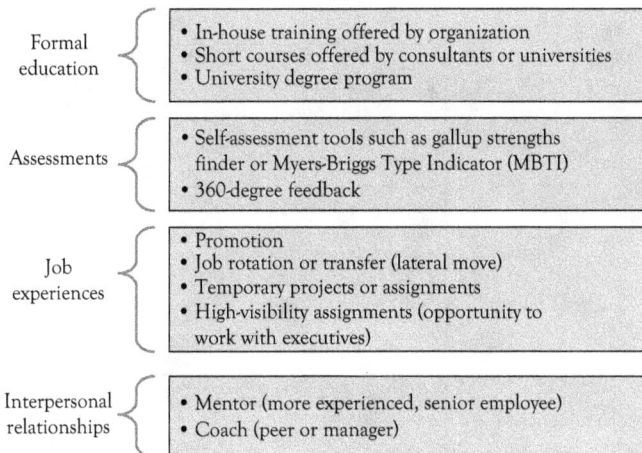

Formal education	• In-house training offered by organization • Short courses offered by consultants or universities • University degree program
Assessments	• Self-assessment tools such as gallup strengths finder or Myers-Briggs Type Indicator (MBTI) • 360-degree feedback
Job experiences	• Promotion • Job rotation or transfer (lateral move) • Temporary projects or assignments • High-visibility assignments (opportunity to work with executives)
Interpersonal relationships	• Mentor (more experienced, senior employee) • Coach (peer or manager)

Figure 14.4 Approaches to employee development

Regarding rewards, an ideal reward program is both internally consistent (i.e., employees perceive that they are rewarded fairly as compared to others within the organization) and externally competitive (i.e., employees perceive that they are rewarded fairly compared to others in similar positions in different organizations). Realize that pay is not the only way to reward employees. "Total rewards" refers to a blend of monetary and non-monetary rewards employees receive in exchange for their time, efforts, and performance, as illustrated in Figure 14.5.[12]

Due to nonprofit organizations' challenge of limited resources, a total rewards approach is necessary. Because employees can generally find higher financial compensation at other employers, they should understand the total rewards package to assess the true value of their employment with the organization. Nonprofit organizations are particularly well-positioned to reinforce the contribution of employees' work to the organization's mission, a significant motivator for many nonprofit employees.

Xavier continues its journey in becoming a high-performing organization. As such, the organization has invested in its people at the same time it is trying to ensure its financial health into the future. Xavier implemented a new market-based compensation system that required campus-wide commitment. Employees submitted updated position descriptions; leadership developed a Total Compensation philosophy statement; HR

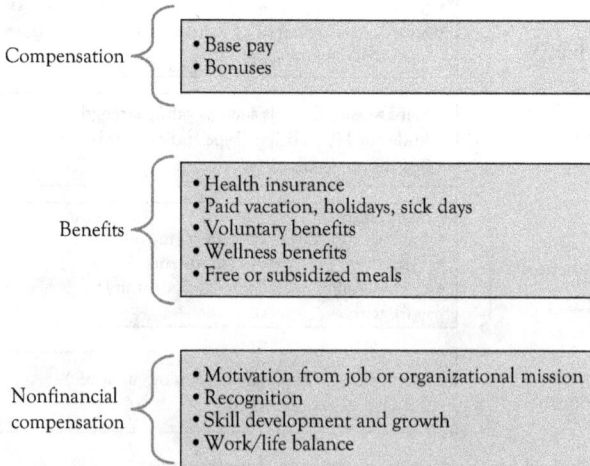

Compensation
- Base pay
- Bonuses

Benefits
- Health insurance
- Paid vacation, holidays, sick days
- Voluntary benefits
- Wellness benefits
- Free or subsidized meals

Nonfinancial compensation
- Motivation from job or organizational mission
- Recognition
- Skill development and growth
- Work/life balance

Figure 14.5 Total rewards

worked with a third-party vendor to gather relevant market data, developed structure using market data points, placed jobs in the new structure, and reviewed all changes with leaders. In cases where an outside firm cannot be used, it is essential to have appropriate peer groups to benchmark salaries with and to use independent third-party surveys for maximum credibility. Within the new structure, employees know their pay grade (and the pay potential within a certain job) as well as know when positions being posted are a lateral move or a promotion. This is designed to ensure a fair pay system that is internally consistent and externally competitive and that supports employee growth and career pathing opportunities. The system provides hard maximums to minimize unnecessary salary creep and encourages continuous development and mobility among its workforce.

Key challenges include low annual salary increases that make it more difficult to motivate performance differentiation on pay alone; many employees also tend to stay in their positions for a long time so, with limited turnover, traditional hierarchical advancement is constrained. Thus, Xavier fosters and communicates a total rewards strategy where compensation is just one important reward component in partnership with benefits, work environment, mission affiliation, and work challenge.

Key steps:

- Be creative with development opportunities; while Xavier offers employees the ability to attend conferences and seminars, cross-functional teams, committee assignments, project assignments, mission-related development, systems training, mentoring, and the opportunity to take classes are available.
- Ensure position descriptions are provided and reviewed annually.
- Nonprofits often do not lead the market in pay, so a total rewards approach is key to offering a variety of reasons for persons to join or stay with your organization. If possible, periodically provide employees with a total compensation statement so that they can see just how much the organization contributes to other benefits.

- Educate managers on tangible and non-tangible rewards and how to communicate the value of each employee and their total compensation package.

Succession

Succession concerns the process of systematically planning for future leadership by identifying and developing employees with the capability to fill key roles. Organizations must first specify the critical positions for which they must have succession plans in place. Although traditionally succession planning has focused on positions at the chief executive level (CEO, CFO, and so forth), efforts should not be limited to this level. Critical positions would include executive leadership positions but should also include broader leadership levels as well as other positions your organization deems significant to its success, whether in development, marketing, or public or government relations. A typical succession process involves preparation, planning, and development, as illustrated in Table 14.5.[13]

Table 14.5 The Succession planning process

Preparation ⟶	Planning ⟶	Development
Goal: Understand the context	**Goal:** Identify positions and talent	**Goal:** Prepare and develop talent
Key Questions:	**Key Steps:**	**Key Processes:**
• How to define key positions? • How to define high potentials? • What is exemplary performance? • How to fill key positions? • Develop or buy for key positions? • How to prepare successors? • HR's and managers' roles and responsibilities? • Level of system transparency?	• Enlist top management support • Identify key positions by function/area • Determine the necessary competencies for roles • Review talent • Develop succession plans by position • Discuss developmental planning	• Determine appropriate development approach • Ensure ongoing support for development (e.g., resources, positive reinforcement)

Organizations with formal succession planning processes in place tend to be more effective than those with informal planning, as they are more proactive in identifying and developing talent, more attuned to diversity issues, and more transparent regarding their process.[14] Although smaller nonprofit organizations may not feel they have sufficient staff or resources to devote to succession planning, leaders should consider doing so as an investment both in their employees and the future of their organization. To maximize chances for success, the process must be tied to the organization's strategic objectives and engage both HR staff and line management/ leadership. Additionally, we recommend informing those individuals identified as high potentials and, therefore, worth additional investment by the organization to help quality talent feel valued, engaged, and motivated to stay with your organization.

This is an area where notable improvement can be made at Xavier. Many exemplary leaders do this naturally, but with competing demands and leadership shortages this has been an area of emerging focus. Xavier is establishing an intentional framework that supports its new strategic planning efforts. This process includes identifying critical talent pipelines to ensure succession planning for critical roles, taking into account strategic workforce planning principles. In addition, the executive team is identifying persons they believe to be upwardly mobile. From these steps, Xavier will focus its limited resources on preparing and developing talent in the roles most critical to the organization, as well as determine whether a "build or buy" strategy (i.e., develop talent internally or recruit externally) for the necessary talent is appropriate.

Key steps:

- Identify and focus on the critical positions that are necessary to deliver upon your strategy.
- Get leadership involved in assessing the talent within the organization, identifying gaps, and developing talent with potential.
- Design opportunities to build competencies or identify the external sources to seek talent upon need.
- Monitor the activities, obtain feedback from leaders and participants, and refine as needed.

There are other necessary HRM activities that we did not cover here, such as employee relations, compliance, benefits administration, and transition of employees out of the organization.

However, we offer several key lessons from Xavier's experience:

- It is in understanding where the organization is headed that HR can be a true business partner and add strategic, value-added services to the organization.
- HR communications need to be intentional and direct on why changes to HR policies, systems, or structures are necessary, answer what is trying to be accomplished, and demonstrate alignment with the university direction.
- HR must continually monitor the metrics, policies, systems, and structures, as they will need to evolve in support of an ever-changing organization.

Volunteer Management

Most nonprofit organizations rely on both volunteer and paid staff. To address the challenge of limited staff and resources, many nonprofit organizations are increasing the number of volunteers who they use and expanding the scope of the work volunteers do. Volunteers can and do contribute to strategic planning as well as daily operations, and thus, are vital to most nonprofit organizations. However, a full discussion of volunteer management is outside the scope of this chapter. We would refer the reader to comprehensive resources on volunteer management.[15] That being said, much of what we have discussed in this chapter is also relevant to volunteer resource management.

For example, organizations sometimes struggle with recruitment and retention of volunteers. During recruitment, potential volunteers, like prospective employees, want to understand the work and your organization. Analyzing the roles volunteers will play in your organization—their tasks and responsibilities, the knowledge, skills, and abilities volunteers need to perform them successfully—can help you effectively and realistically communicate volunteer opportunities. A volunteer selection process will ensure you place volunteers in roles which are a good fit for their interests, abilities, and desired time commitment. Communicating a compelling value proposition to volunteers will be valuable in helping individuals understand why they should want to volunteer with your organization.

Onboarding is critical for volunteers as well. Like employees, they also require clear expectations regarding their roles and relevant policies and laws (clarification and compliance). However, culture and connection may be even more significant for volunteers. Some organizations experience issues with volunteer–staff relations (e.g., staff may feel threatened by volunteers' skills or roles, view the training and management of volunteers as a burden, be fearful of managing volunteers when they have no experience doing so, or wonder if they can depend on volunteers to be professional and reliable). Resources focused on volunteer management will address the topic of volunteer–staff relations in depth.[16] Effective onboarding, though, will facilitate productive working relationships between volunteer and staff and enable volunteers to understand and successfully function within the organization's culture. Ongoing performance feedback can help volunteers to fulfill their role more efficiently and effectively; soliciting volunteers' input during this process can help staff to understand if volunteers need additional tools, resources, or skills to fulfill their roles. Development and reward strategies are perhaps even more relevant for volunteers. Individuals crave growth and challenge in their work; providing opportunities for volunteers to work on a variety of tasks, or develop new skills (which they may also leverage for paid employment opportunities) can enhance motivation and retention. As volunteers are unpaid, emphasizing the nonfinancial compensation component of total rewards is obviously essential. Organizations must ensure volunteers are recognized and shown how their efforts contribute to fulfillment of the organization's mission. Volunteers who feel overwhelmed, unequipped to fulfill their role, bored, unappreciated, or socially segregated within the organization will quickly find another organization with which to volunteer. Thus, effective volunteer management draws on many of the same practices as effective HRM.

Conclusion

As we previously stated, effective HRM creates an environment in which employees can do their best work. The focus is not only on employees' performance, but also on their well-being. Hence, this chapter fits well in this section on *Developing Your Team*. Effective HRM also provides value to the organization by helping the organization achieve its mission, vision, and strategic objectives. Thus, HR can enable the other key processes in the virtuous cycle: *Living the Mission, Making Good Decisions*, and *Getting Things Done*. The next chapters in this section offer additional strategies—for example, employee empowerment, process improvement, a strengths-based management approach, and creating a sense of employee ownership—that can contribute to effective HRM.

Key Assessment Questions

1. How do your fundamental HR activities—selection, onboarding, performance, development and reward, and succession—contribute toward achievement of your organization's mission and strategic objectives?
2. How do your fundamental HR activities respect the dignity of your employees and volunteers as human beings?
3. What measures does your organization use to assess the HR function?
4. Is the HR function positioned as a credible and critical component for achievement of the organization's mission and strategic objectives? Consider where HR is placed within your organizational structure (i.e., reporting relationships) and whether you have the right leader in place.
5. Where in the organization should you facilitate the presence of HR "at the table?" Consider key meetings/events, decision-making committees, and so forth.

Resources for Additional Information

- **Society for Human Resource Management** (SHRM; www.shrm.org). This professional society offers many templates and samples (e.g., interview guides, performance appraisals) and other resources (SHRM Foundation's *Effective Practice Guidelines* series) free online.

- *HR from the heart: Inspiring stories and strategies for building the people side of great business*, by Libby
Sartain, in which the former top HR executive for Southwest Airlines and Yahoo! reveals how HR professionals create synergy between business objectives and employees' needs and wants.
- Any work by **Dave Ulrich**, an HR thought leader. His most recent book (co-authored with Younger, Brockbank, and Ulrich) is *HR from the Outside In: Six competencies for the future of human resources.*
- *Managing to change the world: The nonprofit manager's guide to getting results*, by Alison Green and Jerry Hauser, focuses on the fundamental skills of effective management.
- **HR Leadership Council** (www.hrleadershipcouncil.com) is a member-based advisory company focused on mid-size organizations. Memberships are offered on a subscription basis and include access to best practices, peer benchmarks, information sessions, and advisory support. Xavier has found membership, although not inexpensive, to be worthwhile.

Notes

1. Cascio and Boudreau (2012).
2. Kotter (1996).
3. Lawler and Boudreau (2009); Lawler, Levenson, and Boudreau (2004).
4. Carlson and Kavanagh (2012).
5. Pulakos (2005).
6. Bauer (2010).
7. Bauer (2010).
8. Noe (2013).
9. Pulakos (2004).
10. Noe (2013).
11. Esen and Collison (2005).
12. Heneman (2007).
13. Day (2007).
14. Day (2007).
15. McCurley and Lynch (2010).
16. McCurley and Lynch (2010).

References

Bauer, T. N. (2010). *Onboarding new employees: Maximizing success.* Alexandria, VA: SHRM Foundation.

Carlson, K. D., & Kavanagh, M. J. (2012). HR metrics and workforce analytics. In M. J. Kavanagh, M. Thite, & R. D. Johnson (Eds.), *Human resource information systems: Basics, applications, and future directions* (pp. 150–174). Thousand Oaks, CA: Sage Publications.

Cascio, W. F., & Boudreau, J. W. (2012). *Short introduction to strategic human resource management.* Cambridge: Cambridge University Press.

Day, D. V. (2007). *Developing leadership talent.* Alexandria, VA: SHRM Foundation.

Esen, E., & Collison, J. (2005). *Employee development.* Alexandria, VA: SHRM Research.

Heneman, R. L. (2007). *Implementing total rewards strategies.* Alexandria, VA: SHRM Foundation.

Kotter, J. P. (1996). *Leading change.* Boston, MA: Harvard Business School Press.

Lawler III, E. E., & Boudreau, J. W. (2009). What makes HR a strategic partner? *People & Strategy 32,* 14–22.

Lawler III, E. E., Levenson, A., & Boudreau, J. W. (2004). HR metrics and analytics: Use and impact. *Human Resource Planning 27,* 27–35.

McCurley, S., & Lynch, R. (2010). *Volunteer management: Mobilizing all the resources of the community* (3rd ed.). Plattsburgh, NY: Interpub Group.

Noe, R. A. (2013). *Employee training and development.* New York, NY: McGraw-Hill Irwin.

Pulakos, E. D. (2004). *Performance management.* Alexandria, VA: SHRM Foundation.

Pulakos, E. D. (2005). *Selection assessment methods.* Alexandria, VA: SHRM Foundation.

CHAPTER 15

Total Quality

Integrating Customer, Employee, and Process Voices

Timothy J. Kloppenborg

Timothy J. Kloppenborg is a Professor Emeritus from Xavier University. He has published books on leadership and project management. Tim is a Certified Project Management Professional (PMP®). He has worked with over 150 volunteer organizations, directly and through supervising student projects. He has hands-on and consulting experience in six continents.

Introduction

Organizations that want to consistently deliver excellent quality to their clients and continuously improve can use guidance from the Malcolm Baldrige and ISO frameworks. In this chapter, we cover the tactical responsibilities of listening to and integrating three sets of voices identified in those frameworks. Customers, both external and internal, have needs and desires to be understood and served. Employees are the lifeblood of organizations and need to be developed so that they are engaged and effective. Work is accomplished through processes which can be studied and improved. This chapter introduces all three voices in the context of total quality and describes how to incorporate each into an effective management system.

The strategic leadership components of quality were covered primarily in the Living the Mission section. The data-based decision components were covered in Chapter 7: Making Good Decisions Using Data. Some of the employee development and engagement is covered in the other chapters in this section: Developing Your Team.

Purpose

The purpose of this chapter is to help you

- describe what would be included in a leadership system based upon customers, employees, and processes and why it is so powerful;
- lead capturing of customer voices and using that knowledge in your management systems;
- use employee empowerment, engagement, and teamwork in your management competency;
- describe, measure, understand, control, and improve your work processes;
- describe how this three-voice system can help you achieve your objectives.

Introduction to the Congregation of Saint Joseph

In 2007, after several years of conversation and interaction, seven independent groups of Sisters of Saint Joseph, all tracing their origins back to 1650 France, joined to become the new Congregation of Saint Joseph with a membership of more than 800 sisters over a wide geographic spread in the Midwest.

Two central questions facing the first leadership team were

- how to honor the voices of all the members, associates, and employees as the seven groups merged; and
- how to plan for appropriate downsizing of large motherhouses and properties to best serve their dwindling, aging population.

The Two Dominant Quality Approaches

This chapter shares the essential concepts and techniques of the dominant quality management methods. Then these frameworks are systemically used to improve the methods and culture of your organization. We also describe how several of the more useful additional approaches provide guidance in understanding how customers, employees, and processes interact.

Table 15.1 summarizes the two approaches to achieving quality that dominate globally: Malcolm Baldrige (a national quality award in the United States) and ISO also known as International Organization for Standards (a certification in the European Union) with the demands each place on executives. One concept common to all quality frameworks is that leadership from the top is required to set the tone and create tangible examples for the organization to follow. We cover the three leadership responsibilities of dealing with customers, employees, and processes in this chapter.

Table 15.1. Combined ISO and Baldrige principles and leadership responsibilities[1]

Level	Principles	Leadership responsibilities
Strategic	Strategic Leadership	Establish and communicate vision and values Develop and lead implementation of strategy Provide necessary resources for implementation
Tactical	Customers and Other Stakeholders	First seek to understand all stakeholders Develop relationships with all stakeholders Ensure stakeholder satisfaction
	Employees	Ensure employees are empowered Ensure employees are engaged Ensure employees are developing and working together
	Processes	Describe and measure processes Analyze and understand processes Improve processes
Both Strategic and Tactical	Data-Based Decisions	Gather accurate and reliable customer, employee, and process data Use data to understand interdependencies and integrate them Make decisions based on factual analysis, judgment, and intuition

Customers and Other Stakeholders

Customers are individuals or groups who will use the outputs of a process. They can be internal (within) the producing organization or external to it. External customers are the traditional definition of customers—clients who use your products, services, or both. They are the ultimate judge of the quality of your products and services. Internal customers are your employees, volunteers, and suppliers who play a role in the work processes you employ to make and deliver your products and services. When you see work as a process, internal customers are the people who receive the output of the work tasks that precede them. By focusing on both types of customers, you are developing an organization culture that first understands what customer expectations are and then sets about meeting or exceeding these expectations on a consistent basis.

Stakeholders are often persons or groups that are actively involved in the work of an organization. However, individuals and groups whose interests may be positively or negatively impacted by the organization, or who may exert influence over the organization are also stakeholders. In nonprofits, stakeholders can include clients, donors, and other interested parties. First you seek to understand who your stakeholders are and then work with them to achieve the best possible outcome that considers their interests.

Customers and other stakeholders today sometimes seem more powerful than ever since they can learn about us and freely share their opinions through the Internet and social media. If we displease a customer, they can let the entire world know about it quickly and in an emotional manner. It has always been important to listen to our customers, but in some ways it is more critical now.

Understanding Customers and Other Stakeholders

The voice of the customer is the stated and unstated customer needs or requirements.[2] One primary reason we listen to customers and other stakeholders is to obtain actionable information. This information can be used to satisfy their wants and needs, but it can also be to help identify and select potential projects to improve our organizations. While it is widely understood that customer input is important, all too often customer research tells us one thing, but then the customers behave in a different manner. The key is to obtain customer information that accurately predicts their future behavior.

One way to gain customer information is during normal interactions with them. When you provide products and services, make sure you obtain customer feedback as quickly as possible. This can be informal. When seeking customer input more formally through surveys, consider asking questions related to the following five areas:

1. Overall relationship (your importance to them, their satisfaction, and loyalty to you)
2. Touch points (where your employees and processes impact customers)
3. Drivers (where you're doing well or poorly that has a large impact on them)
4. Ad hoc (changing customer preferences and current strategic needs)
5. Latent requirements (things you can offer that the customer never considered).[3]

Developing Relationships With All Stakeholders

Relationships with customers can range from superficial to quite intense. The depth and quality of customer relationships can be expressed at four levels:

1. Confidence—trust in the organization and knowing they will always deliver on their promise
2. Integrity—fair treatment and fair problem resolution
3. Pride—proud to be a customer and feeling of respect
4. Passion—the nonprofit is perfect and the world would be less without it[4]

As you begin to develop a relationship with a customer, you need to start at the first level—demonstrating to that customer that they can have confidence in you. As you satisfy one level in the relationship, you can move to higher levels. There is no substitute for attention and hard work when it comes to developing excellent relationships with customers.

Careful supplier selection makes life easier in many ways. A supplier that can already produce consistently what we need will help us immediately. A supplier that is willing to invest in improvements and learn with us will help us to continually improve. Great suppliers offer improvement suggestions we can use.

Ensuring Stakeholder Satisfaction

Most successful organizations have many stakeholders and a challenge is to treat them all well. At the organizational level, one needs to develop a sense of balance by not treating one group especially well at the expense of another group. It may be tempting to treat paying customers very well, but this causes difficulties for other groups in the process. While this may yield short-term results, it is often counterproductive toward building sustainable capacity. At the project level, sponsors often determine which stakeholders are relatively more important. That still does not give an excuse to completely ignore less important stakeholders.

When we treat our stakeholders (customers, employees, suppliers, and community) well, many of them develop a sense of ownership in our organization. That does not mean they receive monetary profits, but it means they have a desire for us to succeed and they feel they benefit when we succeed.

Acting Upon Customer Voices and Relationships

Once we have heard the customer's voice, we need to describe it in a requirements statement. That is, considering the customer's environment, what is the functional or performance requirement to fulfill the stated need? The customer's requirement will often dictate both enhancements needed in the competencies of our employees and in the capabilities of our processes. Thus, customers, employees, and processes are intertwined and the gaps identified by studying them identify needed improvements. In the remainder of this chapter, we discuss employee and process voices.

Employees

When understanding and acting appropriately upon the voice of employees, leaders use empowerment, engagement, and teamwork. In nonprofit organizations, volunteers are often as critical as employees and everything stated in this section applies equally to volunteers.

Employee Empowerment

Employee empowerment is trusting in, investing in, and inspiring employees; recognizing their accomplishments; and decentralizing decision making.[5] To truly empower an employee, she needs to be given enough information, training, and confidence to progressively make more important decisions. As an employee develops the judgment and confidence to make more decisions, the supervisor is free to spend more time on higher level issues. Thus both the employee and the supervisor benefit.

Employee Engagement

Employee engagement occurs when workers are emotionally and psychologically committed to the organization; feel a strong sense of ownership in the organization's success; and want to contribute to its improved performance.[6] Great organizations recognize that their employees are an exceptional asset. The employees are encouraged to provide ideas on how their work should be improved and are given the freedom and resources (within reason) to recommend and act on ideas that can help meet or exceed customer expectations.

Another aspect of employee engagement is the investment the organization makes in communicating with and training their people so that they have the skills and knowledge they need to solve customer problems effectively. Just as customer relationships can be measured and developed at four levels, so can employee engagement by having each employee progressively answer these sets of questions:

1. Do I know what is expected of me and do I have the equipment I need?
2. Do I get to do what I do best, do I get recognized, and does someone care about me and help me develop?
3. Does my opinion count, do I feel aligned with the mission of my nonprofit, do my co-workers want to improve, and do I have a best friend at work?
4. Is someone measuring my progress and giving me opportunities to grow?[7]

Employee Development and Teamwork

There are many aspects to employee development. One of the most important is teamwork. Teamwork occurs in a work group that possesses a clear mission, effective leadership, shared values and behavior norms, trust, openness, and commitment.[8] Teamwork means that cross-functional teams are common places to solve far-reaching organizational problems and work on new ideas from multiple functional perspectives. Teamwork also extends beyond the four walls of your own organization to include your key suppliers, customers, as well as other stakeholder organizations such as neighborhood groups and educational institutions. Working with an end-to-end perspective with many parties actively involved provides better and more holistic solutions to challenging opportunities.

Process

A process is usually thought of as a series of activities executed and decisions made to perform specific tasks, such as paying a bill, shipping a product, and even more complex processes like that of developing a new product or service.

Describe and Measure Processes

When studying a process, in addition to the activities performed and decisions made, people often also consider the inputs that are needed and who supplies each at the front end and the outputs created and who the customers of each are at the back end as shown in Figure 15.1. By

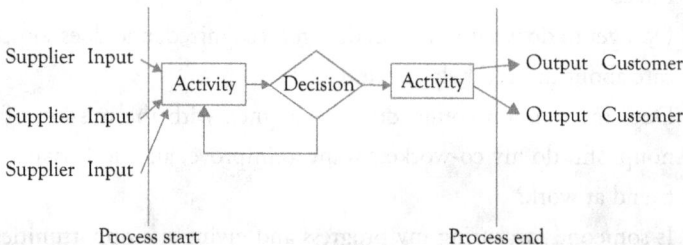

Figure 15.1 Process illustration

seeing work as a process, one is able to analyze how things are done now and, through objective data, identify where improvements are needed. Another reason seeing work as a process is so effective is that many work processes today cross multiple parts of the organization and are cross-functional. By analyzing cross-functional work processes (vs. analyzing by function), you are examining your organization much more holistically and developing insights at a deeper level.

Analyze and Understand Processes

The voice of the process is the data describing actual performance that can be used to predict the future average and natural process limits that define the range of outputs that can be expected from a process.[9] We gather data concerning the inputs, activities, and outputs of our processes so that we can understand, control, and improve them. If we continue to perform our processes in the current manner, we can expect the same range of results. Thus, the range of current results predicts the expected range of future results, unless we make changes. This current process result along with our knowledge of how the process currently operates is the voice of the process. Controlling a process means monitoring it to ensure we continue to receive the predicted range of outputs that it is normally capable of producing. If that normal range fully satisfies all of our customers, we might be content with how that particular process is performing. However, in most nonprofit organizations, some processes are in need of improvement at any point in time.

Improve Processes

Process improvement includes both incremental and large, breakthrough changes to a process to enhance customer value, reduce problems, increase productivity, and improve responsiveness,.[10] Process improvement is sometimes called continuous improvement. The term continuous improvement can be challenging because it implies you are never done! You must find ways to improve your work processes to meet your customer's evolving needs. The changes you make can be small, incremental, and gradual changes or changes can be breakthrough, large, and rapid changes that result in significant improvements. Most organizations have both small and large changes most of the time. Deciding which processes need change the most is a prioritization decision covered in Chapter 8.

One common approach advocated today is **Six Sigma**. Six Sigma has two meanings. The literal meaning is you want your quality to be so good, that the variation in your process results from the average to the customer's tolerance limit is six standard deviations. For example, if you were supplying rehabilitation service to clients, you would have no more than a handful of service encounters out of every million that were not good enough! Even many people who are strong advocates of Six Sigma will tell you candidly that achieving true Six Sigma results on all of their processes all of the time is an aspirational goal—not easily achieved. The second meaning of Six Sigma is a dedication to continuous improvement in an effort to improve process performance in the direction of Six Sigma or near perfection.

Six Sigma has multiple themes just as ISO and Baldrige do. In practice, the larger focus is often on process improvement—and especially on reducing cost and time in work processes. Six Sigma major themes can be envisioned as follows:

- Fact-driven management with top-down metrics and rigorous statistical analysis.
- Process understanding, control, and improvement particularly to save time and money.
- Goal setting to objectively select improvement projects and set stretch goals.
- Defined project sponsors and experts and collaboration during each project.
- Use of the define, measure, analyze, improve, and control (DMAIC) process to guide the projects.

How do you go about analyzing your work processes to make changes? One of the most common models to guide improvement is the DMAIC model (see Figure 15.2).

The DMAIC model is based on the scientific process. That is, it starts with a hypothesis—an educated guess during the define and measure

Define
Understand voice of
the customer
Describe the process at an
overview level
Charter the improvement
project

Control
Create procedures
and documentation
Train workers and
monitor performance
Share learnings

Measure
Describe the process in detail
Define needed
data and the collection plan
Baseline current
performance

Improve
Develop possible
solution for root cause
Select and pilot
solution
Analyze
and confirm results

Analyze
Identify possible root causes
Collect data
Confirm root causes
through data analysis

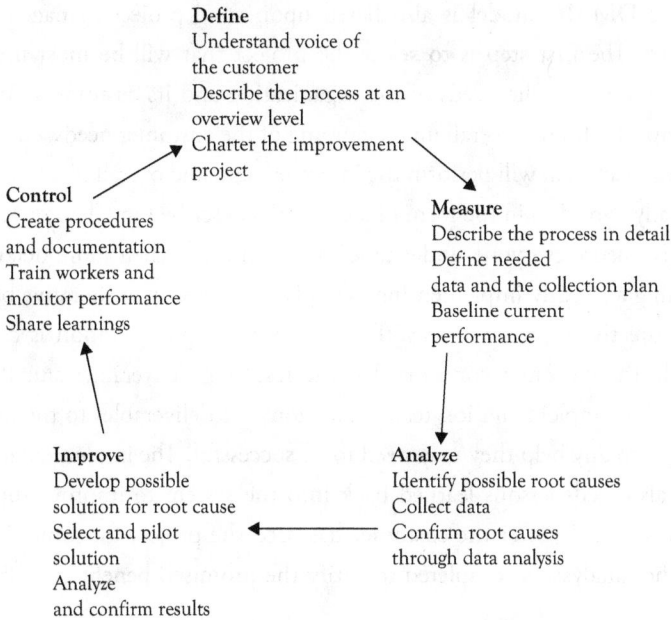

Figure 15.2 Define, measure, analyze, improve, and control
(DMAIC) model

steps. That implies both knowledge of how the current process works and supporting data. Next in the scientific process is to try an experiment while collecting data. Analyze, improve, and control are the remaining DMAIC steps that correspond to the remainder of the scientific process. When you analyze the current situation, you describe what is going on in the process(es) as well as the end results of the process(es). These two types of measures are called in-process measures and outcome measures. In-process measures help you see the process activity such as how many transactions are flowing, how long in time it takes for each step in the process, and so forth. Outcome measures quantify the final results such as the total costs of this transaction, and final quality measures relevant to this process.

The results of the experiment are compared with the previous results to determine any impact. Finally, if the results look promising, the experiment is often conducted multiple times under varying circumstances before confirming a theory. Likewise, with improvement models, an experiment is often repeated and expanded prior to instituting an organization-wide implementation with full controls.

The DMAIC model is also based upon solid project management practice. The first step is to select the project that will be most useful based upon both the needs of the organization and its customers. Then develop a high-level overall understanding of the customer needs, current process, team that will perform the improvement, and overall plan. This is normally agreed to in the form of a charter as described in Chapter 12 to quickly ensure everyone understands and commits. Then more detailed planning and early implementing take place—often on an iterative basis to ensure the approach works. The remaining implementation is completed. The customer confirms that the resulting deliverables suit their needs. The implementation team transitions the deliverables to the users along with any help they may need to be successful. The implementation team also feeds lessons learned back into the system to improve future projects. Finally, after the customer has used the project for some time, a further analysis is completed to verify the promised benefits are being delivered.

A process improvement team is usually chartered and empowered by management of the organization. The charter may specify which process they want improved and why. The charter should specify your problem boundaries, and any constraints you have as you go after this problem. If you have not been "given" a problem/process to solve, then you will need to select what problem to go after. A simple but effective way to do this is to get input on key processes that people in your organization and your customers believe could be and need to be improved and then evaluate these problems using criteria such as the following:

- How important is this process to your customers? (1–10 scale)
- Do you believe you have the skills and resources to improve this process? (1–10 scale)
- How difficult will it be to improve this process? (1–10 scale)

Combining Customers, Employees, and Processes

A key aspect of making your organization's strategy come to life is the selecting and implementing of strategic projects that will deliver the best short- and long-term business results. Customer satisfaction, employee development, and process improvement needs can be used in selecting the best work portfolio. Once you select a project to implement, you need to execute it with excellence by using proven project management principles to achieve an on time and on budget execution that delivers the promised business benefits.

Portfolio management is used to link your organization's strategy to specific projects. The best portfolio decisions are made based upon key quantitative measures that are meaningful to your key customers.

Individual projects are better when using a customer-focused approach to ensure desired results are delivered. Many projects are undertaken to significantly improve existing work processes. Projects are guided by objective in-process and outcome measures.

Improving your organization's culture and operating methods takes a concerted effort. This use of these principles to lead the organization needs to be driven both top-down and bottom-up. Top-down implementation needs to come from making clear strategic choices and communicating them by explaining why these strategies were chosen. Leadership can demonstrate their commitment to quality by setting measurable goals for each strategy and holding quarterly reviews to assess progress. Those in leadership roles can examine their own work processes. Chartering process improvement teams will also empower people to apply these quality principles where they live and work each day.

Bottom-up change can be seen when people at each level in the organization focus on the customer of their work and make changes to delight those customers. Making decisions based on well-defined and objective data is another way people can live by these quality principles. Employees can form process improvement teams that focus on the most important and impactful work processes. This will make significant and lasting change and provide momentum to the widespread and successful use of these quality approaches.

An executive can do several things to build the project culture. She can insist that all managers stay close to their customers. She can ensure all projects have signed charters to ensure they are initiated well. She can insist on adequate documentation so that decisions are made based upon facts. She can develop a management community of practice within the nonprofit to promote continual improvement of processes. She can join an external community of practice for executives. She can work with executives and managers throughout the organization to ensure they understand what a good project culture looks like.

How the Congregation of Saint Joseph Integrates Customer, Employee, and Process Voices

The following illustrates how the leadership of the Congregation of Saint Joseph listened to many voices and included them in their decision making. At the first major gathering (Chapter) in 2007, over 400 sister delegates elected a Congregation Leadership Team (CLT) of seven from the whole (not one from each original group), replacing 29 leaders from the historic groups. They worked to develop relationships among the members ("customers"), and created minimal structures. The structures now in place are circular as shown in Figure 15.3.

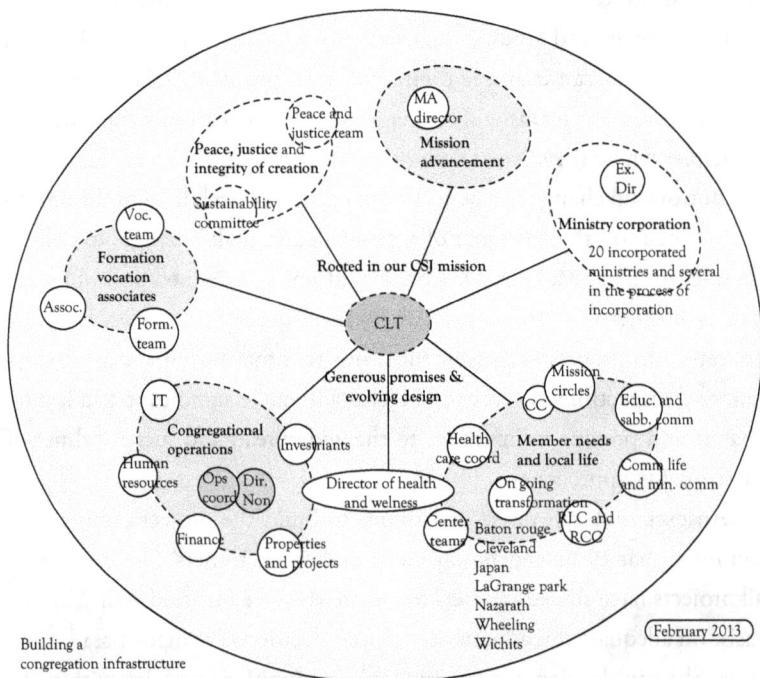

Figure 15.3 Congregation of Saint Joseph leadership circles

At the chapter, the delegates wrote and accepted a set of "Generous Promises," or goals, for the coming years. They committed to be faithful to their own internal growth as individuals and as a group, to deepen their mission of unity. They articulated four areas to pursue, in whatever ministry they engaged: collaboration in changing oppressive systems, networking to shift the global culture to inclusivity and mutuality, claiming oneness with Earth in ways that heal and renew Earth, and recognizing that all are leaders.

They know that they are creating a different way of being Catholic sisters, relying on their evolving consciousness. They focus on relationships, inclusion, and mutuality rather than on efficiency, using interfacing circles for communication of both factual information and continually probing the meaning of them being together. Reflecting together on their experience in light of their mission leads us to the next step together. They believe that the vision and mission of the congregation are the primary leaders; those elected to leadership choreograph and coordinate movement within the vision and mission; every member is committed to the vision, and is thus a leader wherever she is. They have developed a sense of themselves as a learning community, and a discerning community, as partners who share the values of empowerment, engagement, and teamwork.

They have seven former motherhouses, where sisters who need care reside, and where administrative functions are carried out. They have approximately 350 employees and 500 associates (individuals who commit to living their mission and vision in their daily lives—a more formally committed type of long-term volunteer), who are also stakeholders who embody the mission. The sisters, employees, and associates all contribute in meaningful ways to discussions and are privy to both internal and external communications. Employees and associates also serve in leadership roles.

In their various ministries, thousands of clients are served through the generous efforts of volunteers and donors. The clients, volunteers, and donors receive external communications and have their opinions solicited in multiple ways. The leaders know understanding all of these stakeholders more completely will continue to be a challenge.

Because this congregation began with everyone as equals, they are consciously building a culture together that differs from the internal culture of any of the founding groups. Listening to the voices of members, employees, and associates has been complemented by listening to the voice of the process. The mechanisms for listening to one another have enabled them to develop appropriate structures as they were needed. Relationships are key: they are more consistent, more lasting, and more effective for the discernment style of decision making the sisters have chosen to live. An unusual characteristic of this organization is that they are committed to a lifestyle rather than to a work, although the two are not mutually exclusive.

The leadership team members did not move to a central location. They meet face to face one week out of every month, traveling to every center at least once a year, learning faces, names and histories—building relationships. They have built a capacity for electronic communication to ensure the ability to offer and receive information and insight as needed. They communicate monthly through an e-mailed newsletter, highlighting the current foci of attention. Each is liaison with several community committees. When an urgent situation arises, they either travel in pairs, or set up videoconferences with all centers to apprise all members (and, when appropriate, employees and associates) of the situation and their vision for addressing it, as well as receiving the insights of these stakeholders.

They periodically gather various groups of employees with similar positions to deepen their understanding of the mission, to introduce them as support systems to one another, and to encourage their sharing of ideas for greater efficiencies as they live the Generous Promises together. One center has been resourceful in finding biodegradable disposable cups and plates; another is advertising positions in publications read by minorities; another is involved in improving the lives of the very poor.

Gradually, they are leaving the sense of "my founding community" and "my Center" behind and grasping that all are one: what they have belongs to all; they are all responsible together for their future. The question of transitioning some or all of the former motherhouses is being addressed in this light. Sisters have discussed core values for the use of the properties that will carry on their legacy. The hope is that all properties will be used in a manner that is comprehensive, realistic, implementable, and sustainable. They have begun discussions and surveys about where members will live as they decrease in number. The sisters have engaged dozens of "thought leaders" in conversation concerning that the needs of the most vulnerable in each location could most readily be addressed in the former motherhouses. And the leaders know that, no matter how thoughtfully, prayerfully, carefully they plan and prepare, turning over of buildings that have been home to some for generations will be accompanied by the pain of loss. Future steps in total quality management will include finding ways to honor grief without being consumed by it.

Some Key Learnings

1. Relationships are everything! Trusting, open, honest, transparent relationships of partners in mission build cohesiveness in the group.
2. Communications are key. Confidentiality can be maintained while being transparent about the processes and procedures of the organization.
3. How the congregation organizes and uses their resources is an expression of values and mission. True collaboration with all stakeholders creates a strong infrastructure that enhances and supports the work of all those involved.
4. Expressed appreciation for jobs well done contributes to the forward movement of the organization.

Summary

The Malcolm Baldrige and ISO frameworks provide much advice for executives leading their organizations. This chapter focuses on the tactical portions of listening to and acting appropriately upon voices of customers, employees, and processes. Combining that knowledge with strategic leadership and data-based decision making is needed to consistently deliver excellent service to clients and continuously improve to better meet tomorrow's challenges. The next chapter expands upon engaging your employees by describing how to use a strengths-based approach.

Key Assessment Questions

1. Describe the core quality principles exhibited in your organization.
2. What does your organization specifically do to understand the expectations of your external and internal customers?

3. How do you engage your employees, volunteers, and suppliers to work collaboratively to meet the expectations of your external and internal customers?

4. Describe how people in your organization work individually to improve their specific work and collaboratively to improve cross-functional work.

5. How do improvement goals get set and progress toward them get reported?

Notes

1. Baldrige Performance Excellence Program (2011); International Organization for Standards (2011).
2. Crow (2011).
3. Evenson (2011).
4. Fleming and Asplund (2007).
5. Manning and Curtis (2012).
6. Fleming and Asplund (2007).
7. Fleming and Asplund (2007).
8. Manning and Curtis (2012).
9. Wheeler (2000).
10. Evans and Lindsay (2011).

References

Baldrige Performance Excellence Program. (2011). *2011–2012 criteria for performance excellence.* Gaithersburg, MD: National Institute of Standards and Technology.

Collier, D. A., & Evans, J. R. (2012). *OM³.* Mason, OH:South-Western Cengage Learning.

Crawford, J. K. (2004). *Project management roles and responsibilities.* Noida, IN: Center for Business Practices.

Crow, K. (2011). *Voice of the customer.* Retrieved October 25, 2011, from http://www.npd-solutions.com/voc.html

Daft, R. L. (2010). *Management* (9th ed.). Mason, OH: Southwestern Cengage Learning.

Evans, J. R., & Lindsay, W. M. (2011). *Managing for quality and performance excellence* (8th ed.). Independence, KY: South-Western Cengage learning.

Evanson, R. (2011, July 25). *How to design an effective Voice of the Customer (VoC) insights program.* Forester Research, Inc.

Fleming, J. H., & Asplund, J. (2007). *Human sigma: Managing the employee-customer encounter.* New York, NY: Gallup Press.

http://blog.vovici.com/blog/bid/75840/Welcome-to-the-Listening-Post

International Organization for Standards. (2011). *ISO 9000 quality management.* Retrieved October 26, 2011, from http://www.iso.org/iso/iso_9000_essentials

Kloppenborg, T. J., & Laning L. J. (2012). *Strategic leadership of portfolio and project management.* New York, NY: Business Expert Press.

Manning, G., & Curtis, K. (2012). *The art of leadership* (4th ed.). New York, NY: McGraw-Hill Irwin.

Wheeler, D. J. (2000). *Understanding variation: The key to managing chaos* (2nd ed.). SPC Press.

CHAPTER 16

A Strengths-Based Approach for Managing Your People

Leisa Anslinger and Stephanie Moore

Leisa holds a Bachelor's degree from Saint Mary-of-the-Woods and master's degrees from Purdue University and the Athenaeum of Ohio. She is an author, speaker, and consultant who specializes in Catholic parish leadership. She is a founding member of the Catholic Strengths and Engagement Community.

Stephanie brings her passion and years of leadership, facilitation, and speaking experience to helping leaders build vibrant and engaged organizations and communities. Over the past 20 years, she has held various senior leadership positions and is currently a master trainer, facilitator, and executive coach in the areas of engagement, team development, and leadership development. She is a founding member of the Catholic Strengths and Engagement Community.

Introduction

In the previous chapters, you have learned that one of the keys to an organization's success is how well that organization empowers, engages, and develops their employees. As we have learned in the previous chapter on Total Quality Management, empirical data demonstrates that when an organization focuses on their employees' talents and strengths, overall engagement increases and productivity is enhanced.

In this chapter, we will look at one of the factors that contribute significantly to employee engagement. The primary driver of engagement is the ability to give people the opportunity to do what they do best.[1] Identifying, developing, and leveraging your employees' talents and strengths are the key to retaining your most precious resource, your people, resulting in huge returns for your nonprofit organization.

Purpose

In this chapter, we will

- describe the importance of a "strengths-based" approach for management and leadership with staff, key volunteers, and board members, grounded in years of research and empirical data;
- identify the relationship between strengths-based leadership and organizational engagement;[2]
- describe how to utilize the Clifton StrengthsFinder© assessment as a primary tool to assess an individual's top talent themes, using this as a foundation of strengths-based teams and individual development plans;
- illustrate the impact of leveraging team strengths in workforce planning, collaboration, and partnering;
- describe the first steps in making the shift to a strengths-and-engagement organizational approach.

Introduction to the Catholic Strengths and Engagement Community

The Catholic Strengths and Engagement Community (CSEC)[3] was founded as a grassroots organization to support faith leaders as they build engagement and foster strengths development within their faith communities. The first initiative of CSEC was to offer an online "connected community." The CSEC connected community provides leaders with a platform for networking, sharing, and discussions. Everything that is shared is stored in libraries that are searchable by topic and content. The response to the connected community was surprisingly robust, with over 200 members joining in the first quarter the community was offered, providing strong evidence of the need for this and future initiatives through CSEC.

The leadership team that came together to form CSEC faced challenges that are common to many nonprofit organizations:

- How would we capitalize on the people resources of members to fulfill the mission of CSEC?
- How will we draw upon the talents of our leadership team to make this possible?

From the beginning, CSEC was founded with the principles of strengths-based leadership in mind. In sharing our story with you, we will demonstrate the difference this approach can make for any company, particularly your nonprofit organization.

Overview of *Strengths-Based Leadership*

Being an effective leader requires not only knowing your own strengths as a leader but also knowing and investing in the strengths of the people you lead—whether they are paid staff or key volunteers. Research conducted by the Gallup organization and captured in the bestselling book *Strengths Based Leadership*[4] highlights the science that shows that engagement and strengths are far more powerful when managed and supported in tandem. Building on the Gallup research of interviews with over 20,000 senior leaders, Rath and Conchie went on to interview over 10,000 "followers." In their interviews they asked these individuals "why they followed the most influential leader in their life" and three key findings emerged:

- The most effective leaders are always investing in strengths.
- The most effective leaders surround themselves with the right people and then maximize their team.
- The most effective leaders understand their followers' needs.

But why would a company invest in a "strengths-based" approach versus the traditional "weakness-based" approach? Many organizations implicitly

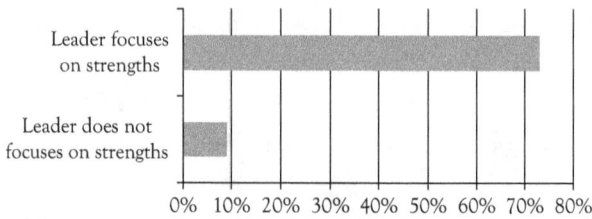

Figure 16.1 Chances of employees being engaged at work

or explicitly adhere to a style of management that says "let's figure out what you are NOT doing well and focus on that for improvement." The bottom line in Gallup's research is that when companies focus on building on an employee's strengths it has a direct tie to overall engagement, leading to productivity and contribution to the mission of the organization. Figure 16.1 shows that leaders who focus on strengths as opposed to weakness have 73% chance of having employees who are engaged at work versus the manager who does not focus on strengths has only a 9% chance of employees being engaged at work.[5]

The Items of Engagement and the Connection to Strengths

"In the 1990s, Gallup concluded a decade-long study on employee engagement." One of the key findings of the study is that employees need 12 essential elements to thrive in their workplaces. These elements— measured by Q12, Gallup's 12-item assessment of engagement—reflect a sense of "belonging, growth, and contribution" among staff or key volunteers. Staff members' responses to these items "are deeply emotional. If workers' emotional needs are met, they become engaged with their companies, and their productivity, profitability, retention rate and safety rate increases."[6]

Having led dozens of introductions to engagement among faith community leaders, we know how challenging it may be at first to internalize and integrate a strengths-and-engagement approach to organizational leadership. Leaders often manage through their own perspective, focusing on tasks that must be accomplished and the bottom line of mission and financial solvency. Often, those who are in leadership in organizations manage the way they have experienced the management of others, for better or for worse. Quite frankly, some leaders approach employee management from the perspective that "It's their job, and they ought to do it," regardless of whether staff experience satisfaction in the process or not.

Gallup's research helps us understand why engagement is important, and how deeply connected strengths development is in establishing this important organizational environment. Employees and key volunteers need to have a sense that their contributions matter, and that the organization provides the materials and affirmation needed in order for them to not only get by, but thrive. Establishing such a quality environment ensures the effectiveness of the staff and volunteers, and therefore the organization.

Embracing employee engagement as a means to the organization's thriving can initially leave one feeling unsettled. One of our CSEC founders, a Catholic priest and pastor, recalls the day he was first introduced to engagement, "I had such a headache! I kept trying to fit what I was being told into my old way of doing things, and the presenter kept forcing us to think about things differently!"

Yet the research on engagement is striking. The way employees and key volunteers *experience* the organization dramatically impacts the extent to which the organization will *thrive*. And remember, the studies are clear: one of the primary ways to build engagement is to develop the strengths of your people. That is where StrengthsFinder© comes in.

Strengths Finder 2.0 + Four Domains of Leadership

StrengthsFinder 2.0[7] is an online talent assessment created by Gallup in over 50 years of study of people and organizations. A talent, the research describes, is "a natural way of thinking, feeling, or behaving that can be productively applied."[8] "We are at our best when we do what we do best,"[9] the research demonstrates. Why would we not organize our people in ways that provide opportunities for them to use their greatest talents, combining them with skills, knowledge, and the investment of time which produce strengths?

Work with StrengthsFinder 2.0 is useful in determining how all team members can maximize their contribution to the group's collective goals.

The research upon which StrengthsFinder 2.0 is based has identified 34 themes of talent that people possess to one degree or another. Upon completion of the StrengthsFinder© assessment, participants receive a list of their Top 5, or Signature themes of talent. These themes represent the person's primary areas of talent, and provide insight into the ways those talents are experienced, developed, and can be used to contribute with success.

Strengths-based leadership builds on the talents of team members in staff interactions, task assignments, roles and responsibilities, and in the general spirit of collaboration and cooperation. Team members learn how to leverage their talents to approach situations, and they form stronger team relationships by forming complementary partnerships. They become better able to balance strong talents through careful self-management, and they learn to appreciate the talent and potential of others.

Gallup found through additional research that these 34 themes of talent could naturally be categorized into four domains of leadership strength. Their studies demonstrate that the most effective teams are ones in which a variety of talents are represented, and in which team members have the opportunity to use their talents regularly:[10]

> *Executing*—These themes "make things happen." Individuals with these themes will work tirelessly to get it done.
>
> *Influencing*—These themes help to reach a broader audience. They sell ideas inside and outside of the organization.
>
> *Relationship Building*—These themes are the "glue that holds a team together."
>
> *Strategic*—These themes focus on what "could be." Individuals with these themes analyze and synthesize information to inform the team and make better decisions.[11]

Over time, as teams learn to leverage the strengths of their members, their productivity, creativity, and growth increase exponentially. Their appreciation for their own talents and those of their teammates creates an environment in which every person has something to contribute, providing an effective means for time management, personnel allocation, and project development and management.

Using Strengths to Manage at the CSEC

As highlighted earlier, our nonprofit organization, the CSEC was founded by a number of individuals who were already "strengths" practitioners. One of our founders, Fr. Bill Hanson, after attending the first Gallup summit on Engagement and Strengths for church leaders, was the first Catholic pastor to implement this strategy in his faith community, St. Gerard Magella Parish in Port Jefferson Station, NY. Over the course of the next 6 years, his parish went from being severely in the red and stagnant to being in the black, growing, and thriving. The St. Gerard's experience provides a success story that highlights the validity of focusing on engagement and strengths for other church leaders. St. Gerard's story is captured as a key case study in Gallup's faith-based book *Growing an Engaged Church*. Along with Fr. Bill Hanson, there were a number of early adopters forging ahead to implement these strategies in their parish communities. Namely, Leisa Anslinger at Immaculate Heart of Mary in Cincinnati, Ohio; Don Garbison of St. Matthews in Charlotte, NC; and Stephanie Moore, with St. Anne Parish in Byron, CA. All four of us worked independently in our various regions, not only implementing them in our own parishes but also being asked to consult and mentor many surrounding parishes. While still in the early stages of application of these concepts in our own parishes, we were invited to speak nationally and regionally on the subject at Stewardship and Leadership Conferences.

As the four of us shared our experiences and learned from one another, it became apparent that there were many parishes, dioceses, universities, and campus ministries who were just getting started in their own implementations from across the country and beyond. They needed support and the opportunity to learn from and share with one another. Establishing engagement and developing strengths is a dynamic process that requires a common vision and understanding of the process. Our team had experience that would enhance the shift to engagement- and strengths-based leadership for others, as did those whose experience was developing at that time.

Early in the process, Leisa, Fr. Bill, Don, and Stephanie met to discuss the possibility of forming a "connected community" for networking and sharing, and in addition had just stumbled upon some leading edge software that could give us the platform to implement this international network for faith community leaders. In late 2010, we launched the "Catholic Strengths and Engagement" Connected Community. As mentioned earlier, the site took off quickly and continues to grow.

From the beginning, our founding team decided to model the principles of an engaged community focused on the strengths and talents of our team and our members. One of the first things we did was to make sure we had our "talent chart" always present at our meetings. We established ground rules that would allow us to say no to those tasks and activities that did not align well with our talents, and we discussed the ways each of us would tap into talents as roles and responsibilities emerged. For our membership, it was important to give people the opportunity to share their Top 5 in their profiles, which was accomplished through a special feature of the online platform. We created search engines so that if you wanted to connect with people who had similar talents, you could immediately do so.

Over the past few years, we have leveraged the talents and strengths of the team in order to create our strategic plans, our key objectives, and our committees to implement these objectives. Our goal is that committees will use a strengths-based approach in the recruitment, planning, and operation of the committee. The bottom line is that every member be given the opportunity to do what he or she does best. This does not mean that there will not be moments in which we must do things that we do not initially feel talented to do. Rather, consistent with the strengths approach, we leverage the talents we do have in order to accomplish what needs to be done.

As an example, when we formed our first board of directors, we created the following grid that would not only highlight our Top 5 talent themes but also our dominant areas of leadership. As you can see in Table 16.1, the team has a nice representation of all four leadership domains.[12] The talents and domains of team members are assessed as roles and responsibilities are assigned.

One experience will illustrate how the strengths-based approach works in the management of projects. Prior to the development of our first formal board of directors, our founding team invited a dozen people to join us in an advisory capacity. The Advisory Council met via web-based

Table 16.1 CSEC Founders and board of directors' top five signature themes with domains of leadership

Name	Theme 1	Theme 2	Theme 3	Theme 4	Theme 5
Leisa	Ideation (strategic)	Input (strategic)	Futuristic (strategic)	Connectedness (relationship)	Arranger (executing)
Stephanie	Maximizer (influencing)	Relator (relationship)	Individualization (relationship)	Adaptability (relationship)	Connectedness (relationship)
Don	Arranger (executing)	Maximizer (influencing)	Individualization (relationship)	Responsibility (executing)	Learner (strategic)
Rick	Self-Assurance (influencing)	Activator (influencing)	Focus (executing)	Achiever (executing)	Significance (influencing)
Fr. Bill	Connectedness (relationship)	Ideation (strategic)	Learner (strategic)	Self-Assurance (influencing)	Responsibility (executing)
Kirsten	Input (strategic)	Woo (influencing)	Adaptability (relationship)	Connectedness (relationship)	Maximizer (influencing)
Scott	Input (strategic)	Learner (strategic)	Analytical (strategic)	Discipline (executing)	Consistency (executing)
Shelley	Arranger (executing)	Connectedness (relationship)	Positivity (relationship)	Maximizer (influencing)	Futuristic (strategic)

conferencing once per month to share experiences, ideas, and practices, allowing us to learn from the Council and to consider new initiatives for CSEC. We began hearing common themes and tracked emerging best practices that deserved sharing with the wider membership. The group decided to offer a few webinars to expose our members to these emerging practices and share with them continuing thought development.

"CSEC Live" is the webinar series that resulted. By using our talents, the process of developing, communicating, and hosting this webinar series was remarkably effective, so much so that membership doubled in the first year that CSEC Live was offered. Drawing on the strengths of our team, one member strategically mapped out potential offerings; another high in relationship-building themes contacted potential speakers and met with them prior to their session; a third member took on additional operational details to free up the two who were coordinating the early webinars, and that pattern has continued into the present. In fact, a new coordinating team for CSEC Live is in development at the writing of this chapter. The new team will learn from prior experience to leverage the talents of the new team members, ensuring that CSEC Live continues to thrive!

One other significant outcome we have observed and experienced over the years during the numerous workshop and presentations we've conducted on the subject of strengths and the impact on team productivity is the exponential affect that it can have on meeting organizational objectives. As an exercise in our workshops, we take groups of individuals (typically 5–7 individuals sitting at a table) and as many as 6–10 groups and assign a hypothetical project for them to complete in an designated amount of time (typically 15–20 minutes). The instructions are that they will be assigned a project and can only use the talents of the individuals at their table to complete the assignment. The assignment is something similar to planning a "welcoming day" for new members to their organization or faith community. The first step is to map out the talents of the team similar to the grid. From there, they come up with the "theme" of the event and start working out some of the initial objectives and assignments of the team members. What is consistent each time we conduct this exercise is the amount of energy, excitement, and enthusiasm that builds as the team coalesces around the assignment and their role. The remarkable outcome is the detail that will come as each team reports out and the sense of accountability and ownership that takes place with each of the members. It's not uncommon to hear participants comment on the power and ease of getting a project defined and objectives created when people approach it from their talent themes. Many will remark that while it is an exercise, they are motivated to carry out the assignment. When asked how long does it normally take a team to figure out projects such as this without focusing on teams strengths, many will remark "months," "years," or "it never ends up happening."

The First Steps

How do nonprofit organizations make the shift to an engagement-and-strengths approach to management? What will your first steps be?

The two key resources that are foundational to understanding engagement and strengths are the following books:

- *The Elements of Great Managing*[13]
- *Strengths Based Leadership*

Both of these books provide insights into the research on engagement-and strengths-based leadership. The books also highlight effective leadership practices from which to learn, adapt, and develop:

1. As the leader or leadership team, you will want to study both of these resources and become familiar with the concepts included in them. Begin with the study of engagement, as this provides the context for the strengths-based approach. If you read them with a team, take time to discuss the content in sections, and again at the conclusion of your study. Share with each other key concepts learned, potential areas of application, and how the concepts of engagement challenge your current vision, practice, or style of management.
2. Following your familiarization with engagement, read *Strengths Based Leadership* and complete the StrengthsFinder© assessment. A StrengthsFinder 2.0 code is included in the back of the book. Use the following worksheet to reflect on your experience of your Top 5 talent

themes; give your theme description report to one or two close friends or colleagues and ask them to share ways they have seen you using those talents; create an action plan for the development of the talent themes into strengths using the suggestions included in the report.

3. Now it is time to share the vision of engagement- and strengths-based leadership with others. If a team shared your reading and study of the resources, now is the time for them to complete StrengthsFinder©. Additional codes may be purchased at www.gallupstrengthscenter. com. A team grid will be prepared for all who complete Strengths-Finder© through codes purchased on that site, or you may create a grid like the one we provided as a sample. Invite each team member to reflect on his or her talent themes using the process described in number 2 on the previous page.

4. As the staff and key volunteers complete StrengthsFinder©, ask each to share his or her Top 5 and schedule a meeting with you. Invite each person to ask how you see his or her talents in action in your organization. This will provide beneficial insight for the staff person, and for you as you recognize the impact of the person and his or her talents. Affirming the staff and their contribution to the organization not only creates a sense of meaningful contribution. You are also setting the stage for future partnership and collaboration among staff members.

Questions the leader may use for this conversation include the following:

• What do you see as your top 2–3 areas of strength?
• How do you see your strengths aligning with top priorities?
• What do you see as one area of weakness that you need to address? How might you leverage a talent in order to address this weakness?

5. Discuss engagement- and strengths-based leadership with your staff and key volunteers. Create a strategic plan for incorporating strengths into personnel goal setting and evaluation; begin meetings with a brief go-around in which each person shares one way he or she has used a talent theme since the last meeting; assign new tasks or build new teams with talents and the domains in mind; affirm one another whenever possible.

That is a start! There is much more to learn and share. For example, organizations that become very serious about engagement can give their staff and key volunteers the Q12 assessment from Gallup that measures employee engagement. The process includes a visit with a Gallup consultant who will help the organization develop a strategic plan to increase engagement.

A strengths coaching kit is available on the Gallup Strengths Center website, as is the ability to order one's full 34-theme report, with all themes listed in the person's individual rank order based on his or her responses on StrengthsFinder©. Those who wish to become more proficient in strengths can be trained through Gallup via web-based or in-person training.[14]

Key Learnings

- Engaging your staff and key volunteers creates an environment in which your organization will thrive and grow.
- Building a strengths-based team is a key component of the engagement process.
- Focusing on strengths rather than weaknesses provides the foundation for effective management of people and projects.
- The most effective teams are not ones in which everyone has similar talents. Rather, the most effective teams have many talents represented and draw on the talents of everyone.
- Becoming an engagement- and strengths-based leader is a dynamic process of personal and professional growth and development.

People sometimes struggle to recognize one or more of their talents identified in StrengthsFinder© in positive ways. One pastor tells the story of his initial misgivings about his talent themes, until an ah-ha during a discussion at the Pastoral Council meeting. Each member of the Council had completed StrengthsFinder© and had their Top 5 listed on a table tent in front of them. As the discussion continued, the pastor experienced an insightful moment. In the past, he explained, when new ideas were being explored, his reaction would be to ask, "How does this fit within the big picture?" and he felt like the wet blanket, squashing the new idea. Looking at his Top 5 at this meeting, however, he understood. His #1 talent theme is Strategic, a talent that leads the person to see how elements contribute to the whole. Now, he is grateful to offer his talent by saying, "The strategic part of me is wondering." He and his community are now on their strengths journey together. Are you ready to begin yours?

Key Assessment Questions

1. How would you describe the strengths, specific contributions, or both of each of your employees?
2. In reviewing the importance of developing strengths as a key element of building an engaged team, what strategies emerge as next steps for you, your team, or both?
3. Which of the four domains of leadership is most represented by your team?
4. How can you leverage the talent of your entire team as part of your workforce planning strategy?
5. In what ways do you use a strengths-based approach to conduct meaningful strengths-based development discussions as part of your overall development process?

Notes

1. Rath and Conchie (2008), p. 14.
2. Wagner and Harter (2006).
3. www.csec.info; this site includes a link to the CSEC Connected Community. Create a login and password to access member-only content and to contribute.
4. Rath and Conchie (2008).
5. Rath and Conchie (2008), p. 14.
6. Asplund and Blacksmith (2011).
7. Rath (2007).
8. Rath (2007), p. 20.
9. Rath (2007).
10. Rath and Conchie (2008), p. 22.
11. Rath and Conchie (2008), p. 23.

12. www.csec.info/resources
13. Wagner and Harter (2006).
14. www.gallup.com

References

Asplund, J., & Blacksmith, N. (2011, April 7). How strengths boost engagement. *Gallup Business Journal*.

Rath, T. (2007). *StrengthsFinder 2.0*. New York, NY: Gallup Press.

Rath, T., & Conchie, B. (2008). *Strengths based leadership*. New York, NY: Gallup Press.

Wagner, R., & Harter, J. K. (2006). *12: The elements of great managing*. New York, NY: Gallup Press.

CHAPTER 17

Creating a Sense of Employee Ownership

Lessons From Worker-Owned Cooperatives

Ray West and Rebecca Luce

Carl Raymond (Ray) West is Executive Director and a founder of Interfaith Business Builders, Inc. (IBB) in Cincinnati, Ohio. He has 30 years of experience developing and managing social enterprises, especially community-based, employee-owned worker cooperatives. He holds a BA from St. Louis University. Prior to IBB he was a community organizer.

Rebecca Luce is an Associate Professor on the faculty of the Management and Entrepreneurship Department at Xavier University. Prior to obtaining her PhD in Management from Michigan State University, Luce was an HR executive for over 20 years. She is a board member of Interfaith Business Builders.

Introduction

Employees' intrinsic motivation toward a job arises from the nature of the work itself and its meaningfulness to the individual. Work is intrinsically motivating when an employee experiences satisfaction and enjoyment from his or her performance, such as completing an interesting, challenging project. Intrinsic motivation is more effective in driving individual performance than extrinsic motivation, which originates from external sources (such as money or other rewards).

Intrinsic employee motivation is fueled all the more when employees feel a sense of ownership within their organization. The employee-owned cooperative business model, also known as the worker cooperative model, illustrates the intrinsic motivation and power of actual ownership to fuel organizational and individual performance. The model is noteworthy for the loyalty, levels of engagement, opportunities for employee input, and efficiency it generates within such enterprises.

Employee-owned cooperative businesses are a growing phenomenon around the globe. Outstanding examples of these organizations are found in the Emilia-Romagna area of Italy and the Basque region of Spain. In both these areas, tens of thousands of people are employed in good paying jobs in co-op enterprises ranging from grocery stores to machine tool manufacturing. Worker cooperatives, with the special strengths and benefits they can bring to small businesses, are an emerging niche sector in the market economy.

Purpose

This chapter will provide suggestions on how you can build a sense of ownership within and among the employees of your organization. There are structural and behavioral strategies nonprofit organizations can institute to elicit managerial and employee benefits similar to those which accrue from the ownership by employees in cooperative enterprises. These approaches include the following:

1. Educating managers regarding the benefits of involving employees in organizational decision making
2. Actively and consistently soliciting and respecting employee participation in meaningful organizational decisions at multiple levels within the organization
3. Reaping the benefits of higher quality decisions and enhanced organizational performance
4. Realizing a newfound level of appreciation and passion for the organization and its mission among managers and employees alike.

Introduction to Interfaith Business Builders and Its Cooperatives

Interfaith Business Builders, Inc. (IBB) is a small faith-based community organization in Cincinnati, Ohio developing and promoting community-based, employee-owned worker cooperatives that create jobs and business ownership opportunities for low-income people. Cooperative Janitorial Services, Inc. (CJS) launched by IBB in 1995, is a successful worker-owned cooperative business offering commercial janitorial services. Community Blend, an IBB-sponsored worker-owned cooperative coffee shop, will open shortly.

The objectives of worker-owned cooperatives, such as those developed by IBB, encompass more than simply providing a paying job and ownership opportunities for employees. A key question faced within these cooperative businesses is "How do we work with the employees' initial primary desire simply to have a paying job and develop that, through the employees' ownership stake and the distinct structure and culture of the business, into a healthy feeling of engagement and passion for the job and the organization?"

About the Sense of Ownership in Employee-Owned Cooperatives

The most obvious statement of direct ownership for an employee in an employee-owned worker cooperative is the piece of stock, called a membership share, which is purchased by the employee. Significantly, each worker/owner (member) in the cooperative corporation owns one and only one such voting membership share. This membership share stands as clear evidence that the person has an ownership stake and, therefore, a voice in running the cooperative. It is also clear evidence that the person is an equal among his or her peers, that is, fellow worker/owners in the cooperative business.

Worker/owners commonly engage in participative decision making and even elect the board of the cooperative corporation. Among the members of successful worker cooperatives, there emerges an awareness of the implications of the members' ownership, followed by behaviors of responsibility, accountability, cooperation, and efficiency. Over time, members develop the sense that what is most important about being an owner is not the piece of stock and not even the potential for profit sharing. As important as these are, an employee's primary motivation becomes the fact that the person is in a setting where he or she has an actual voice and is treated seriously and with respect as an important contributor to organizational success.

For managers, an obvious result is the reduced need for middle-level management supervision over the workforce. Management and role distinctions are still part of normal operations, but less need for supervision is the norm. The motivation among employees to "do it right" accelerates with that feeling of having a real ownership stake. The motivation among employees to build the capacity of co-workers also accelerates.

The member's ownership paired with his or her intensive involvement in the cooperative business evolves over time into a commitment to organizational mission and success that typically has positive impacts both for the person individually and for the organization as a whole. The cooperative ownership structure conveys the message in a much more dramatic fashion than in the typical corporation that worker/owners can impact their work and the company providing them with employment. When employed in a well-functioning cooperative setting, a member gradually realizes that working there is different. With this comes a release of very healthy energy and a newfound commitment to the mission and success of the organization, that is, to the entity which is affording the individual these very affirming experiences. Benefits of worker-owned cooperatives are shown in Figure 17.1.

Creating a Sense of Employee Ownership in Your Nonprofit

While it may seem that it would be the ownership in the company that is the primary driver of the typical benefits realized in worker-owned cooperatives, research studies conducted on employee-owned businesses have reached a different conclusion. Findings suggest that it was primarily participative decision making and employees' perceptions of influence on change in their enterprises, not the fact of ownership per se, that led to desirable employee outcomes, such as increased commitment to the

Employees

- provide input into decision making;
- have a higher level of intrinsic motivation to perform well;
- experience increased job satisfaction;
- display more organizational commitment and reduced turnover;
- feel an enhanced sense of responsibility and accountability;
- demonstrate increased productivity and efficiency;
- identify with organizational goals, values, and mission;

Resulting in

- enhanced likelihood of employee and business success;
- improved organizational performance and sustainability.

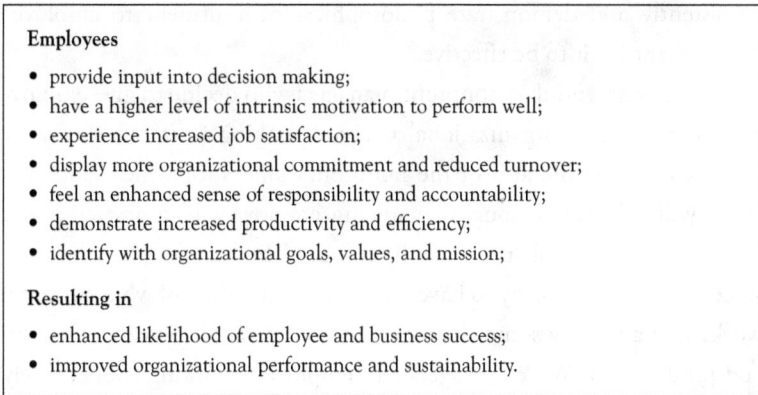

Figure 17.1 Benefits of worker-owned cooperatives

company, greater job satisfaction, and lower voluntary turnover.[1] In other words, the direct employee involvement which accompanies *financial* ownership in cooperative businesses can translate into employees experiencing *psychological* ownership in the organization[2] as indicated in Figure 17.2.

While the participative decision making observed in cooperatives flows directly from employees' ownership of shares in the enterprise, employees in all types of organizations express their desire to be included in the decision-making process of their organizations, especially where their work is concerned. Research shows that greater levels of employee influence in organizations are positively linked with organizational performance.[3] This may occur because when employee input is actively solicited and incorporated, there is a richer background for decision making, leading to higher quality organizational decisions. Higher quality decisions lead, of course, to improved organizational performance.[4] Managers who sincerely solicit the input of employees prior to making meaningful organizational decisions thus stand to benefit in a variety of ways. It is critical, however, that managers who venture down the path of seeking employee participation in making organizational decisions act

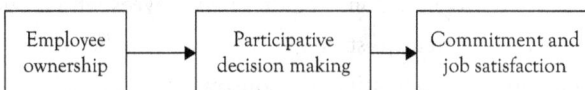

| Employee ownership | → | Participative decision making | → | Commitment and job satisfaction |

Figure 17.2 Employee/owner perceptions

consistently and demonstrate philosophical commitment to employee involvement for it to be effective.[5]

We recommend that nonprofit managers who decide to give employees more voice in organizational decision making start out slowly by identifying a specific area of the nonprofit's affairs for which employee input will initially be sought. Involving employees to a greater extent in designing their job responsibilities would be a good place to start, since employees are likely to have a solid understanding of what currently works well and how some changes could be made to increase efficiency and productivity. With managers and employees working cooperatively regarding the employee's job responsibilities, there is likely to be an increased level of trust and respect developed between the employee and his or her manager. This, in turn, can provide a good foundation for increasing the level of employee participation in broader organizational decisions later on.

It is important to first ensure that employees' managers or supervisors in nonprofits understand how to effectively handle such interactions with their employees. To ask employees for their input and then ignore it without explanation or to treat employees' ideas as unworthy of implementation is apt to create morale problems, rather than achieve the desirable outcomes being sought. A short training session including some role-playing could be a way to prepare managers for this undertaking.

As employees gain confidence in their ideas and can see that their input is valued in making organizational decisions, nonprofit managers will likely find that employee motivation increases since employees will find their jobs more rewarding and meaningful as a consequence of their ability to exercise their voices.[6] This is the intrinsic type of motivation often observed in cooperatives, as noted at the beginning of this chapter. Since empowerment and autonomy go hand in hand with intrinsic motivation, managers may find they can reduce the level of their supervision of employees and give them more freedom to make decisions regarding the performance of their jobs, a win–win situation for the employee and the organization. For those employees who demonstrate the aptitude, involvement in strategic decisions may be an opportunity to consider. Worker cooperatives demonstrate the capacity of employees to rise to the level of strategic decision making, usually associated exclusively with boards and their committees. It is critical to the success of empowering employees to participate in making organizational decisions that managers constantly reinforce the value of employees' voices being heard.[7]

The psychological ownership that results from meaningful and substantial inclusion of employees' input in making workplace decisions often leads to an increase in their sense of identification with organizational goals, values, and mission.[8] When employees identify with their organizations in this way, they realize a greater intrinsic motivation for their work[9] and, therefore, increased productivity.[10] Employees' work becomes the organization's work and vice versa, leading to a reinforcing cycle that reaps benefits for both the employee and the organization.

Employee Ownership at Cooperative Janitorial Services—An IBB Cooperative

Cooperative Janitorial Services, Inc. (CJS) is a successful worker-owned cooperative. CJS currently has 15 members and 28 customers. Those customers include small businesses, condominiums, credit unions, social service agencies, churches, and individuals. The company was originally developed by IBB, and CJS purchases some management and training services from IBB.

Becoming a Member Owner

Each CJS employee is eligible to become a member in the cooperative after a 6-month trial period. The decision rests with the cooperative's board and is dependent upon the board sense that the new employee understands and is ready to take on the responsibilities of being a member in a cooperative business. Employees are told when hired that if they are not accepted for membership, their job with CJS ends after 6 months. If accepted for membership, the new member then begins paying $500 for a membership share. This is typically paid through a payroll deduction plan. The full rights of membership are bestowed on the new member at the time of acceptance into the cooperative, rather than waiting until the full membership share fee has been paid.

Board Membership and Meetings

Given the current size of the membership, all CJS members are at this time members of the board of the company. That will change as the workforce grows. At that point in time, the members will annually elect their board from the ranks of CJS worker-owners for the coming year.

Meetings of the board, members, and workers still in their trial period are held monthly. The monthly meetings are inclusive in order to gain input from the full workforce, practice transparency and accountability, and provide on-the-job orientation and training to the new employees. The monthly meetings review customer accounts, performance, monthly sales data, sales work under way, general operations, use of cooperative principles and methods, and policy questions that arise.

Committee meetings and customer site-specific meetings are held as called for. Meetings of the board or officers exclusively are held as appropriate. Final hiring and firing decisions ordinarily rest with the board officers.

Management

The CJS General Manager is in many respects a General Coordinator. While the General Manager (GM) is expected to make management decisions on a daily basis as needed, the GM is also expected to do this in a collaborative manner that involves the appropriate stakeholders as per the issue at hand. The Operations Coordinator makes operations decisions related to customer sites on a daily basis as needed and by acting in consultation with the relevant CJS employee(s). Decisions of the GM and the Operations Coordinator are reported at the monthly meetings and are subject to review when a member questions a decision.

Decision Making

Decisions made in the monthly meetings are based upon consensus as much as possible. More formal voting is the fallback position in order to ensure decisions are made in a timely fashion. While use of the consensus approach risks domination of the group by inflexible members, the members as a whole have become adept at calling out such inflexible behavior and negotiating reasonable tradeoffs that address the variety of concerns presented in any given situation.

Decision making within a healthy cooperative fundamentally rests upon the questions, "Who are the relevant stakeholders?" and "How do we practice transparency and achieve accountability?"

Employee Satisfaction and Intrinsic Motivation

Overall employee satisfaction within the cooperative is one of the results of these structures and methodologies. While each employee does not always get his or her way, members have a sense that they have been heard and made a difference. The time invested in communications and inclusive decision making proves to be time well spent. Evidence of this is reflected in the very low rate of employee turnover. The average CJS employee has been with the company for over 5 years. That is unheard of in the janitorial industry, where workers are ordinarily moving from job to job in search of better pay and working conditions. In companies where steady turnover occurs, the result is added personnel screening, hiring and training expenses, along with loss of institutional knowledge for the company.

In CJS, overall employee satisfaction not only shows in low turnover. It also shows in employee demonstrations of loyalty to their co-op as they strive to appreciate and meet customer's needs and produce top quality services. Personal commitment is followed by greater collective commitment to the institution's mission. The commitment of the whole clearly becomes greater than the sum of its parts. In turn, CJS has had an unusually high rate of retention of its customers. The average CJS customer has been with the company for over 4 years. This is much higher than is typical in the commercial janitorial field.

The higher levels of intrinsic motivation within CJS come from the reality of and consequences of ownership. When asked what is most rewarding about working in CJS, members most often respond, "I am an owner. I am finally working someplace where I have a voice." Significant decision making, that part of being a human being which is craved but too often denied to the average person, is more often made available within the cooperative structure. Where it is present, it is appreciated. It is a motivator. The job becomes a chance to exercise ownership and make reasoned decisions in the workplace, decisions benefiting the employee and the organization. It becomes a chance to hone one's abilities and develop a greater appreciation for quality activity.

Responsibility and Accountability

An enhanced sense of responsibility and accountability regularly shows itself in the monthly CJS meetings. A clergyman with a business background once commented after sitting in on a CJS meeting that he had never seen a meeting like it before. He said it was a combination of a standard business board meeting and a group therapy session where people were freely offering each other both criticism and positive reinforcement. The outcome was a focused group of people.

One of the most obvious ways by which CJS members show their understanding of business and exercise their responsibilities toward their business has to do with their review and establishment of wage scales. They sometimes joke that "We can pay ourselves whatever we want." And they do in fact use a wage scale slightly higher than the industry norm. They hold that wage level there, though, recognizing that short-term gain in hourly wages can result in long-term pain for the co-op's bottom line. They know that losses for CJS can ultimately mean loss of the business and then loss of their jobs. They know they have to act responsibly and be accountable to each other.

Being accountable also means retaining customer contracts. Employees are expected to become good problem solvers at their customer job sites. That means identifying potential cleaning-related problems and resolving them. That may mean something that can be handled on the spot. It may mean a phone call to the Operations Coordinator. It definitely means learning how to listen and talk effectively with the customer. The CJS employee handbook is full of rules the employees voted on themselves. Failure to follow the rules and use good judgment makes it likely the employee will be called on the carpet by one or more of his or her peers, either in private or in a meeting.

Building a Multidimensional Sense of Ownership

As indicated, that feeling of ownership increases productivity and efficiency. Less time is spent killing time. Less managerial time is required supervising every move of employees. Experienced employees who understand the culture of the co-op regularly coach newer employees in best work skills and operations of the business. Time is spent in the monthly meetings reviewing best practices learned out on the job. That in turn reduces the likelihood of errors and inefficiencies out on the job. Everyone understands that, should an employee need time off from work, the person's co-workers will be asked if they can step in and cover for the person. The two-way street of reciprocity comes to be appreciated.

With employees holding a clear ownership stake in the organization, the vision of the organization performing as an effective and balanced machine becomes the overall vision and desire of the workforce. Awareness and respect build for the multitude of functions required for the business to be successful. It takes some people longer than others to fully get it, but the realization grows. For each person and for the organization itself, it is an evolutionary process. The need for disciplinary actions shrinks. Disciplinary matters are more easily resolved.

Autonomy is often viewed as one of the things people desire the most in their work environment. That is certainly true in CJS. People appreciate a boss not constantly breathing down their neck. Something else is true, though. People come to see the benefits of working in an environment where they share in the ownership. Helping each other becomes the logical thing to do. Testing each other and learning how to trust each other becomes the logical thing to do. Working together becomes a more attractive exercise. Words like team, collaboration, trust, community, and cooperation begin to take on new and more real meanings. An understanding and respect builds for the co-op's constituencies: the members themselves, their customers, suppliers, the community, and the co-op developer, IBB. That feels good, and it improves the overall organizational performance.

In the case of CJS, that sense of a cooperative community has even manifested itself through hundreds of hours volunteered by CJS members in the research and development processes required for opening the next worker cooperative, Community Blend, a fair trade worker co-op coffee shop opening in Cincinnati in 2013.

Summary

The environment for success within CJS and other employee-owned cooperative businesses builds steadily, thanks in no small part to the crucial element of the sense of ownership felt by the employees. It is a seedbed for both personal and organizational success. Nonprofits seeking to create this type of environment within their organizations can readily adopt many of the managerial practices of employee-owned cooperative businesses, particularly by offering capable employees the opportunity to participate in organizational decision making. Giving employees a meaningful voice in your nonprofit can create a similar sense of ownership to that of employee-owned cooperative businesses. While the sense of ownership in the nonprofit setting will be derived from psychological ownership rather than financial ownership, research and experience show that it is no less effective in leading to results that are beneficial to employees and organizations alike.

Key Assessment Questions

The overarching question within cooperative businesses that you can apply to your nonprofit organization is "How do we work with employees' initial desire simply to have a paying job and create an environment where they develop a sense of ownership in the organization as well as a passion for achieving the organization's mission?" Putting it more specifically:

1. Within our nonprofit organization, what steps can we take to appropriately structure employees' genuine input and voice into the decision-making components of our organization's structure, whether at the operational, committee, strategic, or board levels?
2. How can we demonstrate to employees that the organization's management and board respect and take them seriously?
3. How can we develop systems of transparency and mutual accountability that work to the real benefit of all stakeholders?

4. How do we build appropriate levels of information sharing, so that employees are more thoroughly informed, better able to weigh in on decisions as appropriate, and thereby more motivated and passionate about taking on responsibility for the success of the organization and its mission?

5. How do we move in such directions with eyes wide open? It's an evolutionary process for management and employees alike. How do we systematically discern, implement, and evaluate the steps in a continuous, self-reinforcing, positive cycle?

Addressing these questions clearly takes vision, boldness, patience, and humility, but the fruits of the process can be most beneficial.

Notes

1. Bakan et al. (2004), pp. 231–241; Long (1978), pp. 29–48; Rhodes and Steers (1981), pp. 1013–1035.
2. Pierce, Rubenfeld, and Morgan (1991), pp. 121–144.
3. McHugh et al. (1997).
4. Mowday, Porter, and Steers (1982).
5. Long (1981), pp. 847–876; Rosen and Quarrey (1987), pp. 126–128.
6. Webb (1912).
7. Rosen, Klein, and Young (1986).
8. Hammer and Stern (1980), pp. 78–100.
9. Webb (1912).
10. Bernstein (1979).

References

Bakan, I., Suseno, Y., Pinnington, A., & Money, A. (2004). The influence of financial participation and participation in decision making on employee job attitudes. *International Journal of Human Resource Management 62*, 231–241.

Bernstein, P. (1979). *Workplace democratization: Its internal dynamics*. New Brunswick, NJ: Transaction Books.

Hammer, T. H., & Stern, R. N. (1980). Employee ownership: Implications for the organizational distribution of power. *Academy of Management Journal 23*, 78–100.

Long, R. J. (1978). The effects of employee ownership on organizational identification, job attitudes and organizational performance: A tentative framework and empirical findings. *Human Relations 31*, 29–48.

Long, R. J. (1981). The effects of formal employee participation in ownership and decision making on perceived and desired patterns of organizational influence: A longitudinal study. *Human Relations 34*, 847–876.

McHugh, P. P., Cutcher-Gershenfeld, J., & Polzin, M. (1997). Ways in which structure and process matter: Employee influence, plan design and communication in ESOP companies. *Academy of Management Proceedings*, 154–158.

Mowday, R. T., Porter, L. W., & Steers, R. M. (1982). *Employee organization linkages: The psychology of commitment, absenteeism, and turnover.* New York, NY: Academic Press.

Pierce, J. I., Rubenfeld, S. A., & Morgan, S. (1991). Employee ownership: A conceptual model of process and effects. *Academy of Management Review 16*, 121–144.

Rhodes, S. R., & Steers, R. M. (1981). Conventional versus worker-owned organizations. *Human Relations 34*, 1013–1035.

Rosen, C. M., Klein, K. J., & Young, K. M. (1986). *Employee ownership in America.* Lexington, MA: Lexington Books.

Rosen, C., & Quarrey, M. (1987). How well is employee ownership working? *Harvard Business Review 65*, 126–128, 132.

Webb, C. (1912). *Industrial cooperation: The story of a peaceful revolution.* Manchester, England: Cooperative Union.

Concluding Comments

This book is designed to provide basic, yet solid techniques on how to perform many of the most essential management and leadership tasks needed to successfully run a nonprofit organization. We used a structured research process to identify the four essential areas of living the mission, making good decisions, getting things done, and developing your team. Then we recruited experts in each area to capture the most essential skills and knowledge of their field in concise chapters, with examples from non-profit organizations. So, how do you as a busy person effectively use this?

For many organizations, there are pain points at any moment in time. One approach is to consider the pain points you have, find a chapter that addresses one of those points, and assess your organization using the five questions at the end of the chapter. Pick one thing you can do quickly and give it a try. Consider the lessons learned from the example organization along with the suggestions in the body of the chapter for ideas. Many pain points have multiple causes, so you may not solve the entire problem on the first try. Nevertheless, get started, make progress, and then determine what you can do next to make more progress.

If your organization either has multiple or no pain points, you may use a different logic on how to start. You can pick a chapter that represents an important area, but one in which you believe you have good prospects of making a difference. Again, follow the assessment questions to determine exactly what you wish to improve. This approach is a balancing act. On the one hand, you wish to pick something in which the probability of success is high, but on the other hand, you wish to improve something that is significant. If in doubt, it is frequently a good idea to start with something that is easily doable to get on a roll and, with experience, tackle larger challenges.

Regardless of the approach you take, you do not need to do it alone! Distribute copies of this book to your leadership team, your board, or other key stakeholders. You can call attention to particular topics or case examples. This can then become your "book club" for improving your nonprofit organization. Many heads are better than one!

Finally, please let us know how you are doing. We love to hear specifics of how leaders implement our ideas and what their results are. Nonprofit organizations provide so many valuable services to so many worthwhile clients and causes. Keep up the good work!

Dr. Timothy J. (Tim) Kloppenborg   **Dr. Laurence J. (Laurie) Laning**

kloppenborgt@xavier.edu   ljlcincy@aol.com

APPENDIX

Our Research Process

This appendix briefly explains the research processes we used to identify the topics and sections for this book. The two co-editors first performed **literature searches** of books, journals, the Web, and so forth. (Sources appear in our references.) We found well over 100 ideas suggested that were either important in creating or measuring success in faith-based and other nonprofit organizations.

The second research step was to conduct a **focus group**. We facilitated 10 active participants who ranged from executive directors, board members, volunteers, and a retired CEO of United Way of Greater Cincinnati. The members ranged in age from one person under 30 who had just established her own agency to those past normal retirement age. The focus group began by removing duplication of similar ideas and tightening up the wording. They also used the Method for Priority Marking to delete items that all focus group members thought did not apply.[1] The focus group participants then created an affinity diagram to group ideas that were similar in some way (had an affinity for each other) and used the resulting factors to form an interrelationship diagraph (ID) as shown in Figure A.1. The ID helps understand complex cause and effect relationships among the groups of ideas that emerged.[2]

One interprets the results by recognizing that item groups with many inward arrows such as financial management and impact are primarily effects. To impact those effects, one looks for groups with many outward arrows such as leadership principles, ethics, and values, as those are primarily causes. One also looks at item groups with many arrows both inward and outward such as stakeholders and expectations, as those are interrelated with many other things. The knowledge gained from our focus group constructing these tools was used first to help us build our surveys and then to interpret the results.

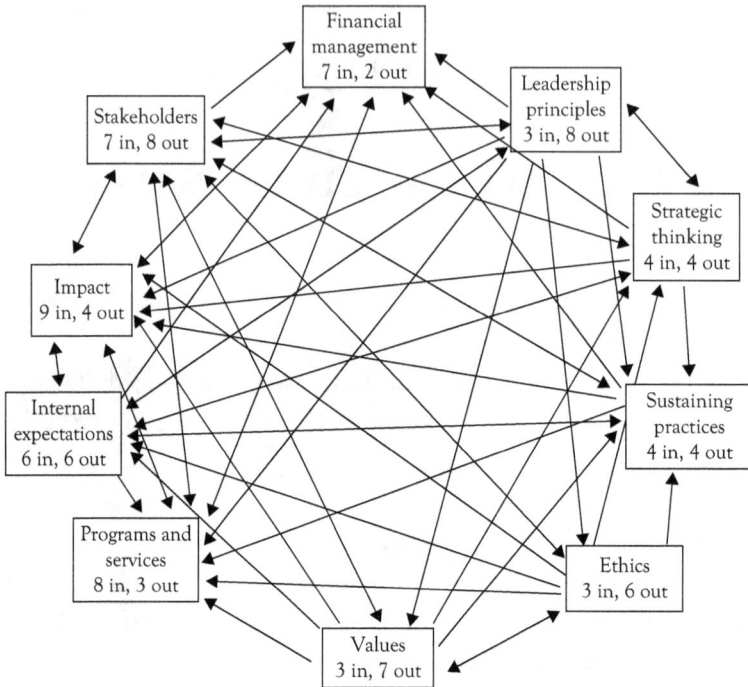

Figure A.1 Cause and effect relationships in nonprofit success

We also had our focus group members multivote for the individual items that constituted each group.[3] This was used to limit the number of questions we would later ask in our surveys. Each member was given a limited number of votes and asked to vote for the items that he or she personally thought might be most helpful for leaders of nonprofit, faith-based organizations, or both. For the sake of simplicity, we only show the items that received multiple votes, in Table A.1. They are listed by number of votes each received (out of 10 possible votes).

Armed with the focus group results, the third step in our research was to create a **pilot survey**. After receiving responses, we tightened up the language on a number of our questions and constructed a **large-scale survey**. Nearly 200 leaders of various nonprofit and faith-based organizations across the United States responded by rating the value of each suggested item on a scale of 1 to 5 with 5 being the most important. We performed **factor analysis** on the survey responses, and are using the results from the survey as justification for our book. Many of the items in

Table A.1 Individual items receiving multiple votes in focus group

10—Bring about change in individuals and society
10—Build value-added collaborations
10—Client needs are met
10—Needed outcomes are created
7—Build your constituency over the long term
7—Document outcomes
7—Pragmatic, well-understood vision for both short- and long-term
5—Board development: includes succession, continuity, and governance
5—Clients use products and services
5—Clients are satisfied
5—Share leadership empowering others
5—Transparency: provide accurate information that is accessible
4—Attract more people to support the organization
4—Leave ego out
4—Superior performance and efficiency assessed relative to mission
3—Able to carry out their missions
3—Articulate and operationalize clear and comprehensive values and standards of ethics
3—Powerful mission drives organization
3—Shared ownership: create mutually acceptable expectations and hold people accountable to them
3—Volunteer and staff are committed to mission
2—Focus on development needs of individuals
2—Fund-raising is adequate
2—Good and timely decisions are made and executed
2—Exceptional results last beyond any individual, idea, or business cycle
2—Strategic leadership guides direction, rigorous decision making, and capacity creation

the survey did not cluster into reliable factors and so we did not use them. There are four reliable factors and these form the four major sections of our book and are described in detail in those sections.

- **Living the Mission**
- **Making Good Decisions**
- **Getting Things Done**
- **Developing Your Team**

These four factors form what we termed a "Virtuous Cycle in Nonprofit Organization Success." As you do things well in one section, it helps to do other things well in other sections. Instead of the negative vicious cycle, this is a positive or virtuous cycle.

Notes

1. Center for Quality of Management (1997).
2. Brassard and Ritter (2008).
3. Brassard and Ritter (2008).

References

Brassard, M., & Ritter, D. (2008). *The memory Jogger II healthcare edition: A pocket guide for continuous improvement and effective planning*. Salem, NH: GOAL/QPC.

Center for Quality of Management. (1997). *The method for priority marking*. Cambridge, MA: Center for Quality of Management.

Carver, J. (2006). *Boards that make a difference: A new design for leadership in nonprofit and public organizations*. San Francisco, CA: Jossey-Bass.

Collins, J. (2005). *Good to great and the social sciences*. Boulder, CO: Jim Collins.

Crutchfield, L. R., & McLeod Grant, H. (2012). *Forces for good: The six principles of high-impact nonprofits*. San Francisco, CA: Jossey-Bass.

Denhardt, R. B., Denhardt, J. V., & Aristiguenta, M. P. (2013). *Managing human behavior in public and nonprofit organizations* (3rd ed.). Los Angeles, CA: Sage.

Drucker, P. F. (2006). *Managing the nonprofit organization principles and practices*. New York, NY: Harper Collins Publishers.

Gordon, G., & Crabtree, S. (2006). *Building engaged schools: Getting the most out of America's classrooms*. New York, NY: Gallup Press.

http://www.cultureofaccountability.ca/index.html

http://www.jeanroberts.com.au/non-profit/critical-success-factor-checklist/

Kloppenborg, T. J., Tesch, D., & King, B. (2012). *21st century project success measures: Evolution, interpretation, and direction*. Proceedings, Project Management Institute Research and Education Conference. Limerick, Ireland.

Lowney, C. (2006). *Heroic leadership: Best practices from a 450 year old company that changed the world*. Chicago, IL: Loyola Press.

Morino, M. (2011). *Leap of reason: Managing to outcomes in an era of scarcity*. Washington, DC: Venture Philanthropy Partners.

Rowe, W. G., & Conway Dato-On, M. (2013). *Introduction to nonprofit management text and cases.* Los Angeles, CA: Sage and Ivey Publishing at the Richard Ivey School of Business.

Tschirhart, M., & Bielefeld, W. (2012). *Managing nonprofit organizations.* San Francisco, CA: Jossey-Bass.

Useem, M. (2011). *The leader's checklist. Philadelphia*, PA: Wharton Digital Press.

Winseman, A. L. (2006). *Growing an engaged church: How to stop "Doing Church" and start being the church again.* New York, NY: Gallup Press.

Worth, M. J. (2012). *Nonprofit management: Principles and practices.* Los Angeles, CA: Sage.

Index

OTHER TITLES IN THE STRATEGIC MANAGEMENT COLLECTION

William Q. Judge, Old Dominion University, Editor

- *Business Intelligence: Making Decisions Through Data Analytics* by Jerzy Surma
- *Designing the Networked Organization* by Ken Everett
- *Successful Organizational Transformation: The Five Critical Elements* by Marvin Washington, Stephen Hacker, and Marla Hacker
- *Top Management Teams: How to Be Effective Inside and Outside the Boardroom* by Annaloes M.L. Raes
- *The Family in Business: The Dynamics of the Family Owned Firm* by Bernard Liebowitz
- *A Stakeholder Approach to Issues Management* by Robert Boutilier
- *The Strategic Management of Higher Education Institutions: Serving Students as Customers for Institutional Growth* by Hamid Kazeroony
- *Managing for Ethical-Organizational Integrity: Principles and Processes for Promoting Good, Right, and Virtuous Conduct* by Abe Zakhem
- *Corporate Bankruptcy Fundamental Principles and Processes* by William J. Donoher
- *Learning Organizations: Turning Knowledge into Action* by Marcus Goncalves
- *Moral Leadership: A Transformative Model for Tomorrow's Leaders* by Cam Caldwell
- *Knowledge Management: The Death of Wisdom: Why Our Companies Have Lost It—and How They Can Get It Back* by Arnold Kransdorff
- *Intellectual Property in the Managerial Portfolio: Its Creation, Development, and Protection* by Thomas O'Connor
- *Strategy and Training: Making Skills a Competitive Advantage* by Philippe Korda
- *Business Models and Strategic Management: A New Integration* by Francine Newth
- *Business Model Design and Learning: A Strategic Guide* by Barbara Spencer
- *Leading Latino Talent to Champion Innovation* by Vinny Caraballo, Greg McLaughlin and Heidi McLaughlin

Announcing the Business Expert Press Digital Library

*Concise E-books Business Students Need
for Classroom and Research*

This book can also be purchased in an e-book collection by your library as
- a one-time purchase,
- that is owned forever,
- allows for simultaneous readers,
- has no restrictions on printing, and
- can be downloaded as PDFs from within the library community.

Our digital library collections are a great solution to beat the rising cost of textbooks. e-books can be loaded into their course management systems or onto student's e-book readers.

The **Business Expert Press** digital libraries are very affordable, with no obligation to buy in future years. For more information, please visit **www.businessexpertpress.com/librarians**. To set up a trial in the United States, please contact **Adam Chesler** at *adam.chesler@ businessexpertpress.com* for all other regions, contact **Nicole Lee** at *nicole.lee@igroupnet.com*.